GUIDE TO MISSOURI CONFEDERATE UNITS, 1861–1865

GUIDE TO MISSOURI CONFEDERATE UNITS, 1861–1865

James E. McGhee

The University of Arkansas Press
Fayetteville
2008

Copyright © 2008 by The University of Arkansas Press

ISBN-10: 1-55728-940-9
ISBN-13: 978-1-55728-940-7

14 13 12 11 10   5 4 3 2 1

First Paperback Edition

Designed by Liz Lester

The Library of Congress has cataloged the hardcover edition as follows:

McGhee, James E., 1939–
    Guide to Missouri Confederate units, 1861–1865 / James E. McGhee.
        p.   cm.   — (The Civil War in the West)
    Includes bibliographical references and index.
    ISBN-13: 978-1-55728-870-7 (cloth : alk. paper)
    ISBN-10: 1-55728-870-4
    1. Missouri—History—Civil War, 1861–1865—Regimental histories.
    2. United States—History--Civil War, 1861–1865—Regimental histories.
    3. Confederate States of America—Armed Forces. 4. Confederate States of
    America—Armed Forces—Officers—Registers. 5. Missouri—History—Civil
    War, 1861–1865—Registers. 6. United States—History—Civil War, 1861–1865—
    Registers. 7. Missouri—History—Civil War, 1861–1865—Regimental histories—
    Bibliography. 8. United States—History—Civil War, 1861–1865—Regimental
    histories—Bibliography. I. Title.
        E569.4.M38   2008
        973.7'478—dc22

                                        2008000697

For my father, the best man I have ever known.

CONTENTS

ILLUSTRATIONS
(after page 176)

Major General Sterling Price

Major General John S. Bowen

Brigadier General Mosby M. Parsons

Brigadier General M. Jeff Thompson

Major James Harding

Sergeant Robert E. Young

Colonel Solomon G. Kitchen

Colonel William L. Jeffers

Colonel David Shanks

Major James M. Parrott

Lieutenant Washington L. Watkins

Men of the 12th Missouri Cavalry Regiment

Men of the 13th Missouri Cavalry Regiment

Colonel John B. Clark Jr.

Lieutenant William H. Dunnica

Lieutenant John E. Wright

Private Henry Clay Luckett

Lieutenant William H. Mansur

Lieutenant Colonel Lebbeus A. Pindall

Captain Elbert Feaster

Captain David Thompson

Brigadier General Daniel M. Frost

SERIES EDITORS' PREFACE

The Civil War in the West has a single goal: to promote historical writing about the war in the western states and territories. It focuses most particularly on the Trans-Mississippi theater, which consisted of Missouri, Arkansas, Texas, most of Louisiana (west of the Mississippi River), Indian Territory (modern-day Oklahoma), and Arizona Territory (two-fifths of modern-day Arizona and New Mexico) but encompasses adjacent states, such as Kansas, Tennessee, and Mississippi, that directly influenced the Trans-Mississippi war. It is a wide swath, to be sure, but one too often ignored by historians and, consequently, too little understood and appreciated.

Topically, the series embraces all aspects of the wartime story. Military history in its many guises, from the strategies of generals to the daily lives of common soldiers, forms an important part of that story, but so, too, do the numerous and complex political, economic, social, and diplomatic dimensions of the war. The series also provides a variety of perspectives on these topics. Most important, it offers the best in modern scholarship, with thoughtful, challenging monographs. Second, it presents new editions of important books that have gone out of print. And third, it premieres expertly edited correspondence, diaries, reminiscences, and other writings by participants in the war.

It is a formidable challenge, but by focusing on some of the least familiar dimensions of the conflict, *The Civil War in the West* significantly broadens our understanding of the nation's most pivotal and dramatic story.

Anyone engaged in Civil War research appreciates a good reference work. Not surprisingly, there are as many different types of guides as there are possible topics. Equally unsurprisingly, genuinely useful reference works are rare. It is especially hard to find reliable and comprehensive guides to Civil War military units. Both *reliable* and *comprehensive* should be emphasized. A variety of guides for Union and Confederate units exists, but few satisfy all of a researcher's needs. Most merely list commanding officers, engagements, mustering dates, and when units disbanded. They rarely provide information below the battalion or regimental level for cavalry and infantry, and far too many are slapdash affairs riddled with errors and contradictions.

James E. McGhee's book on Missouri Confederate military units avoids these usual pitfalls while realizing all of the benefits of a model guide. He is a highly respected and widely published authority on the Civil War in Missouri, and his expertise is evident on every page of this book. The scope of the work is startling, the depth of detail gratifying, its reliability undeniable, and the unit narratives highly readable. While a departure from the usual format of the volumes in this series, it fits the purpose of the series extremely well. It is a signal contribution to our knowledge of the War in the West.

T. Michael Parrish
Daniel E. Sutherland
SERIES EDITORS

ACKNOWLEDGMENTS

No one undertakes a project of this magnitude without the assistance of others. Certainly I did not, for many individuals helped bring this history of the Missouri Confederate units to fruition.

Danny Odom, Southaven, Mississippi, who has conducted extensive research on the Confederate units of the Trans-Mississippi and Western Departments, initially urged me to undertake the project. He then made his voluminous notes available to me without my asking, read the manuscript with a critical eye, offered useful suggestions, and encouraged me to continue when I tired of the undertaking. In many respects this book is as much his as it is mine.

Billy J. Gurley, Little Rock, Arkansas, an authority on the war in the Trans-Mississippi, provided invaluable assistance. He generously shared his research and made many manuscripts available for my use. He noted mistakes in the first draft of the manuscript that saved me from myself in several instances. Bill also insisted that the manuscript merited publication when I had doubts in that regard. His interest in the project has been most gratifying, and I offer him my sincere appreciation.

John F. Bradbury Jr., an old friend, is widely known for his many fine historical endeavors regarding the war in Missouri, including articles, books, and maps. He always provides encouragement, constructive criticism, and wise counsel regarding my historical efforts. He helped with this one as well by reading the manuscript and making images from his collection available. I thank him for his continued support, and I value his friendship.

Many other individuals generously provided information and images for the project, including Bruce Allardice, Des Plaines, Illinois; Greg Biggs, Clarksville, Tennessee; Walter E. Busch, Site Director, Fort Davidson Historic Site, Pilot Knob, Missouri; John E. Fayant, Camdenton, Missouri; Janae Fuller, Site Director, Battle of Lexington Historic Site, Lexington, Missouri; Margaret Harmon, Cape Girardeau, Missouri; Bryan Howerton,

Searcy, Arkansas; John Livingston, Basalt, Colorado; Charles Machon, Director, Missouri National Guard Museum, Jefferson, Missouri; James R. Mayo, Bloomfield, Missouri; Mark Meatte, Jacksonville, Florida; Kay White Miles, Clinton, Missouri; Alinda M. Miller, President, Friends of Historic Lone Jack, Inc., Lone Jack, Missouri; Bruce Nichols, St. Louis, Missouri; Ray Nichols, Arnold, Missouri; Richard C. Peterson, Memphis, Tennessee; Bob Schmidt, French Village, Missouri; Wayne Schnetzer, Independence, Missouri; Mark and Deborah Schreiber, Jefferson City, Missouri; Joe F. Webb, Gulf Shores, Alabama; J. Dale West, Longview, Texas; Ronald K. Wright, rural South Carolina; and Edward Ziehmer, St. Louis. I thank them all for the help they provided.

The good people at the Missouri State Archives in Jefferson City, Missouri, merit special recognition. During my numerous research visits, Patricia Luebbert and her excellent staff invariably offered a warm welcome and cheerful assistance. They went the extra mile to locate needed documents, suggested sources, and exhibited remarkable patience with an often demanding patron. Likewise, Lynn Morrow, director of the local records program, deserves the gratitude of all for constantly expanding the Civil War holdings at the archives.

Other repositories that answered my numerous requests for documents include the Arkansas History Commission, Little Rock, Arkansas; the Missouri Historical Society, St. Louis, Missouri; the Missouri National Guard Museum, Jefferson City, Missouri; and the State Historical Society of Missouri, Columbia, Missouri.

Finally, my wife Kathy demonstrated remarkable patience while I spent countless hours researching and writing. She cares little for history but understands my love for it, and I appreciate her more than she knows.

While many people obviously helped along the way, I bear the ultimate responsibility for the end result. Any errors or omissions discovered in the pages that follow are mine alone.

INTRODUCTION

Tracing the origins and history of Missouri Confederate military units that served during the American Civil War is nearly as difficult as comprehending the divisive politics that produced them. Deeply torn by the issues that caused the conflict, some Missourians chose sides with enthusiasm, others with reluctance, and a number from sheer necessity, for fence straddling held no sway in the state after the fighting began. Those that sided with the Confederacy, several thousands in number, formed a variety of military organizations, some of which earned reputations for hard fighting exceeded by few other states, north or south. Unfortunately, the records of Missouri's Confederate units have not been adequately preserved, officially or otherwise.

During the period 1861–65, Missouri furnished the Confederacy the equivalent of 20 artillery batteries; 26 regiments, 7 battalions, and 3 squadrons of cavalry; and 12 regiments and 1 battalion of infantry. Missourians organized most of these units outside their state since the Federals overran Missouri in the first year of the war. Some organizations included a number of Arkansans, especially the cavalry units recruited in the late summer of 1864. The batteries, battalions, and regiments seldom consisted entirely of soldiers from the same geographical region of Missouri; indeed, the companies that composed the units often consisted of men from widely separated counties. Most Missouri units thus lacked the geographic homogeneity common to the majority of Confederate outfits.

The Missouri units formed as a result of three discernible recruitment cycles. With the exception of the 1st Missouri Infantry Regiment, which organized in mid-1861, most Missouri units did not muster into the Confederate army until early 1862. These early units soon combined to establish the 1st and 2nd Missouri Brigades. After the battle of Pea Ridge, Arkansas, in early March 1862, these brigades transferred east of the Mississippi River and remained there until most of the men received paroles in 1865 at Jackson, Mississippi. In the summer of 1862, a second wave of recruitment began when numerous recruiters entered Missouri. They collected hundreds of men and organized them into units in northern Arkansas. Those recruits eventually composed Brigadier General Mosby M. Parsons's infantry brigade and the cavalry brigades of Joseph O. Shelby and Colton Greene. These latter units fought primarily in Arkansas and Louisiana, although the cavalrymen occasionally raided deep into Missouri. The last major recruiting effort took place in northeast Arkansas in the summer of 1864 before Major General Sterling Price's raid into Missouri, when both Missourians and Arkansans joined newly formed cavalry outfits; a few thousand more enlisted or were conscripted during the course of Price's disastrous expedition. Soldiers remaining west of the Mississippi River took paroles at Alexandria or Shreveport, Louisiana, or at Jacksonport or Wittsburg, Arkansas, in the spring of 1865; others simply disbanded and went home or to other locales.

The quality and combat experiences of the units in any army tend to vary, and such is also the case with the Missouri units in the Confederate forces. It is difficult to accurately compare the Missouri Confederate units owing to the disparity of existing records. Certainly the batteries, dismounted cavalry, and infantry organizations of the 1st Missouri Brigade fought magnificently in several major campaigns and ranked among the elite Confederate forces; they likewise suffered fearful losses in sustaining their stellar reputation. Fatality rates exceeding 30 percent for most brigade units reflected their valor and devotion to duty. Parsons's Missouri brigade (later increased to a division) enjoyed high marks for its fighting ability as well; its soldiers suffered high casualties in four major battles in the Trans-Mississippi Department. Although the cavalry brigades generally experienced fewer losses in combat than their infantry counterparts, the Missouri troopers executed perilous raids deep into enemy territory that tested men and beasts in the extreme. They also often fought dismounted in several major engagements. Sufficient documentation to determine losses is lacking for some units, particularly those raised in 1864. Obviously, they fought considerably less than their comrades in the earlier-formed organizations.

Missouri's Confederates deserve recognition for the extent of their sacrifice if for no other reason. Exiled from home and family for years, they fought primarily beyond the state's border, where they survived on short rations, lived in primitive camps, often fought with inferior arms, and seldom knew true victory. Missouri blood flowed generously at the great battlefields of Pea Ridge, Prairie Grove, and Helena, Arkansas; Allatoona and Kennesaw Mountain, Georgia; Pleasant Hill, Louisiana; Corinth, Champion Hill, Port Gibson, and Vicksburg, Mississippi; Shiloh and Franklin, Tennessee; Lone Jack, Pilot Knob, and Westport, Missouri; and Mine Creek, Kansas, as well as in numerous lesser battles and a multitude of skirmishes. At least 7,000 Missourians made the ultimate sacrifice for the cause they embraced, and the recorded deaths are very incomplete.

The purpose of this guide is to give the neglected Missouri Confederates their due by providing brief sketches of each regiment, battalion, squadron, and separate company they organized for Confederate service. Units of the Missouri State Guard are not included, for although the Guard often fought in tandem with the Confederates, it nevertheless remained strictly a state organization throughout its existence. The irregular units that fought a bloody guerrilla war in the state are likewise not covered. The guerrilla bands most often did not swear allegiance to the Confederacy and thus hardly qualify as Confederate troops by definition. Besides, much has already been written regarding the guerrilla operations.

This guide is divided into sections for artillery, cavalry, and infantry. In each section are short histories of every unit of that branch of service. Each unit history provides a listing of field officers and company commanders, along with a list of companies for battalions, regiments, and squadrons. The counties of origin of the companies are included in parentheses after the company names if that information could be ascertained. A historical narrative follows the company listing and includes the date and place where the unit was organized; brigade assignments; the battles the unit participated in and the losses suffered in those battles; the date and place of parole, if known; and a recitation of overall numbers and losses during the unit's existence when those numbers could be reliably determined. A short bibliography for further reading regarding the unit follows each historical sketch, and a more general supplemental bibliography completes the study.

My primary guide in determining the units to include in this study was the list contained in *Organization and Status of Missouri Troops, Union and Confederate, in Service during the Civil War,* a 1902 publication of the United States Record and Pension Office. Another useful source in identifying units was the pamphlet *Compiled Service Records of Confederate Soldiers Who Served in Organizations from the State of Missouri,* issued by the National Archives. More obscure units, whose history can be found only in unofficial sources, such as diaries, letters, and memoirs, are included, as well as those units that failed to complete their organization.

I

ARTILLERY

1st Field Battery (Roberts's/Ruffner's)

Captain: Westley F. Roberts, resigned January 6, 1863; Samuel T. Ruffner

This battery organized near Van Buren, Arkansas, about September 7, 1862, under the command of Captain Westley F. Roberts. In October the battery acquired two 12-pounder James rifles captured from the enemy at Lone Jack, Missouri, the previous August, and two bronze 6-pounder smoothbores for its armament. The battery members, largely untrained in artillery matters, had limited time to drill before experiencing their first engagement at Prairie Grove, Arkansas, on December 7. Assigned to Colonel Robert G. Shaver's Arkansas infantry brigade at the battle, the battery initially deployed with the reserve to defend against attacks on the flank or rear. Brigadier General John S. Marmaduke soon summoned the battery forward and placed it with Colonel Joseph O. Shelby's cavalry brigade on a ridge fronting Brigadier General Francis J. Herron's Federal division. Because of the terrain, Roberts deployed only one section of the battery, the James rifles. After enemy artillery fixed the range of the battery's position on the ridge, Lieutenant Samuel T. Ruffner advanced the guns down the incline closer to the Federal position. The section received a punishing fire from the enemy in that position and soon moved back up the ridge. For two hours the section endured heavy shelling from opposing artillery but suffered few casualties. It continued to rain conical shells on the Union line, creating havoc in Battery L, 1st Missouri Artillery, which had two guns disabled. The battle ended as darkness descended on the field, and at midnight the Confederates retreated to Van Buren. The artillerymen wrapped the wheels of the artillery pieces and caissons in blankets to muffle the noise on the retreat. Colonel Shelby praised the battery's battle performance.

Captain Roberts resigned his commission on January 6, 1863, when the battery moved to Little Rock; Lieutenant Ruffner thereafter assumed command. The battery remained in garrison at Little Rock until transported on the steamer *Granite State* to Fort Pleasant, near Pine Bluff, Arkansas, where it arrived on February 22. At Fort Pleasant it guarded the river approach to Little Rock as part of Brigadier General Daniel M. Frost's infantry brigade. In mid-June, the battery accompanied a mixed force led by Colonel John B. Clark Jr. to attack shipping on the Mississippi River. The battery participated in actions on June 22 and 27, doing considerable damage to Federal transports and a tin-clad gunboat before returning to Fort Pleasant.

The battery moved with the brigade to Little Rock in late July to contest a Federal offensive led by Major General Frederick Steele but did not engage the enemy before the capital fell on September 10. Ruffner's Battery helped elements of Shelby's brigade repulse Federal pursuit on the retreat from Little Rock and received honorable mention for that service.

The company temporarily joined Brigadier General John S. Marmaduke's Missouri cavalry division after the fall of Little Rock. It participated in the attack on Pine Bluff, Arkansas, on October 25, serving on the right of the Confederate line, and fought well without casualties. The battery's assignment with the cavalry ended December 2, 1863. When the unit departed Marmaduke's command three days later, it transferred its guns to Captain Joseph Bledsoe's artillery company of Shelby's brigade. Ruffner's men returned to Fort Pleasant and after arrival took charge of four guns of Lieutenant Benjamin Von Phul's artillery company, including two 10-pounder Parrott rifles and two 12-pounder howitzers.

Assigned thereafter to an infantry brigade commanded by Colonel John B. Clark Jr. as part of Brigadier General Mosby M. Parsons's Missouri division, the battery accompanied the division in March 1864 to support General Richard Taylor's army near Pleasant Hill, Louisiana, during the Red River Campaign. The battery remained in reserve when the division entered combat at Pleasant Hill on April 9.

The battery's final engagement occurred at Jenkins's Ferry, Arkansas, on April 30, 1864, the last fight of Major General Frederick Steele's Camden Expedition. One section under Lieutenant John O. Lockhart followed a brigade of Parsons's division onto the field of battle but became separated from the command because of delayed orders and rain-soaked terrain. Suddenly confronted by the enemy in force, and without infantry support, the section deployed and fired a few rounds of canister before being overwhelmed by two Federal regiments. In addition to losing two guns, its horses, and its caissons, the section of 22 men suffered casualties of 4 killed, 6 wounded, and 7 captured. African American troops executed some prisoners in retaliation for the massacre of black troops by Confederate cavalrymen at Poison Spring, Arkansas, on April 18. The captors also took three miniature flags from the guns, apparently of the first national pattern; one bore the inscription "God and Our Native Land." The battery received new guns after the battle at Jenkins's Ferry, which consisted of four 6-pounder smoothbores captured during the Red River Campaign.

Ruffner's Battery spent the remaining months of the war in southern Arkansas and northern Louisiana without further action. Although the unit was invariably known as Roberts's or Ruffner's Battery, Special Order No. 290, Headquarters, Trans-Mississippi Department, dated November 19, 1864, designated it as the 1st Missouri Field Artillery and assigned it to the 5th Artillery Battalion under Major William D. Blocher, although it remained attached to Parsons's division. The men of the battery received paroles at Alexandria, Louisiana, on June 7, 1865. About 170 men served in the battery during the war. Known fatalities include 6 soldiers lost in battle and 4 to disease.

BIBLIOGRAPHY

Edwin E. Harris Correspondence. Gilder Lehrman Institute of American History, New York Historical Society, New York, New York.

Ruffner, S. T. "Sketch of First Missouri Battery, C.S.A." *Confederate Veteran* 12 (1912): 417–20.

Trans-Mississippi Order and Letter Book, Brigadier-General John S. Marmaduke. Transcribed by Carolyn M. Bartels. Independence: Two Trails, 2000.

1st Light Battery (Wade's/Walsh's)

Captain: William Wade, killed April 29, 1863; Richard Walsh

The 1st Light Artillery Battery, recruited from elements of the Missouri State Guard at Osceola and Springfield, Missouri, mustered into Confederate service at the latter place on December 28, 1861, under the command of Captain William Wade. Many soldiers from St. Louis joined the company. The battery became part of the 1st Missouri Confederate Brigade shortly after organization. Artillery pieces assigned to the unit included two 6-pounder bronze smoothbores and four 12-pounder howitzers.

The battery's first combat occurred during the retreat of Major General Sterling Price's army from Springfield, when it engaged pursuing Federals on February 15, 1862, near Flat Creek, Missouri. Wade's Battery fought at Pea Ridge, Arkansas, March 7–8, providing counterbattery fire from near Elkhorn Tavern and supporting several infantry assaults. On the second day of the battle, the battery depleted its ammunition and retreated from the field with the army. Wade's artillerymen suffered casualties of 2 killed, 6 wounded, and 1 missing at Pea Ridge.

As part of Major General Earl Van Dorn's Army of the West, the battery crossed the Mississippi River to Memphis in mid-April and then moved to Corinth, Mississippi, where on May 5 it mustered 107 men. Although present at Farmington on May 9, it did not participate in the fight. Likewise, the battery saw no action at Iuka on September 19, because it could not find a favorable position to deploy. Wade's Battery engaged in heavy fighting at Corinth on October 3, 1862, supporting the 1st Missouri Brigade and dueling with enemy artillery. The next day, it served on the left of the line with Brigadier General Frank Armstrong's cavalry brigade but fired only a few rounds that dispersed enemy cavalry probing the Confederate flank. Wade's Battery suffered casualties of 5 killed, 13 wounded, and 2 missing at Corinth.

In December, Captain Wade became acting chief of artillery for Major General John S. Bowen's division; 1st Lieutenant Richard Walsh took command of the battery. When the 1863 spring campaign opened, the 1st Light Battery, equipped with four 10-pounder Parrotts, occupied Fort Wade at Grand Gulf on the Mississippi River. Artillerymen of the

1st Light Battery, together with Guibor's Missouri Battery, eventually served four large guns at the fortification, including a 100-pounder Blakely rifle, an 8-inch Dahlgren, and two rifled 32-pounders. On March 19, before the heavy ordnance could be emplaced, the cannoneers used their field pieces to shell two Union naval vessels, scoring several hits and inflicting 10 casualties on the enemy crewmen. One of the battery's Parrotts burst while engaging the enemy on March 31, killing 2 and wounding 8 Missourians.

On April 29, seven Federal gunboats attacked Fort Wade and another stronghold dubbed Fort Cobun. Fort Wade suffered severely as the gunboats poured massive amounts of heavy ordnance onto the position. Enemy fire dismounted the two rifled 32-pounders, badly damaged the fort's parapet, and inflicted casualties of 1 killed and 6 wounded on the 1st Light Battery. The rebel artillerymen, though badly outgunned, continued to bombard the Union fleet until the damaged ships withdrew to their anchorage at Hard Times after five hours of intense fighting.

The battery, along with infantry support, guarded Bayou Pierre at the beginning of the battle at Port Gibson to prevent Federal gunboats from ascending the Big Black River. Thus, it did not participate in the May 1 fight, for the army commenced withdrawing before it could deploy. Battery members destroyed a bridge on the anticipated line of the Union advance after Port Gibson fell to the Federal army.

At the battle of Champion Hill, on May 16, the 1st Light Battery deployed near the Champion House, engaged in counterbattery fire, and forced the 17th Ohio Battery to abandon its position. The Missouri artillerymen lost 3 men wounded and 2 missing in the battle. Following the retreat from Champion Hill, the unit occupied a position on the east bank of the Big Black River south of a railroad bridge. The battery deployed its guns but sent the horses across the river per orders. On May 17, Federals broke the Confederate line, causing a rush of troops across the river to escape capture. Personnel of the 1st Light Battery spiked their guns with files, fled to safety over the railroad bridge, and retreated to Vicksburg. Inside the Vicksburg defensive perimeter the cannoneers helped complete fortifications and took charge of a 32-pounder rifled gun.

Walsh's artillerymen often engaged in sniping with rifles. They fired their assigned cannon very little, although constantly exposed to enemy artillery fire. Battery members began digging a tunnel for the purpose of exploding a mine beneath a nearby Federal position in late June, but the garrison surrendered before they completed the tunnel. During the extended siege the 1st Light Battery lost 2 killed and 5 wounded; 52 battery members accepted paroles at the Vicksburg capitulation on July 4. The parolees reported to an exchange camp at Demopolis, Alabama, and learned of their exchange on September 12. Owing to heavy losses in the Missouri units to death and desertion, the battery consolidated with Guibor's and Landis's Missouri batteries on October 3 to form a new organization that was also known as the 1st Missouri Light Artillery, although typically referred to as Guibor's Battery. See the entry for Guibor's Battery for the further service of the men of this unit.

BIBLIOGRAPHY

Martin, John L. "Price's Men." *Daily Missouri Republican,* St. Louis, Missouri, January 1, 1887.

Truman, W. L. "Battle of Elk Horn—Correction." *Confederate Veteran* 12 (1904): 27–28.

———. "Gallant William Wade—His Battery Flag." *Confederate Veteran* 19 (1911): 419.

———. "The Greatest Artillery Duel." *Confederate Veteran* 29 (1921): 328.

———. "The Missouri Brigade at Franklin." *Confederate Veteran* 11 (1903): 273–74.

———. "With the Missouri Artillery." *Confederate Veteran* 31 (1923): 425.

1st Light Battery

This is a designation often applied to the unit formed by the consolidation of the batteries of Captains Henry Guibor, John Landis, and Richard Walsh. It is also a designation sometimes used to describe Captain Hiram M. Bledsoe's artillery company.

2nd Field Battery (Joseph Bledsoe's/Collins's)

Captain: Joseph Bledsoe, resigned December 11, 1863; Richard A. Collins

Undoubtedly the best-known Missouri artillery unit in the Trans-Mississippi Department, this battery formally organized for Confederate service about September 20, 1862, at Camp Coffee near Newtonia, Missouri. The battery included many recruits from the west central counties of the state. Attached to Colonel Joseph O. Shelby's Missouri brigade, and sometimes referred to as a "mountain battery," the unit served as horse artillery throughout its existence. Although initially equipped with two 12-pounder James rifles captured from the enemy at Lone Jack, Missouri, the battery transferred those guns to Roberts's Missouri Battery and received three iron 6-pounder smoothbores as replacements. The battery later transferred one of those guns to another artillery company in late November, leaving Bledsoe's unit with only two pieces.

Bledsoe's Battery experienced initial combat at Newtonia on September 29, when sent forward to help disperse a threatening Union patrol. A battle soon developed (First Newtonia), and the battery spent much of the day exchanging fire with Union artillery, sending shot and shell into the enemy ranks until it depleted its ammunition. It then went into battery behind the Confederate line and endured heavy fire until the Federals withdrew. The mere presence of the battery behind the line discouraged a Union flank attack.

Following the Confederate victory at First Newtonia, Bledsoe's unit next engaged in battle on November 28 near Cane Hill, Arkansas. Initially deployed in a cemetery, the battery then fought in several ambuscades in a running cavalry fight that covered twelve miles. On December 7, the battery participated in the battle of Prairie Grove, Arkansas, where it dueled with enemy artillery and opposed enemy infantry attacks. Bledsoe's Battery deployed at various locations on the field at Prairie Grove, generally on the right of the Confederate line, but heavier Union rifled cannons eventually outgunned the Missourians.

A section of the battery, under 1st Lieutenant Richard A. Collins, accompanied Shelby's brigade on Brigadier General John S. Marmaduke's raid into southwest Missouri in January 1863. It fought at Springfield on January 8 and at Hartville three days later, with light casualties. It earned accolades from both Marmaduke and Shelby for its "distinguished services."

During Marmaduke's raid into southeast Missouri in late April 1863, the battery manned two 6-pounder smoothbores and two 10-pounder Parrotts. It fought at Cape Girardeau on April 26 and at Chalk Bluff on May 1, losing 4 wounded and 6 missing in the engagements. The battery joined the attack on Helena, Arkansas, on July 4, 1863, where broken terrain mandated that the guns be moved into position by hand. Bledsoe's men endured a punishing enemy crossfire for five hours that caused casualties of 1 killed, 6 wounded, and 1 missing. Volunteers dragged the guns from the field under heavy fire rather than abandon them as the battle ended. The battery played a role in the defense of Little Rock, fighting at Brownsville on August 25, at Reed's Bridge on August 27, and on September 10 at Bayou Fourche.

One section of Bledsoe's Battery, commanded by Lieutenant David Harris, accompanied Colonel Shelby's raiding party into western Missouri on October 2. At Neosho the artillerymen placed well-directed shots into the courthouse used by the enemy for a fort that caused a quick Union surrender. During the balance of the raid, the battery played only a minor role, skirmishing with Union forces at Tipton, Boonville, and Salt Fork Creek, until October 13, when the enemy caught up with the raiders near Marshall. In a prolonged fight at that place, the battery fired a shot "every two minutes for four hours," but the Federals described the fire as largely ineffective. When Shelby's troopers eluded the Federals and headed south for Arkansas, the trail on one gun broke and it had to be spiked and abandoned. The Confederates likewise spiked and left the remaining gun near Humansville when the battery horses gave out.

The battery acquired four guns formerly assigned to Ruffner's Missouri Battery in early December; this included the two 12-pounder James rifles captured at Lone Jack, Missouri, previously part of the battery, and two 6-pounder bronze smoothbores. Captain Bledsoe resigned his commission on December 11, 1863; Richard A. Collins replaced him as commander.

The battery next confronted the advance of Major General Frederick Steele's Federal army in Arkansas during the Camden Expedition of 1864. Collins's unit engaged the enemy on April 2 near Okolona and a week later fought an artillery duel for six hours at Prairie D'Ann as Shelby strove to delay Federal progress. The battery lost 2 killed and 3 wounded during these actions. The battery fought little at the battle at Marks's Mill on April 25 but benefited from the fight, for it acquired two James rifles captured by Shelby's men.

Collins's company accompanied Shelby's brigade to northeastern Arkansas in May for operations against the enemy. The cannoneers participated in various actions, the most significant occurring on June 24, when the battery and 400 cavalrymen launched a dawn attack on the tin-clad *Queen City* near Clarendon. The artillery fire damaged the gunboat to the extent that it quickly surrendered. The Confederates then burned the boat. Thereafter, Collins's cannoneers engaged three other gunboats that appeared on the scene until General Shelby ordered a withdrawal. The battery also performed important service at Ashley's Station on August 24, when the rebels overpowered and captured the entire Federal garrison.

Collins's Battery divided into two sections for Major General Sterling Price's Missouri Expedition of 1864, with one section remaining with Shelby's brigade while the other joined Colonel Sidney D. Jackman's brigade of Shelby's division. The section with Shelby's brigade shelled Glasgow from across the Missouri River for two hours on October 15 in support of an attack by troops on the opposite side.

The battery fought hard on October 23 at the battle of Westport, assisting in driving back repeated Federal attacks and dueling with several enemy batteries. During the course of the day, one gun burst and the enemy disabled two others in heavy combat, but the artillerymen saved all except the one that burst. While encamped near Newtonia on October 28, pursuing Federals under Major General James G. Blunt attacked the Confederates (Second Newtonia). Shelby's division, including Collins's artillery, drove the Federals back and kept the enemy at bay until the army could safely withdraw. Collins reported losses of 2 killed and 3 missing during the Missouri raid.

After the Confederates retreated into Arkansas, the battery participated in Major General James F. Fagan's fruitless attack on Fayetteville on November 3. Collins's unit thereafter rejoined Shelby's brigade and proceeded through Indian Territory to Texas. Special Order No. 290, Headquarters, Trans-Mississippi Department, dated November 19, 1864, designated the battery the 2nd Missouri Field Artillery and assigned it to the 2nd Artillery Battalion, commanded by Major Joseph H. Pratt, but it remained attached to Shelby's brigade until the end of hostilities. The Missouri cannoneers of Collins's Battery spent the remainder of the war in Texas and were included in the surrender by General Edmund Kirby Smith on May 26, 1865. Some of the artillerists traveled to Shreveport, Louisiana, and received paroles in early June; others simply went home, while a few accompanied General Shelby into exile in Mexico. At the end of the war the battery possessed two rifled cannons and two 12-pounder howitzers that General Shelby sold to Mexican forces opposed to the monarchy imposed by the French. The battery enrolled some 180 artillery-men during its existence, suffered 22 battle deaths, and lost 5 men to disease.

BIBLIOGRAPHY

Joseph Bledsoe Papers. Barker Texas History Center, University of Texas, Austin, Texas.

"Collins' Battery." In *History of Lafayette County, Missouri*, 373. St. Louis: Missouri Historical Co., 1881.

Crabb, R. W. "Cavalry Fight against Gunboats." *Daily Missouri Republican,* St. Louis, Missouri, July 3, 1886.

Edwards, John Newman. *Shelby and His Men; Or the War in the West.* Waverly: Joseph Shelby Memorial Association, 1993.

Smith, Coleman, "Capture of Gunboat 'Queen City.'" *Confederate Veteran* 22 (1914): 120–21.

Francis Coleman Smith Diary. Francis Coleman Smith Civil War Collection. Fitzgerald Collection. Research Library and Archives, Jackson County Historical Society, Independence, Missouri.

2nd Light Battery "Clark Artillery" (Clark's/King's/Farris's)

Captain: Samuel Churchill Clark, killed March 8, 1862; Houston King, transferred to Trans-Mississippi October 1864; James L. Farris

Recruited at Osceola and Springfield, Missouri, from the Missouri State Guard, the 2nd Light Battery mustered into Confederate service at Springfield on January 16, 1862. Most recruits for this unit had prior serv-ice with Clark's Battery of the 4th Division, Missouri State Guard, which performed distinguished service at the siege of Lexington, Missouri, in

September 1861. Captain Churchill Clark, who left West Point to fight for the South, trained his battery personnel to a very high level of proficiency. At the time of organization, the battery's armament consisted of one iron 6-pounder, one brass 6-pounder and two 12-pounder howitzers.

During the retreat of Major General Sterling Price's army from Springfield in mid-February 1862, the 2nd Light Battery generally served as part of the rear guard, often skirmished with the pursuing Federals, and assisted in checking the enemy at Sugar Creek, Arkansas, on February 17. Clark's Battery supported the 1st Missouri brigade near Elkhorn Tavern on March 7–8 at the battle of Pea Ridge. The last unit fighting when the battle ended, it had two guns disabled during the engagement. A shell decapitated Captain Clark just as the battery abandoned the field to the Federals on March 8. Captain Clark Kennerly temporarily replaced Clark as battery commander.

The unit accompanied the 1st Missouri Brigade to Memphis, Tennessee, in mid-April 1862, and Houston King assumed permanent command of the battery there on April 26 by election. The army moved to Corinth, Mississippi, where in early May the 2nd Light Battery numbered 91 artillerymen present. The battery became part of Brigadier General Martin E. Green's infantry brigade. While stationed at Corinth, the battery typically served on outpost duty. King's unit engaged the enemy at the battle of Iuka on September 19; it did good service and lost 3 wounded during the action. The 2nd Light Battery served with the cavalry during the battle of Corinth, being only slightly engaged on October 3, and then helped cover the retreat the day following.

In January 1863 the battery transferred to Major General Earl Van Dorn's cavalry division. At that time the battery possessed two 3-inch brass rifles and two 12-pounder howitzers. The 2nd Light Battery performed signal service at the battle of Thompson's Station, Tennessee, on March 4, 1863. King's cannoneers repulsed two Federal charges and, in conjunction with another battery, drove the Union artillery from the field. Following the engagement the cannoneers received Van Dorn's compliments for their "heroic courage" and the "admirable manner" in which they handled their guns.

King's Battery mustered 89 artillerymen on June 4. During the summer months the battery often skirmished with the Federals in back-and-forth fighting in the vicinity of Columbia and Franklin, Tennessee. One section of the battery, under Lieutenant Henry S. Johnson, accompanied Colonel Thomas Woodruff's cavalry command to raid shipping on the Cumberland River near Clarksville, Tennessee, resulting in the destruction of transports and the capture of large quantities of supplies.

In July, the battery acquired four 10-pounder Parrotts. King's artillerymen joined General Joseph E. Johnston's army near Jackson, Mississippi, during the Vicksburg Campaign. When Johnston relinquished all hope of relieving embattled Vicksburg, the battery helped cover the Confederate withdrawal. In the fall of 1863, the battery welcomed a remnant of McNally's Arkansas Battery to its ranks, together with a 10-pounder Parrott that belonged to the Arkansans. The battery acquired new weapons in late November, consisting of two 3-inch rifles and two 12-pounder howitzers.

In January 1864 King's artillerymen began service with Brigadier General Sullivan Ross's Texas cavalry brigade. In February and early March, the battery often skirmished with elements of Major General William T. Sherman's Federal army during the Meridian Campaign, with the most serious contacts occurring on February 28 and 29 near Canton, Mississippi. In March, King's cannoneers helped rout the enemy near Yazoo City, Mississippi. The division commander reported, "all praise is due [the cavalry and King's Battery] for the noble defense of the Yazoo country." In May the battery acquired four 3-inch Rifles as replacement armament.

In mid-May the King's company joined General Joseph E. Johnston's Army of Tennessee in opposing Sherman's advance on Atlanta. The 2nd Light Battery engaged the enemy several times as the Confederates gradually fell back before the Federals, particularly at Kingston, Georgia, on May 18 and at Kennesaw Mountain on June 19. During August, the battery helped Ross's cavalry brigade contain a raid by Brigadier General Judson Kilpatrick's cavalry on Confederate supply lines south of Atlanta. After the fall of Atlanta in early September, King's Battery guarded fords along the Chattahoochee River line, often skirmishing with Federal foraging parties.

Captain King left the battery due to a promotion and transfer in October; James L. Farris assumed command of the unit on November 18. The battery skirmished with Federal cavalry raiders at Egypt Station, Mississippi, in late December 1864, which ended the unit's combat career.

Near the end of hostilities the 2nd Light Battery joined Lieutenant General Nathan Bedford Forrest's cavalry corps at Gainesville, Alabama.

General Richard Taylor surrendered the department, including the battery, on May 4. When learning of the Confederate surrender, the men threatened to throw their artillery pieces into the Alabama River. Forrest quelled this near mutiny by surrounding the unit's camp with a guard. About 150 men served in the Clark Artillery during its term of service, and its known losses are 7 battle deaths, 1 murdered, and 6 men lost to disease.

BIBLIOGRAPHY

"Second Missouri Artillery." In *History of Lafayette County, Missouri,* 371–73. St. Louis: Missouri Historical Co., 1881.

Tucker, Phillip Thomas. "Captain Samuel Churchill Clark: The West's Forgotten Battery Commander." *Confederate Veteran* (September–October 1990): 14–20.

Wilson, Joseph A. "Clark's Battery." *Daily Missouri Republican,* St. Louis, Missouri, November 28, 1885.

Winter, William C. "'Amidst Trials and Troubles': Captain Samuel Churchill Clark, C.S.A." *Missouri Historical Review* 92 (October 1997): 1–17.

3rd Field Battery (Also known as the 8th Light Battery) (Gorham's/Tilden's/Lesueur's)

Captain: James C. Gorham, dropped November 10, 1862; Charles B. Tilden, failed election December 18, 1863; Alexander A. Lesueur.

Captain James C. Gorham organized a replacement company for Captain Henry Guibor's battery in the 6th Division, Missouri State Guard, on November 6, 1861, at a camp near Cassville, Missouri. The new unit included nearly two dozen soldiers from Guibor's old battery. At the time of organization the battery manned four Model 1841 6-pounder smoothbores captured at Lexington, Missouri, on September 20. Gorham and his men fought with the 6th Division at Pea Ridge, Arkansas, on March 7–8, 1862, in the engagement near Elkhorn Tavern. During the battle the battery moved forward to support the 1st Missouri Brigade. At one point it advanced too near the enemy lines, and only a valiant cavalry charge by

Captain Rock Champion's cavalry company prevented the battery's capture. The battery had 3 men wounded during the fight.

Following the battle of Pea Ridge, Gorham's unit retreated to Frog Bayou near Van Buren and in mid-April accompanied the Confederate Army of the West to Memphis, Tennessee. The battery stayed at Memphis for a short time and then proceeded to Corinth, Mississippi, on May 2, remaining there during the siege of that place by Major General Henry W. Halleck's army.

The battery counted 43 men on its roll while at Corinth in early May. Members of the battery that elected Confederate service transferred to Guibor's Missouri Battery on June 17 at Baldwyn. Gorham's Battery constituted part of the remnant of the Missouri State Guard that returned to the Trans-Mississippi Department on July 31, 1862, under the command of Brigadier General Mosby Monroe Parsons. The battery, sometimes known as the 8th Light Battery, mustered into Confederate service about September 22, 1862, at Des Arc, Arkansas. It became part of General Parsons's Missouri infantry brigade on November 9 and received an influx of men from the disbanded battery of Captain William B. Foster that same day. The unit's armament consisted of two bronze 6-pounder field guns and two 12-pounder bronze howitzers at that time.

For reasons unknown, Major General Thomas C. Hindman replaced Gorham as battery commander with Charles B. Tilden on November 10. Although deployed in several positions at the battle of Prairie Grove, Arkansas, on December 7, the battery did not engage in the fighting but remained in reserve until the Confederates retreated to Van Buren. The cannoneers used blankets to cover the wheels of the artillery pieces and caissons to muffle the noise of the guns on the retreat. The artillerymen marched toward Little Rock on December 28, where they established winter quarters after their arrival at the capital.

From early January until June 1, 1863, the unit remained in garrison at Little Rock. At Helena, on July 4, 1863, the battery could not be deployed effectively because of unfavorable terrain. Consequently, 32 artillerymen, under command of Lieutenant Alexander A. Lesueur, accompanied Colonel James D. White's Missouri Infantry Regiment (then designated as the 9th Infantry) in the attack on Graveyard Hill to turn captured artillery on the enemy. The Federals disabled their guns before they yielded to Parsons's charging Missourians; the artillerymen thus continued the fight as infantry. Thirteen of the thirty-two volunteers became casualties before the Confederates retreated after nearly five hours of combat. Afterward, the battery encamped for several days at Des Arc on the White River, with one section (Lieutenant Edward Chappell's) taking position at Taylor's Bluff. After leaving Des Arc the cannoneers continued on to Little Rock, where they built and occupied fortifications, until the city fell to the enemy on September 10.

Following the retreat to Arkadelphia, Arkansas, the battery went into winter quarters near Camden and Spring Hill, spending the balance of 1863 in southern Arkansas. On November 26, the artillerymen mutinied and refused to perform duties unless permitted to elect officers to replace those previously appointed. The standoff ended when Major General Sterling Price promised an election, but only after the men ended the mutiny. As a result of an election on December 18, 1863, Alexander A. Lesueur assumed command of the battery.

Lesueur's Battery accompanied Parsons's Missouri infantry division to Louisiana in April 1864 to bolster General Richard Taylor's army during the Red River Campaign. It remained in reserve during the battle at Pleasant Hill on April 9. The battery then returned to southern Arkansas with Parsons's division to pursue Major General Frederick Steele's command after it evacuated Camden and retreated toward Little Rock. Lesueur's Battery briefly engaged the enemy at Jenkins's Ferry on April 30, 1864, until ordered off the field by Brigadier General John S. Marmaduke because of its position in a boggy field.

On September 10, the battery participated in a brief skirmish with Federal cavalry near Monticello, Arkansas, which ended the unit's limited combat experience. For the remainder of the war, the battery occupied different camps in southern Arkansas and northern Louisiana.

Generally known by the name of its commander, on November 19, 1864, the battery became the 3rd Missouri Field Artillery per Special Order No. 290, Headquarters, Trans-Mississippi Department. Some 170 men served in the battery during its existence; about 70 received paroles at Shreveport, Louisiana, on June 8, 1865, and boarded the steamer *E. H. Fairchild* for Missouri. The 3rd Field Artillery suffered 4 battle fatalities during its service, while another 9 artillerists died of disease.

Bibliography

Alexander A. Lesueur Diary. Wilson's Creek National Military Park Collection, Republic, Missouri.

Banasik, Michael E., ed. *Missouri Brothers in Gray: The Reminiscences and Letters of William J. Bull and John P. Bull.* Iowa City: Camp Pope Bookshop, 1998.

William N. Hoskins Diary. Western Historical Manuscript Collection, University of Missouri, Columbia, Missouri.

McNamara, James H. "A Scrap of Civil War History: The March from Cove Creek and the Battle of Pea Ridge." *Daily Missouri Republican,* St. Louis, Missouri, January 19, 1884.

John D. Waller Diary. Wilson's Creek National Military Park Collection, Republic, Missouri.

Young, R. E. "The Battle of Helena." In *Pioneers of High, Water and Main: Reflections of Jefferson City,* by Young. Jefferson City: Twelfth State, 1997. 113–18.

3rd Light Battery "St. Louis Artillery" (MacDonald's/Dawson's/Lowe's)

Captain: Emmett MacDonald, dropped September 10, 1862;
William E. Dawson, died of disease March 26, 1864; Schuyler Lowe

Recruitment for this battery began October 6, 1861, from various units of the Missouri State Guard near Osceola, Missouri. A large contingent of St. Louisans joined the battery, resulting in the unit's informal designation as the "St. Louis Artillery." The battery's initial armament consisted of three 6-pounder smoothbores. It joined McBride's Division (7th Division) of the Guard at Cassville, Missouri, on November 1, 1861, and converted to Confederate service at Springfield, Missouri, on January 28, 1862.

At the battle of Pea Ridge, Arkansas, the unit reported to Brigadier General Daniel M. Frost. Commanded by Captain Emmett MacDonald during the Pea Ridge Campaign, the battery fired seven hundred rounds during two days of fighting near Elkhorn Tavern on March 7–8. It lost at least 2 men killed and an unknown number wounded in the battle, and received compliments for its service from Major General Earl Van Dorn, commander of the Confederate Army of the West. Thereafter, MacDonald's Battery received another 6-pounder captured from the Dubuque (Iowa) Light Artillery at Pea Ridge.

The battery accompanied the army to Memphis, Tennessee, and there joined the army's artillery brigade. The unit mustered 100 men present at Corinth, Mississippi, on May 5. It subsequently became part of Colonel Louis Hebert's infantry brigade, engaged the enemy during Major General Henry W. Halleck's advance on Corinth, and then fought at Farmington, Mississippi, on May 9, 1862.

During most of the summer of 1862, the battery remained inactive while it moved to different camps in northern Mississippi. On September 10, 1862, the battery reorganized when Captain MacDonald failed to return from leave after entering cavalry service in the Trans-Mississippi Department; he later died in Missouri leading a charge in early 1863. William Dawson replaced MacDonald as captain of the battery by election at the reorganization. The 3rd Light Battery deployed at Iuka, Mississippi, on September 19, with Hebert's brigade, and lost 1 man wounded, even though it did not fire a round.

The next action for the unit occurred on October 3–4, when one section became slightly engaged at Corinth, Mississippi, while the other section, in the charge of Lieutenant James Olds, covered the Confederate retreat with Colonel John W. Whitfield's Texas cavalry brigade following the battle. The section under Lieutenant Olds fought hard, and abandoned a gun for want of horses, when the army barely escaped Federal pursuit at Davis Bridge on October 5. Olds and his men received praise for their performance in the fight.

After the close call at Davis Bridge, the battery moved to Holly Springs and remained there until it followed Hebert's brigade to Grenada, and then to the Big Black River Bridge east of Vicksburg. During the Vicksburg Campaign in 1863, the battery initially fought at Champion Hill on May 16. Like most batteries, the St. Louis Artillery lost its guns when the Federals routed the Confederates at Big Black River Bridge the following day. Dawson's cannoneers endured the siege of Vicksburg until the garrison surrendered on July 4. During the forty-seven day ordeal of Vicksburg, the unit lost 2 killed and 1 man to disease, while 64 men received paroles. After reporting to a parole camp at Demopolis, Alabama, the men of the battery were exchanged, and on October 2, 1863, the 3rd Light Battery consolidated with the Jackson Battery and joined Brigadier General John C. Moore's infantry brigade.

Although present at the battle of Missionary Ridge, Tennessee, the consolidated unit had not been rearmed and did not participate in the fight. Following the retreat from Tennessee, the battery reported to Meridian, Mississippi, and then subsequently moved to Mobile, Alabama. Battery personnel performed guard duty in 1864, until the battery acquired four 20-pounder Parrotts in late February.

Sent to the eastern shore of Mobile Bay, Dawson's Battery disabled a Federal gunboat in an engagement and then reported to Major General Dabney H. Maury in Mobile. At Mobile a section of the battery picketed the mouth of the Dog River for several weeks. In late March and early April 1865, a section served gallantly at Spanish Fort. During the fighting around Mobile the battery fired some 700 rounds of ammunition. When the Confederates abandoned Mobile on March 10, the battery boarded trains for Meridian, Mississippi, and remained there for the balance of the war. General Richard Taylor surrendered all troops of the Department of Alabama, Mississippi, and East Louisiana on May 4, 1865, including the 3rd Light Battery. The men received paroles at Meridian on May 10. During its war service the battery lost 11 men in combat, while another 18 died of disease.

Bibliography

3rd Missouri Artillery Records. Research Library and Archives, Jackson County Historical Society, Independence, Missouri.

Moss, James E., ed. "A Missouri Confederate in the Civil War: The Journal of Henry Martyn Cheavens, 1862–1863." *Missouri Historical Review* 57 (October 1962): 16–52.

Strode, E. W. "Heroism in the Third Missouri Battery." *Confederate Veteran* 5 (1897): 26.

———. "Recollections of an Artilleryman." *Confederate Veteran* 2 (1894): 379.

4th Field Battery (Harris's)

Captain: Samuel Stanhope Harris

This battery formed from a likely unauthorized reorganization of the 13th Missouri Light Artillery in early 1864. On February 9, 1864, General Edmund Kirby Smith, commander of the Trans-Mississippi Department, inquired why Harris appeared as battery commander rather than Captain Daniel B. Griswold, commander of the 13th Battery, and by what authority he commanded. Regardless of the explanation Smith received, if any, existing records reveal that Harris continued to command the unit despite irregularities that may have occurred in the battery reorganization or his placement in command. The battery's armament consisted of four 6-pounder smoothbores. It served with Brigadier General John S. Marmaduke's Missouri cavalry brigade as horse artillery and eventually constituted a part of Major Joseph H. Pratt's artillery battalion.

Harris's Battery first saw action during Major General Frederick Steele's advance into southern Arkansas in the spring of 1864 as part of the Red River Campaign. Despite a shortage of horses, it participated in the various skirmishes and engagements of the extended campaign, particularly at Prairie D'Ann on April 10 and at Gallups on April 15. At Poison Spring, April 18, the battery occupied the right flank of Marmaduke's brigade and provided support when the brigade charged dismounted and helped rout the enemy. It accompanied the 8th Missouri Cavalry Regiment in pursuit of Major General Frederick Steele's army after the Federals evacuated Camden and retreated toward Little Rock, as well as when Marmaduke's brigade tried to break the Union line at Guesses Creek near the Saline River on the evening of April 29. The battery played no role during the engagement at Jenkins's Ferry the following day.

Colonel Colton Greene, commanding Marmaduke's brigade, initiated action in southeastern Arkansas against Union naval traffic on the Mississippi River in June 1864; Harris's Battery constituted part of the artillery that damaged or destroyed several Union transports and gunboats. During the battle at Ditch Bayou on June 6, the battery and 10th Missouri Cavalry Regiment guarded nearby Lake Village against any Federal advance from Columbia, Arkansas. The unit, under the command of Lieutenant Thomas J. Williams and armed with only three guns, served with Marmaduke's brigade throughout Major General Sterling Price's Missouri Expedition in the fall of 1864. When Price decided to attack Fort Davidson at Pilot Knob on September 27, the first major engagement of the expedition, artillerymen dragged two guns of Harris's Battery to the top of Shepherd's Mountain southwest of Fort Davidson, firing the opening salvo of that engagement before accurate fire from heavy guns inside the fort silenced the battery.

As the Confederates moved west through Missouri, Harris's company engaged in a skirmish at Union on October 1 and helped check the Federal pursuit at California on October 9. The battery took part in the battle of Glasgow on October 15. It performed conspicuous service by repulsing a Federal assault on Marmaduke's brigade at the crossing of the Little Blue River on October 21. On October 23, the battery fought with the brigade to defend the crossing of the Big Blue River at Byram's Ford from attacks by Major General Alfred Pleasanton's cavalry command. At the battle of Mine Creek, Kansas, on October 25, Harris's Battery deployed north of the creek in the center of the Confederate position. A Federal cavalry charge broke the Confederate line and captured the battery's guns. Additionally, the battery suffered losses of 2 killed, 9 wounded, and 24 taken as prisoners at the Mine Creek debacle.

After the Confederates regrouped in Arkansas following the Missouri expedition, the battery moved to Grand Ecore, Louisiana, to man heavy artillery on the Red River. The battery surrendered and the men received paroles at that point on May 26, 1865. Always known as Harris's Battery in the army, General Edmund Kirby Smith designated it the 4th Missouri Field Artillery in Special Order No. 290, Headquarters, Trans-Mississippi Department, on November 19, 1864. The battery, doubtless infused with recruits following the Price Raid, mustered 136 artillerymen at the time of parole, primarily men recruited in southeast Missouri. The battery's known losses included 3 killed or mortally wounded in battle and 9 deaths by disease.

BIBLIOGRAPHY

Coker, J. A. "The Battle of Pilot Knob." Unpublished typescript. Thomas Ewing Family Papers, Library of Congress, Washington, D.C.

Conrad, Howard E. "Samuel Stanhope Harris." In *Encyclopedia of the History of Missouri,* vol. 3, 189–90. St. Louis: Southern History Co., 1901. 189–90.

Cole, Birdie Haile. "The Battle of Pilot Knob." *Confederate Veteran* 22 (1914): 417.

John S. Marmaduke Correspondence. National Archives, Washington, D.C.

4th Light Battery

A designation sometimes used for the 7th Light Battery. See the entry for that battery.

7th Light Battery "Jackson Battery" (Lucas's/Lowe's)

Captain: William Lucas, dropped September 19, 1862; Schuyler Lowe

The "Jackson Battery" originated as a unit in the 8th Division, Missouri State Guard, and took its name from Jackson County, Missouri, the locale of the company's initial recruitment and organization for state service. At the siege of Lexington in September 1861, the battery possessed only one gun but still fired some 200 rounds. The battery, under the command of Captain William Lucas, then retreated with the state army to southwest Missouri. At Cassville it received an additional piece, type unknown. Many battery members mustered into Confederate service at Springfield on January 1, 1862, at which time the unit acquired two additional guns, probably 6-pounder smoothbores.

After the army abandoned Springfield on February 12, the Jackson Battery fought in some skirmishes during the retreat to Cove Creek, Arkansas. About 80 recruits enlisted at Cove Creek, and the battery organized for Confederate service and elected officers there on February 27. On March 7–8 the battery, armed with four 6-pounder smoothbores, engaged in the battle of Pea Ridge, fighting near Elkhorn Tavern. During the battle the unit expended approximately 760 rounds and nearly exhausted its ammunition. Following the defeat at Pea Ridge, the unit became part of the artillery brigade commanded by Brigadier General Daniel M. Frost and moved with the Army of the West to Des Arc, Arkansas, for transport east of the Mississippi River. It arrived at Memphis, Tennessee, aboard the *Ferd. Kennett* on April 12, 1862, and went into camp at Fort Pickering south of the city. In late April the battery moved to Corinth, Mississippi, where it mustered 70 artillerymen present and then held different assignments at various locations in Mississippi.

On September 19, 1862, the battery reorganized by order of acting Brigadier General William L. Cabell, and Schuyler Lowe became battery commander. The Jackson Battery engaged in the battle of Iuka on September 19. It also participated in the battle of Corinth on October 3–4 but did little firing. Following the action at Corinth, Lowe's cannoneers retreated with the army to Oxford, Mississippi. The battery changed locations and assignments several times over the next few months, spending a great deal of time encamped near Grenada and Jackson. On January 20, 1863, the Jackson Battery performed outpost duty on the Big Black River east of Vicksburg. There it remained until early May, when the unit divided, with one section reporting to Brigadier General Francis M. Cockrell of the 1st Missouri Brigade, while the other stayed at a bridge over Big Black River. The sections united on May 12 in time to take part in the battle of Champion Hill four days later, where it fired some 600 rounds and suffered 4 wounded.

Assuming a defensive position on the east bank of the Big Black River following Champion Hill, on May 17, the battery lost 6 men as prisoners, and two 10-pounder Parrott rifles and two 12-pounder howitzers, when Federal troops shattered the Confederate line. Members of the battery then retreated into the fortifications at Vicksburg. Once inside the Vicksburg defenses, Lowe's artillerymen manned one 20-pounder Parrott, called "Crazy Jane" by the men; one 10-pounder Parrott; and one 6-pounder smoothbore. During the entirety of the forty-seven-day siege the battery fired approximately 2,500 rounds of ammunition. Additionally, twenty of Lowe's men, acting as grenadiers, hurled some 1,000 grenades at the enemy; others served as sharpshooters. The battery lost 4 killed, 2 wounded, and 1 to disease before the garrison's capitulation on July 4. Major General John S. Bowen, division commander, complimented the battery for its conduct during the siege.

After the Confederate bastion's surrender, some 62 members of the battery took paroles, while 10 sick and wounded returned to the company after being exchanged. The command reported to parole camp at Demopolis, Alabama. Declared exchanged on September 12, 1863, the Jackson Battery consolidated with the St. Louis Battery on October 2 by order of Lieutenant General William J. Hardee. The batteries served together for the balance of the war, generally as Dawson's Missouri Battery, after the commander of the St. Louis Battery, although Captain Lowe commanded it for an extended period of time. See the entry for the 3rd Light Battery for the remaining service of the Jackson Battery.

BIBLIOGRAPHY

"The Jackson Battery." *Blue and Grey Chronicle* 1 (August 1997): 6; 1 (January 1998): 2.

Moore, John C. "Captain Schuyler Lowe." In *Missouri,* by Moore, vol. 12 of *Confederate Military History,* ed. Clement A. Evans. Wilmington: Broadfoot.

Moss, James E., ed. "A Missouri Confederate in the Civil War: The Journal of Henry Martyn Cheavens, 1862–1863." *Missouri Historical Review* 57 (October 1962): 16–52.

8th Light Battery

An alternative designation for the 3rd Field Battery. See the entry for that battery.

10th Light Battery (Rice's/Barrett's)

Captain: D. A. Rice, no service after battery organization on April 1, 1862; Overton W. Barrett

This battery mustered into Confederate service on April 1, 1862, at Memphis, Tennessee. Initially organized without cannons, the company transferred to Corinth, Mississippi, and acquired two 6-pounder smoothbores and two 12-pounder howitzers on May 19. While present during the siege of Corinth, the battery did not engage the enemy. Several soldiers of a disbanded Louisiana unit, the Orleans Guard Battery, joined the battery on July 21. Attached to Colonel Samuel Powell's infantry brigade, Army of the Mississippi, Barrett's Battery first experienced combat at the battle of Perryville, Kentucky on October 8. The Missourians deployed on the left of the Confederate line there and dueled with Federal batteries during Powell's assault on the enemy. When the attack failed, Barrett's Battery withdrew with the infantry without reported casualties.

After the Confederates retreated from Perryville, Barrett's company moved about Tennessee until the end of December when it engaged in the battle of Stone's River. In that conflict the battery occupied a position in the center of the line in support of Brigadier General Edward C. Walthall's infantry brigade and lost 4 men wounded. The Louisianans of the Orleans Guard Battery left the battery on July 11, 1863, when their unit reorganized. Until the end of August, Barrett's cannoneers garrisoned in Chattanooga and then fell back into Georgia.

During the army's advance to Chickamauga, Georgia, the battery helped repulse an enemy cavalry charge near Lafayette on September 7.

The Missourians saw little combat as part of the reserve artillery of the Army of Tennessee in the battle at Chickamauga on September 19–20. The remnant of Captain Hermann H. Sengstak's Alabama battery, survivors of the Vicksburg Campaign, joined Barrett's company after being exchanged in the fall. The battery next fought at Missionary Ridge during the battle at Chattanooga. Barrett's men manned their guns all day on November 24 and 25, fighting hard on the Confederate right flank with Brigadier General Preston Smith's brigade, then on the left of Major General Patrick R. Cleburne's division, and finally on the right center of the line. The battery abandoned a caisson on the field because of a broken wheel. During the Confederate's retreat from Missionary Ridge, Barrett's company composed part of the rear guard placed at Ringgold Gap, Georgia, to counter Federal pursuit. General Cleburne credited a section of the battery commanded by Lieutenant William Brown with delaying the enemy pursuit, thereby permitting his division to escape to safety.

The battery, armed with four 12-pounder howitzers, fought with the Army of Tennessee in the various engagements of the Atlanta Campaign as part of Major James P. Waddell's battalion of the artillery reserve. By October 31, 1864, the battery possessed only two guns. One had burst during the Atlanta fighting, and another had been condemned. The final fight of the battery occurred at Columbus, Georgia, on April 16, 1865, sometimes described as the last battle east of the Mississippi River. Major General James H. Wilson's Federal cavalry corps completely over-whelmed the 3,000 Confederate defenders, capturing most members of Barrett's Battery, its guns, and unit flag, and the battery ceased to exist. Some 200 men served in the 10th Light Battery during the course of the war, and known casualties, doubtless very incomplete, totaled 2 killed in action and 6 deaths by disease. This unit's flag is held in the collections of the Missouri State Museum, Jefferson City, Missouri.

BIBLIOGRAPHY

Confederate Organizations, Officers and Posts, 1861–1865, Missouri Units. Springfield: Ozarks Genealogical Society, 1988.

"Lieut. Isaac Lightner: Member of the Tenth Missouri Battery, C.S.A." *Confederate Veteran* 4 (1896): 252.

13th Light Battery (Griswold's)

Captain: Daniel B. Griswold

Little is known of this battery, but the evidence suggests that it originated from men recruited in southeast Missouri. The type of weapons initially assigned to the battery has not been determined, although it eventually possessed both howitzers and rifled pieces. One section of the battery, in conjunction with Lieutenant Colonel Merritt L. Young's cavalry battalion, engaged the enemy on June 11, 1863, near Seaborn's Bridge in St. Francis County, Arkansas. On June 17, Captain Griswold received orders to station his battery at Chalk Bluff, Arkansas, and to report to Brigadier General John S. Marmaduke. In July and August, the battery served with Lieutenant Colonel Solomon G. Kitchen's Missouri cavalry battalion on outpost duty in northeast Arkansas.

The 13th Battery subsequently disappears from the records until October 25, 1863, when the unit, as part of Marmaduke's cavalry brigade, deployed on the left of the Confederate line in the attack on the Federal garrison at Pine Bluff. The battery fired for over an hour with little effect and lost 1 killed and an unknown number wounded. The headquarters of the Trans-Mississippi Department inquired about the battery's status, organization, and strength on November 23, 1863, indicating a desire to present the unit with a battery of guns. The intent must have been to offer a replacement battery, for at the time, Griswold's company already manned two 12-pounder mountain howitzers and two rifled pieces.

In early 1864, under clouded circumstances, the battery reorganized as Captain Samuel Stanhope Harris's Battery (4th Field Artillery). About 115 men served in the battery during its short existence, with known losses of 1 killed in action, 1 hanged for desertion, and 3 deaths from disease.

Bibliography

Confederate Organizations, Officers and Posts, 1861–1865, Missouri Units. Springfield: Ozarks Genealogical Society, 1988.

Trans-Mississippi Order and Letter Book, Brigadier General John S. Marmaduke. Transcribed by Carolyn M. Bartels. Independence: Two Trails, 2000.

Bledsoe's Battery (Also known as 1st Light Battery) (Hiram Bledsoe's)

Captain: Hiram Miller Bledsoe

This battery originated as the "Lexington Light Artillery," a unit of the 8th Division, Missouri State Guard. Bledsoe recruited the battery, one of the most storied outfits of the Guard, in Lafayette County in May 1861. The unit served at the skirmish at Rock Creek, Jackson County, on June 13. The battery formally mustered into state service on June 16 at Lexington.

The company's initial armament consisted of one 6-pounder smoothbore manufactured at the Morrison Foundry in Lexington and a 9-pounder smoothbore known as "Old Sacramento" that had been captured in the Mexican War. This latter piece, eventually converted into a 12-pounder, had a distinctive and recognizable ringing sound when discharged. At some point the battery absorbed the "Independence Light Artillery," adding one 6-pounder Model 1841 field gun, called the "Black Bitch" by Bledsoe's cannoneers, that had been seized at the United States arsenal at Liberty before the outbreak of hostilities. Bledsoe's unit subsequently saw heavy action at Carthage and Wilson's Creek. A 6-pounder Model 1841 field gun captured from Colonel Franz Sigel's Union command at Wilson's Creek completed the battery's artillery complement.

The battery subsequently saw combat at Dry Wood, the siege of Lexington, and finally at Pea Ridge, Arkansas. Bledsoe's Battery, commanded by Lieutenant Charles W. Higgins, deployed near Elkhorn Tavern on March 7–8, 1862, providing counterbattery fire and infantry support, losing 4 men wounded in two days of conflict.

Some weeks following the Pea Ridge defeat, Bledsoe and his men crossed the Mississippi River to Memphis with the Army of the West. The battery transferred to Confederate service about April 21 at Memphis, at which time the artillerymen of Captain Francis M. Tull's Missouri State Guard battery joined the company. On May 5, the battery mustered at Corinth, Mississippi, with merely 53 soldiers present for duty. The battery composed part of an ambush on September 20 that blunted Federal pursuit following the Confederate retreat from Iuka. The battery served with Brigadier General John C. Moore's infantry brigade, Brigadier General

Dabney H. Maury's division, at the battle of Corinth on October 3–4, where it lost 1 wounded and 1 missing.

A section of the battery skirmished with Federal troops at Thomas's Plantation, Mississippi, on April 7, 1863. The battery then became part of Brigadier General John Gregg's infantry brigade and briefly served at Port Hudson, Louisiana. Bledsoe's Battery, the only Confederate artillery on the field, supported Gregg's brigade at Raymond on May 12 and lost an iron piece that burst from heavy firing. Two days later, as part of General Joseph E. Johnston's Army of Relief, the battery participated in the battle of Jackson but saw only light action.

The battery next fought at Chickamauga, again in support of Gregg's brigade. Armed with two 3-inch ordnance rifled guns and two 12-pounder howitzers, it fired 125 rounds on September 19, silencing a Federal battery and receiving compliments for its "very efficient and important service throughout the day." The battery suffered known losses of 1 killed and 1 wounded in the battle, leaving 4 officers and 67 men available for duty. On November 4, 1863, the battery received four new 12-pounder Napoleon guns. It engaged in considerable combat during the siege of Chattanooga, losing its guns at the Missionary Ridge disaster on November 25, along with 2 soldiers killed and an unknown number wounded. Bledsoe's artillerymen, rearmed with four Napoleons, fought throughout the Atlanta Campaign of 1864, experiencing hard fighting at Resaca during May 13–16 and at Kennesaw Mountain on June 27. Bledsoe's company suffered casualties of 4 killed, 24 wounded, and 1 missing during the extended campaign (May–September).

The battery accompanied General John Bell Hood's army into Tennessee in the fall of 1864. The Missourians took part in the Confederate debacle in front of Nashville and served in the rear guard as the army reeled in retreat. At Franklin, Tennessee, on December 16, Bledsoe's cannoneers checked Major General James H. Wilson's cavalry command by firing their guns down Front Street and permitted the escape of Brigadier General Randall Gibson's Louisiana brigade from imminent capture. The battery suffered losses of 1 wounded and 3 missing during the retreat from Nashville.

Bledsoe's Battery did not accompany the Army of Tennessee to North Carolina but finished the war in Georgia. Most battery members surrendered at Augusta, Georgia, on May 1, 1865, and received paroles at Nashville two weeks later. During the war Bledsoe's Battery had an enrollment of some 150 men. Known losses are 8 killed or mortally wounded in battle, 2 killed by accident, and 5 men lost to disease.

BIBLIOGRAPHY

Barnett, Hayward. "Hiram Bledsoe Gained Fame with Gun Taken from Mexicans." *The Artilleryman* 8 (Spring 1987): 19–21.

"Bledsoe's Battery." In *History of Lafayette County, Missouri,* 368–71. St. Louis: Missouri Historical Co., 1881.

Eakin, Joanne Chiles. *Our Far Away Boys: The Civil War Letters of the Emily Steele Family.* Independence: Two Trails, 2004.

Everman, W. A. "Bledsoe's Battery." *Confederate Veteran* 28 (1920): 140.

Humphrey, Lorraine A. "Hiram Bledsoe's Hard-Fighting Missouri Battery Stood by Its Guns from Wilson's Creek to Nashville." *America's Civil War* (July 1997): 18, 22, 24.

"Lieutenant Wheatly of Bledsoe's Battery." *Confederate Veteran* 28 (1920): 246–47.

Matson, W. H., "Bledsoe's Battery." *Confederate Veteran* 28 (1920): 292.

Ritter, Capt. William L., "Sergeant Ball and the Yankee Boots," *Confederate Veteran* 28 (1920): 331.

Wilson, Joseph A. "Bledsoe of Missouri," *Confederate Veteran* 7 (1899): 462–63.

Bowman's/Parsons's Battery

Captain: Benjamin Lee Bowman, resigned June 9, 1862; John Denard Parsons

Benjamin L. Bowman recruited and organized this battery at New Madrid, Missouri, on January 22, 1862, from men who had served in the 1st Division, Missouri State Guard. Part of the unit engaged the Federals in a skirmish near Sikeston, Missouri, on February 28, losing 1 man seriously wounded. Bowman's men crossed the Mississippi River with Brigadier General M. Jeff Thompson's Confederate recruit command in April 1862 and moved to Fort Pillow, Tennessee. On April 28, the company transferred its artillery pieces to Colonel Meriwether L. Clark, commander of the artillery brigade of the Army of the West. Thereafter, the men performed infantry service despite the battery designation.

During the assignment at Fort Pillow, the Missourians performed service as "marines" aboard the Confederate River Defense Fleet. The company divided into three detachments for assignment to the *General Sterling Price,* the *General Beauregard,* and the *Colonel Lovell.* The detachments saw action at Plum Point Bend (Plum Run Bend) on May 10, 1862, where the Confederate fleet engaged a Federal flotilla with some success.

A dispute, subject matter unknown, arose between the Missourians and the Confederate naval personnel of the River Defense Fleet at Fort Pillow. Consequently, General Thompson requested that his companies be transferred to either Major General Earl Van Dorn or Major General Sterling Price for assignment to a regiment. On June 9, the company refused to obey Captain Bowman, whom they considered inefficient; the captain resigned his commission the same day. Lieutenant John Denard Parsons succeeded Bowman by election.

The company left Fort Pillow for Grenada, Mississippi, on June 27 and subsequently guarded a railroad at Cole's Station. On July 2, Parsons's unit became a company of Hedgpeth's Missouri Infantry Battalion, which soon merged with Major George H. Forney's 1st Confederate Battalion to form a temporary regiment. The unit thereafter left that organization and on August 28 joined the newly organized 6th Missouri Infantry Regiment as Company I and served the balance of the war in that capacity. When the company joined the 6th Infantry it numbered 54 soldiers, rank and file. See the entry for the 6th Missouri Infantry Regiment for the further service of the men of this unit.

Bibliography

General M. Jeff Thompson's Letter Book, July 1861—June 1862. Transcribed by James E. McGhee. Independence: Two Trails, 2004.

Nichols, Ray. "Conflict of Emotions: The Civil War Times of Benjamin L. Bowman." Unpublished typescript.

Stanton, Donal J., Goodwin F. Berquist, and Paul C. Bowers, eds. *The Civil War Reminiscences of General M. Jeff Thompson.* Dayton: Morningside Press, 1988.

Foster's Battery

Captain: William B. Foster

This unit appears to be a reorganization of Captain James Kneisley's Battery (Palmyra Light Artillery) of the 2nd Division, Missouri State Guard, following that company's brief service east of the Mississippi River. The battery reorganized for state service in Monroe County, Arkansas, on August 31, 1862, and mustered into the Guard with 66 men on the rolls the following day. Despite the objections of some soldiers, the battery transferred to Confederate service about September 18 at the same locale. The armament of the battery is unknown, although on November 9, orders transferred the "extra" howitzer of the unit to Captain Westley F. Roberts's Missouri battery. Also on November 9, Major General Thomas C. Hindman ordered the battery consolidated with Captain James C. Gorham's artillery company. Pursuant to that order, the battery disbanded on November 10 at Camp Mulberry in Franklin County, Arkansas. In addition to those that transferred to Gorham's Battery, several of Foster's men joined the newly formed 9th Missouri Sharpshooter Battalion (Pindall's). Foster's Battery engaged in no known combat during the company's brief existence as a Confederate unit. See the 3rd Missouri Field Artillery and the 9th Missouri Sharpshooter Battalion (Pindall's) for the further service of the men of this company.

Bibliography

William N. Hoskins Diary. Western Historical Manuscript Collection, University of Missouri, Columbia, Missouri.

Guibor's Battery (Also known as the 1st Light Battery)

Captain: Henry Guibor

Doubtless the most noted of all Missouri Confederate artillery units, this battery had strong roots in the prewar Missouri Volunteer Militia, as well as the Missouri State Guard. Captain Henry Guibor organized a battery for service in the 6th Division, Missouri State Guard, in June 1861, which did stellar service at Carthage, Wilson's Creek, Dry Wood, and Lexington.

Guibor resigned his commission in late October 1861 and proceeded to Memphis, Tennessee, where he recruited elements of a provisional battery for the Guard from among the parolees of the Camp Jackson affair of May 10, 1861. Guibor acquired six guns, a mix of 6-pounder smoothbores and 12-pounder howitzers, and moved his recruits to Jacksonport, Arkansas, with other troops commanded by Brigadier General Daniel M. Frost. Guibor drilled his men at Jacksonport for six weeks and then marched to Springfield, Missouri, arriving there on February 11, 1862. The following day the Missouri army, pressed by advancing Union troops, moved south to form a juncture with Confederate forces near Cove Creek, Arkansas. During the retreat, Guibor's Battery participated in a skirmish with the enemy at Crane Creek on February 14.

At the battle of Pea Ridge on March 7–8, Guibor's unit became heavily engaged near Elkhorn Tavern, although it employed only four of its pieces owing to a shortage of crews. On the first day of the battle, Guibor's cannoneers succeeded in driving Welfley's Missouri Battery (Union) from the field with loss; the next day they assisted in delaying the final Federal advance long enough to permit the army to withdraw relatively unmolested. The battery retreated to Frog Bayou near Van Buren, Arkansas, having lost 2 men killed and an unknown number wounded in the fight.

At Frog Bayou the battery mustered into Confederate service on March 25 and shortly thereafter accompanied the Army of the West to Memphis, Tennessee. After a short stay in Memphis, the battery transferred to Corinth, Mississippi, where it mustered 69 men on May 5, and then moved on to Baldwyn when the Confederates abandoned Corinth. On June 17, members of the Missouri State Guard still attached to the battery left, and in turn, Confederate volunteers of Captain James C. Gorham's State Guard battery joined Guibor. Also, on June 30, while stationed at Priceville, Gibson's Louisiana Battery (Miles Artillery) consolidated into Guibor's Battery. The battery deployed at Iuka on September 19 but never discharged its guns. Guibor's men fought hard at the battle of Corinth on October 3–4, supporting the 1st Missouri Brigade, and suffered casualties of 5 wounded. The battery received favorable comment for its service at the battle.

When spring arrived in 1863, Guibor's unit, armed with four 6-pounder smoothbores, held a position at Grand Gulf on the Mississippi River and engaged Federal gunboats on March 19 and 31. On the latter date, while manning pieces in the lower battery, called Fort Wade, a 20-pounder Parrott burst, killing two of Guibor's men and wounding two others, including Guibor. In early April, a section of the battery in the charge of Lieutenant William C. Corkery joined a reconnaissance force sent to Louisiana. The battery engaged the enemy at James's Plantation on April 8 but apparently fought no more before returning to Grand Gulf on April 17.

A long, fierce battle with the gunboats occurred again at Grand Gulf on April 29, which resulted in the gunboats withdrawing after repeated hits from the Confederate gunners. At Port Gibson, on May 1, Guibor's cannoneers arrived on the field in time to help cover the Confederate withdrawal. The battery won praise at Champion Hill on May 16 for preventing the 1st Missouri Brigade from being flanked in the most pivotal battle of the Vicksburg Campaign. When the Federals broke the defensive line at the Big Black River on May 17, the artillerymen of Guibor's Battery offered some resistance before abandoning their pieces and retreating into Vicksburg. During the Vicksburg siege Guibor's unit manned heavy ordnance pieces. It helped repel the Federal offensives of May 19 and 22, inflicting heavy casualties on the Federal attackers. The prolonged siege cost the battery 1 killed and 4 wounded. At the surrender of Vicksburg on July 4, about 53 members of Guibor's Battery received paroles and then reported to the exchange camp established at Demopolis, Alabama.

On October 3, the unit permanently consolidated with Landis's and Wade's batteries under the designation of the 1st Missouri Light Artillery, although it continued to be known as Guibor's Battery. The battery acquired new guns on October 27, consisting of four 12-pounder Napoleons. In the spring of 1864, Guibor's Battery, about 110 in number, and a part of Major George W. Storrs's artillery battalion, began an extended period of combat as Major General William T. Sherman initiated the Atlanta Campaign. The battery fought at New Hope Church, Lost Mountain, and Latimer House, losing in the latter engagement 4 killed and 12 wounded. At Kennesaw Mountain, artillerymen dragged the battery's guns uphill 400 feet to the top of Little Kennesaw and rained down shot and shell on the nearby Federal troops. In an attempt to silence Guibor's guns, the enemy massed its artillery and tremendous exchanges of fire followed, but the battery remained a serious threat to Federal movements.

On June 27, the battery played an important role in defeating Sherman's assault on Kennesaw, inflicting many casualties on the enemy, especially punishing the Federals on Pigeon Hill. When the Confederate commander General Joseph E. Johnston moved to the outskirts of Atlanta, the Federals began a siege operation. Guibor's cannoneers endured another two months of combat before the key city fell on September 2. The entire Atlanta Campaign (May–September) exacted a heavy toll on the battery, with total losses of 12 killed and 39 wounded, the latter including Captain Guibor, disabling him for further service. Lieutenant Aaron W. Harris, formerly of the Landis Battery, assumed command of the company.

The battery accompanied the army when General John Bell Hood invaded Tennessee. On November 30, the men of Guibor's artillery participated in the battle at Franklin. One of only two Confederate batteries present on the field, the Missouri unit divided into three sections for the fight. The first fire of the Missourians signaled the advance of General Alexander P. Stewart's corps, which included the 1st Missouri Brigade. After firing a few rounds, Guibor's guns fell silent as the infantry moved toward the enemy's strong position. A section of the battery advanced behind the infantry, the cannoneers eventually pulling the guns by hand after enemy fire killed all of the battery horses. At least part of the battery moved close to the Federal front line and remained there until the slaughter mercifully ended. Surprisingly, the unit lost only 1 killed and 1 wounded in the horrific combat that day.

The battery advanced with the army to Nashville but never engaged in combat there. The unit left Nashville on December 6 and participated in the action at Murfreesboro the day following. Guibor's Battery retreated with the army to Columbus, Mississippi, and stayed there several months. The battery eventually moved to North Carolina and remained there until General Joseph E. Johnston's surrender on April 26, 1865. Most of the men received paroles at Greensboro on May 2. Guibor's Battery had about 160 men on its rolls during three years of service. The unit suffered 18 battle deaths, while 6 men died of disease. A flag of this battery is located at the Museum of the Confederacy, Richmond, Virginia.

BIBLIOGRAPHY

Barlow, W. P. "Guibor's Battery as Heavy Artillery." *Daily Missouri Republican,* St. Louis, Missouri, July 17, 1886.

"Guibor's Battery in Georgia." *Kennesaw Gazette,* Kennesaw, Georgia, May 15, 1889.

Lehr, Suzanne Staker, ed. *As the Mockingbird Sang: The Diary of Private Robert Caldwell Dunlap.* St. Joseph: Platte Purchase, 2005.

——, ed. *Fishing on Deep River: Civil War Memoir of Private Samuel Baldwin Dunlap, C.S.A.* St. Joseph: Platte Purchase, 2006.

McMahon, Michael. "Guibor's Battle Flag." *Daily Missouri Republican,* St. Louis, Missouri, July 3, 1886.

Storrs, George. "The Artillery on Kennesaw." *Kennesaw Gazette,* Kennesaw, Georgia, June 15, 1889.

"The Story of Guibor's Battery, C.S.A." *St. Louis Republic,* St. Louis, Missouri, April 21, 1895.

Tucker, Phillip Thomas. "Cannons on Little Kennesaw: The Role of the First Missouri Confederate Artillery Battery." *Atlanta History* 33 (Summer 1989): 36–45.

——. "The Roar of Western Guns: Captain Henry Guibor's First Missouri Light Artillery, C.S.A." *Confederate Veteran* (May–June 1989): 24–33.

Wilson, Hunt P. "The Battle of Elkhorn." *Daily Missouri Republican,* St. Louis, Missouri , July 4 and 11, 1885.

——. "Guibor's Battery at Corinth." *Daily Missouri Republican,* St. Louis, Missouri, June 19, 1886.

Hamilton's Battery "Prairie Gun Battery"

Commander: 1st Lieutenant James L. Hamilton, disposition not of record; 1st Lieutenant Charles O. Bell, killed August 27, 1863; 2nd Lieutenant Thomas J. Williams

This rather short-lived unit, commonly known as the "Prairie Gun Battery," organized for service with the cavalry on April 12, 1863, and almost immediately became part of Brigadier General John S. Marmaduke's cavalry brigade. The battery's armament consisted of only three pieces, sometimes referred to as the "Little Teasers." While the type of weapons the unit possessed is not definitely known, it appears the battery manned two Model 1838 bronze 6-pounder smoothbores and a 4-pounder smoothbore.

On June 11, a section of the battery briefly skirmished with Federal scouts at Taylor's Creek, Arkansas. Thereafter, on June 17, the battery moved with a detachment under Lieutenant Colonel Leonidas C. Campbell, 3rd Missouri Cavalry Regiment, to attack Federal shipping from the west bank of the Mississippi River fifteen miles north of Memphis.

Soon, the heavily laden *Platte Valley* came into view. The battery opened fire when the boat drew abreast of its position and scored three hits that killed three crewmen and wounded several others before it steamed out of range. On June 18, the battery directed fire on the supply steamer *Ruth*. As soon as the attack began, the *Ruth* made way to the Tennessee shore, out of range of the Missourians' small guns. Campbell withdrew his force after being attacked by a Federal gunboat, considering the battery's small pieces largely ineffective against river traffic.

While present at the battle of Helena on July 4, the battery never fired its guns. The battery next saw combat at Brownsville, Arkansas, on August 25, 1863, as Brigadier General John S. Marmaduke's cavalry division sought to delay a Federal advance on Little Rock. During these operations Lieutenant Charles O. Bell commanded the battery. The affair at Brownsville consisted of prolonged skirmishing as the Confederates retreated before a numerically superior enemy. The battery engaged the enemy that day with only one gun, generally deployed on the right of the Confederate line. The Confederates made a stand on August 27 at Reed's Bridge across Bayou Metoe. The Federals made a determined effort to breach the rebel line, but the Confederates drove them back with considerable loss. The Prairie Gun Battery reportedly outdueled the Federal artillery during the attack, "driving it from every position by well-aimed shots." Lieutenant Bell and one private died during the exchange with the Federal batteries. Following Bell's death, battery command passed to Lieutenant Thomas J. Williams.

Present at the battle of Bayou Fourche near Little Rock on September 10, the battery did not become closely engaged. It received credit for helping delay the enemy advance into Little Rock while the Confederates evacuated the capital later that day. The Prairie Gun Battery disappears from the records after the fall of Little Rock. It may have been disbanded or possibly incorporated into the 13th Battery (Griswold's), but its fate is uncertain. No muster rolls of the Prairie Gun Battery have been found.

BIBLIOGRAPHY

Burford, Timothy Wayne, and Stephanie Gail McBride. *The Division: Defending Little Rock, Aug 25—Sept 10, 1863.* Jacksonville: WireStorm Publications, 1999.

Trans-Mississippi Order and Letter Book, Brigadier General John S. Marmaduke. Transcribed by Carolyn M. Bartels. Independence: Two Trails, 2000.

Harris's Battery

Captain: Samuel Stanhope Harris

Most volunteers for this company had served in the "McDowell Battery," 1st Division, Missouri State Guard, commanded by Captain Samuel S. Harris during the last four months of 1861. The unit mustered into Confederate service on January 1, 1862, at New Madrid, Missouri. On February 28, Harris and volunteers from his company, in charge of a battery of six Hughes's Portable Defense Guns, engaged a large Federal cavalry force near Sikeston. The enemy overwhelmed the small rebel party and captured three of the guns. Harris's Battery, apparently not armed with artillery pieces, accompanied Brigadier General M. Jeff Thompson's Confederate command to the Cis-Mississippi in April 1862, and after a short stay near Memphis, moved to Fort Pillow, Tennessee.

The men of the battery first saw active service as "marines" with the Confederate River Defense Fleet on the Mississippi River on May 10, 1862, as the rebel cotton-clad boats successfully engaged a Federal flotilla at Plum Point Bend (Plum Run Bend).

On July 2, the company joined an infantry battalion commanded by Major Isaac N. Hedgpeth, which subsequently became part of the 1st Confederate Regiment, a temporary organization commanded by Colonel George H. Forney. Captain Harris led sixty Missouri volunteers detached from the regiment, including men from his company, as gunners aboard the Confederate ironclad *Arkansas* on July 15, 1862, on its famous run from the Yazoo River to Vicksburg, Mississippi. The men handled the ironclad's 100-pound Columbiads. According to Lieutenant Isaac N. Brown, the commander of the *Arkansas,* Harris's men "had never served at great guns, but on trial they exhibited in their new service the cool courage natural to them on land." During what one Missouri volunteer described as "a pretty smart skirmish" with Federal ironclads, and two additional encounters with the Union fleet, the Missourians suffered casualties of 4 killed and 3 wounded as the *Arkansas* fought its way to Vicksburg. Harris's detachment did not continue on with the ironclad after it docked at Vicksburg.

Following service on the *Arkansas,* the unit returned to the infantry, whereupon Harris resigned his commission and left for the Trans-Mississippi Department, where he eventually commanded a battery in a cavalry brigade. The company consolidated with Captain Robert

McDonald's light artillery unit on August 26, 1862, near Guntown, Mississippi, under the command of Captain Albert A. Woodard. The company, along with others, joined with Lieutenant Colonel Eugene Erwin's 3rd Missouri Infantry Battalion to form the 6th Missouri Infantry Regiment. The consolidation of Harris's and McDonald's units resulted in the creation of Company D of the 6th Regiment. This company should not be confused with the 4th Field Artillery, an entirely different unit Harris commanded in 1864–65, which served only in the Trans-Mississippi Department. See the entry for the 6th Missouri Infantry Regiment for the further service of the men of this unit.

BIBLIOGRAPHY

Brown, Isaac N. "The Confederate Gunboat *Arkansas,* by Her Commander." In *Battles and Leaders of the Civil War,* vol. 3, edited by Robert U. Johnson and Clarence C. Buel, 572–79. New York: Thomas Yoseloff, 1955.

Conrad, Howard E. "Samuel Stanhope Harris." In *Encyclopedia of the History of Missouri,* 189–90. St. Louis: Southern History Co., 1901.

Stanton, Donal J., Goodwin F. Berquist, and Paul C. Bowers, eds. *The Civil War Reminiscences of General M. Jeff Thompson.* Dayton: Morningside Press, 1988.

Hunter's Battery

Captain: Jason H. Hunter

This largely unknown battery briefly operated with cavalry units that eventually constituted Marmaduke's Missouri cavalry brigade, and appears to have been only a temporary organization. This may have been the battery that the Confederate recruiter Henry E. Clark reported organizing in southeast Missouri in the fall of 1862. What is certain is that in December 1862, Jason H. Hunter, formerly a battalion commander in the 1st Division, Missouri State Guard, had the battery under his "special control" at Jonesboro, and later at Pocahontas, Arkansas. The battery possessed an iron 12-pounder smoothbore and a bronze 24-pounder howitzer, both captured from the Federals at Bloomfield, Missouri, on September 11, by William L. Jeffers's recruit command. The 12-pounder formerly belonged to the McDowell Battery (Company A) of the 1st Division, Missouri State Guard, and had been captured at the battle of Fredericktown on October 21, 1861. The battery disappeared from the records after December 1862. The unit apparently never engaged in combat. No official record of the battery has been located in any source other than in a Federal government listing of Missouri Confederate units.

Bibliography

Stanton, Donal J., Goodwin F. Berquist, and Paul C. Bowers, eds. *The Civil War Reminiscences of General M. Jeff Thompson.* Dayton: Morningside Press, 1988.

United States Department of War, Records and Pension Office. *Organization and Status of Missouri Troops, Union and Confederate, in Service during the Civil War.* Washington: Government Printing Office, 1902.

Landis's Battery

Captain: John C. Landis

On December 8, 1861, John C. Landis, who had served as chief of artillery, 5th Division, Missouri State Guard, received a commission with authority to raise an artillery company for Confederate service. He began recruiting recently discharged guardsmen at Osceola, Missouri, but failed to enlist sufficient men for a full company. In mid-January, Landis's undersized unit left the army at Springfield for Des Arc, Arkansas, to take charge of a new battery manufactured in Memphis, Tennessee. Landis's party took possession of the battery, consisting of two 12-pounder Napoleons and two 24-pounder howitzers, and then headed west to rejoin the Missouri army.

About the middle of March 1862, too late for the battle of Pea Ridge, Landis's unit found the army encamped near Van Buren, Arkansas, where additional recruits joined the company. The battery became part of the artillery brigade commanded by Brigadier General Daniel M. Frost. It thereafter crossed the Mississippi River on the steamer *Clark Dozier* as part of the Army of the West, arriving in Memphis, Tennessee, on April 16.

The battery officially organized for Confederate service and elected officers in camp near Memphis on May 1. Shortly thereafter, the battery moved to Corinth, Mississippi, and occupied a position in the defensive lines of that place. The unit mustered 62 artillerymen on May 5 after arrival at Corinth. The battery engaged the Federals on May 28 near Corinth, losing 2 men wounded. During the summer of 1862, Landis's Battery camped at various locations, including Baldwyn, Tupelo, and Saltillo, Mississippi. Present at the battle of Iuka, and under fire, the battery did not discharge its pieces. At Corinth on October 3, the battery deployed in an open field and dueled with Federal artillery for some two hours. It then advanced with the infantry of Brigadier General Louis Hebert's division, enduring a heavy fire all day. The battery had 6 men wounded and 4 missing during the battle. It joined the rear guard when the Confederates abandoned the field on October 4 and nearly lost its guns at the battle of Davis Bridge on the Hatchie River the day following.

Because of battle damage suffered at Corinth, the battery proceeded to Jackson for repairs to its equipment. Landis's unit rejoined the army on November 29 and then went into winter quarters near Grenada. On January 27, 1863, the battery reported to Grand Gulf to defend the mouth of the Big Black River. A section of the Landis Battery's 24-pounders hurried to the defense of Port Gibson on May 1 as the Federal army moved east after crossing the Mississippi. It engaged in the battle until late afternoon, losing 3 men wounded, 1 mortally. Landis's artillerymen retreated from Port Gibson with Brigadier General John S. Bowen's division.

On May 16, the battery heavily engaged the enemy at Champion Hill. It supported the infantry on the right of the Confederate line and provided cover fire during the retreat. The battery suffered losses of 6 killed and 3 wounded at that pivotal battle, as well as having its two 12-pounder guns disabled. On May 17 the remaining cannons of the battery deployed on the west bank of the Big Black River, overlooking the Confederate position on the opposite side. When the Federals broke the Confederate line on the east bank and threw the defenders into disorder, the battery provided cover fire that slowed the Federal advance and helped some Confederates escape across the river.

Landis's Battery eventually moved into the Vicksburg defenses, the only Missouri artillery unit with guns to do so. The cannoneers of Landis's unit endured the heavy combat and privations of the siege of Vicksburg. During forty-seven days of nearly continuous fighting, the battery lost 7 killed and 6 wounded. When the Vicksburg garrison surrendered on July 4, only 37 men remained to accept paroles. After reporting to a parole camp at Demopolis, Alabama, and awaiting exchange for several weeks, the Landis Battery consolidated with Guibor's and Wade's Missouri batteries on October 1 and ceased to exist as a separate organization. Approximately 75 artillerists served in the Landis Battery before it consolidated with the other Missouri units. Of that number, 15 were killed in battle, 1 was murdered, and 6 died of disease. See Guibor's Battery for the further service of this company.

BIBLIOGRAPHY

Dunlap, Samuel B. "Experiences on the Hood Campaign." *Confederate Veteran* 16 (April 1908): 187–88.

———. "Hard Times on Hood's Retreat." *Confederate Veteran* 7 (1899): 266

———. "The Missouri Battery in the Tennessee Campaign." *Confederate Veteran* 12 (1904): 389.

———. "The Shoeless Confederates." *Daily Missouri Republican,* St. Louis, Missouri, February 5, 1887.

Landis, John C. "The Landis Battery." *St. Louis Republic,* St. Louis, Missouri, April 28, 1895.

Lehr, Suzanne Staker, ed. *As the Mockingbird Sang: The Diary of Private Robert Caldwell Dunlap.* St. Joseph: Platte Purchase, 2005.

———, ed. *Fishing on Deep River: Civil War Memoir of Private Samuel Baldwin Dunlap, C.S.A.* St. Joseph: Platte Purchase, 2006.

McDonald's Battery

Captain: Robert McDonald

Robert McDonald organized this battery for Confederate service at Camp Defiance, a camp located in eastern Dunklin County in southeast Missouri. Effectively a reorganization of the battery McDonald commanded in the 1st Division, Missouri State Guard, it formally entered the Confederate army about March 13, 1862. Whether the unit possessed artillery pieces is uncertain, but if so, it did not retain them long, for Brigadier General M. Jeff Thompson, commander of the First Military District, as well as the Confederate volunteers from that district, issued an order on April 28, 1862, transferring all the command's artillery pieces to the Arkansas Appeal Battery. The company then moved to Fort Pillow, north of Memphis.

McDonald's unit mustered fifty-five officers and men for service as "marines" aboard a ship of the Confederate River Defense Fleet. The rebel fleet engaged a Federal flotilla on the Mississippi River at Plum Point Bend (Plum Run Bend) on May 10, 1862, with some success. Transferred to Memphis in early June, the company anticipated boarding the cotton-clad *General M. Jeff Thompson* on June 6, but an unexpectedly early attack by the Federal fleet prevented it from doing so. The company then marched to Grenada, Mississippi, for duty. Brigadier General Daniel Ruggles instructed McDonald and his men to report to Lieutenant Isaac N. Brown aboard the ironclad *Arkansas* on June 24 but countermanded the order before the unit could comply. Thereafter, McDonald's men drilled solely as infantry.

On August 26, 1862, McDonald's unit consolidated with Captain Samuel S. Harris's battery, a unit also without artillery pieces, to form Company D of the 6th Missouri Infantry Regiment. Captain McDonald, who failed election to any position at the consolidation, returned to the Trans-Mississippi as a member of General Thompson's staff. During the brief service of the company, it lost 2 men killed and 4 to disease. See the entry for the 6th Infantry Regiment for the further service of the men of this battery.

BIBLIOGRAPHY

Confederate Organizations, Officers and Posts, 1861–1865, Missouri Units. Springfield: Ozarks Genealogical Society, 1988.

Stanton, Donal J., Goodwin F. Berquist, and Paul C. Bowers, eds. *The Civil War Reminiscences of General M. Jeff Thompson Dayton.* Morningside Press, 1988.

Tull's Battery "1st Rifle Battery"

Captain: Francis M. Tull, resigned March 25, 1862.

This company organized for service in the Third Division, Missouri State Guard, and mustered into state service about December 31, 1861, at Springfield, Missouri. Sometimes known as the "1st Rifle Battery" or "Tull's Rifle Battery," in late January 1862, it acquired four guns, two rifled iron 6-pounders, and two 6-pounder smoothbores. The battery first fought on March 7 at Bentonville, Arkansas, during the Pea Ridge Campaign, when it participated in an attack on a roadblock on the Sugar Creek Road manned by elements of Brigadier General Franz Sigel's division. In that fight a shell from Tull's Battery dismounted a cannon of the 1st Missouri Flying Battery (Union). Later that day the battery deployed near Elkhorn Tavern and fought there the balance of that day and the next. The battery is mistakenly referred to as "Teel's Battery" in the reports of the battle of Pea Ridge.

Following the Confederate defeat at Pea Ridge on March 8, the unit retreated with the army to near Van Buren, and there, the battery transferred to Confederate service. Tull's company moved east of the Mississippi River with the Army of the West in early April. It served briefly as part of that army's artillery brigade before being permanently consolidated with Captain Hiram Bledsoe's battery about April 21, thereby ending its service as a separate organization. No muster rolls or casualty lists for this battery have been located.

BIBLIOGRAPHY

Confederate Organizations, Officers and Posts, 1861–1865, Missouri Units. Springfield: Ozarks Genealogical Society, 1988.

Thomas W. Westlake. Memoir. Watson-Westlake Family Papers. Western Historical Manuscript Collection, University of Missouri, Columbia, Missouri.

United States Department of War, Records and Pension Office. *Organization and Status of Missouri Troops, Union and Confederate, in Service during the Civil War.* Washington: Government Printing Office, 1902.

Von Phul's Battery

Commander: 1st Lieutenant Benjamin Von Phul

Soldiers detailed from regiments of Brigadier General Daniel M. Frost's infantry brigade formed this battery on February 3, 1863, likely at Little Rock, Arkansas. Initially armed with one bronze 24-pounder and two 6-pounder Parrotts, it moved with Frost's brigade to Fort Pleasant, near Pine Bluff, later that month, where it eventually served six guns while guarding the river approach to Little Rock. On June 12, a section of the battery accompanied a small mixed force commanded by Colonel John B. Clark

Jr. to operate against Federal shipping on the Mississippi River. Von Phul's gunners, along with two other batteries, attacked three transports and the tin-clad gunboat *Little Rebel* on June 22. Accurate fire knocked out the *Little Rebel's* forward battery, and the supply ship *Prima Donna* and a transport suffered such damage that they had to be towed to a repair depot at the mouth of the Yazoo River. The Confederates then marched south and attacked other ships on June 27, and damaged several transports. After that action, Clark's command returned to Fort Pleasant. Von Phul's artillery experienced no further combat. The battery officially mustered into the army on November 22, per Special Order No. 215, Headquarters, District of Arkansas, but disbanded December 2, under the provisions of Special Order No. 222, same headquarters. No reason for the brief existence of the battery appears in the records. When the company disbanded, the detailed men returned to their original units. After Von Phul's Battery disbanded, Captain Samuel T. Ruffner's Battery acquired four of its guns, two 10-pounder Parrots and two 12-pounder howitzers. During the short life of the unit, Von Phul's Battery mustered about 70 men. Casualties of the unit, if any, are unknown.

BIBLIOGRAPHY

Banasik, Michael E., ed. *Serving with Honor: The Diary of Captain Eathan Allen Pinnell of the Eighth Missouri Infantry Regiment (Confederate).* Iowa City: Camp Pope Bookshop, 1999.

Edwin E. Harris Correspondence. Gilder Lehrman Institute of American History, New York Historical Society, New York, New York.

Gibson, J. W. *Recollections of a Pioneer.* Independence: Two Trails, 1999.

Trans-Mississippi Order and Letter Book, Brigadier General John S. Marmaduke. Transcribed by Carolyn M. Bartels. Independence: Two Trails, 2000.

Woodson's Battery

Captain: William Woodson

This battery is generally unknown, for it does not usually appear in lists of Missouri Confederate units. At a date uncertain in 1863, Major General Sterling Price obtained four Williams' Rapid-Fire Guns that had been manufactured at the Tredegar Iron Works in Richmond, Virginia. These weapons, about four feet in length and operated by a crew of three men, are sometimes described as the first machine guns developed during the war. The crank operated guns fired a 1-pound shell 2,000 yards at a rate of 18 to 20 rounds per minute. Whether Price procured the guns from the Confederate Ordnance Department by requisition or by private purchase has not been established. By General Order No. 6, Headquarters, District of Arkansas, dated April 6, 1863, Price ordered sixteen troopers of his escort company transferred to "Captain Wood's light artillery company." About a month later, on May 9, Captain Robert C. Wood, a former aide to Price, reported to Brigadier General John S. Marmaduke that his "cavalry and light artillery" company consisted of 2 officers and 24 men and that it possessed four Williams' Rapid-Fire Guns along with 1,000 rounds of ammunition, including solid shot and canister. While it may have been coincidental, the timing of the events clearly suggests that Wood received the guns procured by Price, for it is unlikely that another such battery existed in the Trans-Mississippi Department at that time. The provisions of Special Order No. 62, Headquarters, District of Arkansas, dated June 12, 1863, authorized Wood to organize one or more companies of cavalry; he began raising a mounted command immediately afterward.

The battery's next appearance occurs in a Union scout's report of August 3, which indicated that Wood's command consisted of an estimated 150 men and 4 pieces of "flying" artillery. From the meager information available, it is apparent that Captain William Woodson's company of Wood's unit possessed the Williams guns. No record has been found that Woodson's company ever employed the guns in combat. As late as October 27, Wood forwarded correspondence to headquarters showing his unit as "Wood's Cavalry Battalion and Light Artillery," but beginning November 3 and thereafter, the unit appears only as "Wood's Cavalry Battalion." The returns of Marmaduke's Missouri cavalry division listed the unit as an independent outfit unattached to any brigade, from October 31 through December 31, 1863. In those returns, nothing indicates any artillery complement existed in the battalion, so it is likely that the Williams guns had been transferred to some other unit by November 1863, but the final disposition of the company's artillery remains a mystery.

Bibliography

Boatner, Mark M. "Williams' Rapid-Fire Gun." In *The Civil War Dictionary*. New York: David McKay, 1959.

Trans-Mississippi Order and Letter Book, Brigadier General John S. Marmaduke. Transcribed by Carolyn M. Bartels. Independence: Two Trails, 2000.

United States Department of War, Records and Pension Office. *Organization and Status of Missouri Troops, Union and Confederate, in Service during the Civil War*. Washington: Government Printing Office, 1902.

II

CAVALRY UNITS

A. REGIMENTS

1st Regiment (Dismounted) (Gates's)
(Subsequently consolidated with 3rd Cavalry Battalion)

Colonel: Elijah P. Gates

Lieutenant Colonel: Richard Chiles, resigned June 15, 1862;
William D. Maupin, killed October 4, 1862; George W. Law,
reassigned February 22, 1864

Major: Robert R. Lawther, resigned June 15, 1862; George W. Law,
promoted lieutenant colonel October 4, 1862; William C. Parker,
killed November 30, 1864

Companies and Commanders:

Company A: (Buchanan, Platte) William D. Maupin, promoted
lieutenant colonel June 15, 1862; Joseph H. Neal

Company B: (Callaway, Montgomery) George W. Law, promoted
major June 15, 1862; William P. Gilbert, died of wounds June 9, 1863

Company C: (Holt) Hiram N. Upton, dropped June 18, 1862;
Lucian P. Johnson, killed October 4, 1862; David Lanter

Company D: (Ray) William C. Parker, promoted major October 4,
1862; James W. Adams

Company E: (Buchanan, Platte) Henry Clay McGee, deserted
February 15, 1862; John Stokely Holland

Company F: (Andrew, Holt, Platte) John Thrailkill, sent to
Missouri to recruit March 8, 1863

Company G: (Daviess) Logan Enyart

Company H: (Nodaway, Worth) John Patton, taken prisoner May 17, 1863

Company I: (Platte) Silas M. Gordon, deserted February 25, 1863; John N. Archer

Company K: (Callaway, Platte) Charles A. Rodgers, dropped June 11, 1863; Harris Wilkerson

This regiment initially organized December 30, 1861, and formally mustered into Confederate service January 16, 1862, at Springfield, Missouri. The regiment became part of the newly created 1st Missouri Brigade. The 1st Cavalry enrolled men from the Missouri State Guard, particularly veterans of the mounted units of the 4th and 5th divisions of north central and northwestern Missouri. When Major General Samuel R. Curtis's approaching Federal army forced the Confederates to evacuate Springfield on February 12, the 1st Cavalry served in the army's rear guard. Throughout the retreat to Cross Hollows, Arkansas, the 1st Missouri skirmished with the enemy, fighting near Springfield on February 12; at Pott's Hill, Arkansas, on February 16; and on Little Sugar Creek the next day. Major General Earl Van Dorn's Confederate Army of the West advanced toward Pea Ridge, Arkansas, on March 6; the 1st Cavalry rode ahead to Bentonville, where it skirmished with the enemy and captured prisoners and an ammunition wagon. The regiment fought dismounted on the left of the line near Elkhorn Tavern on March 7–8 and helped capture two pieces of enemy artillery. The regimental casualty toll for the Pea Ridge Campaign, from the abandonment of Springfield to the retreat from Elkhorn Tavern, amounted to 18 killed, 41 wounded, and 16 missing.

The regiment retreated with the army to Frog Bayou near Van Buren, Arkansas, and later marched across Arkansas to Des Arc for shipment to Memphis, Tennessee. Van Dorn ordered the regiment dismounted at Des Arc on April 9; the men fought as infantry thereafter. After arrival at Memphis aboard the steamer *Capitol* in mid-April, Gates's command moved to Corinth, Mississippi, where it mustered 536 rank and file in early May. Present at the fight at Farmington on May 9, the regiment did not become engaged. The 1st Cavalry spent the next several months moving about to different camps in northern Mississippi and drilling as infantry. At the battle of Iuka, Mississippi, on September 19, the 1st Cavalry fought only briefly. Sent forward late in the battle, the regiment arrived on the field as darkness fell and fired a single volley that unfortunately struck another Confederate unit.

The regiment's next combat occurred at Corinth on October 3–4. Gates's regiment helped drive the enemy into their inner works on October 3 with few casualties. On the second day of the battle, the men of the 1st Cavalry fought tenaciously as they charged Battery Powell, initially with success, but eventually retreated when subjected to terrific artillery cross fire and an infantry counterattack. The regimental casualties at Corinth tallied 23 killed, 53 wounded, and 15 missing. General Price proposed remounting the regiment in November, but Van Dorn denied the request, as he desired no additional cavalry.

The regiment passed the winter months of 1862–63 encamped in northern Mississippi, performing routine military duties. The coming of spring signaled the initiation of Major General Ulysses S. Grant's final effort to capture Vicksburg. The regiment missed the fighting at Grand Gulf and Port Gibson while it performed guard duty elsewhere. As part of Brigadier General Martin E. Green's 2nd Missouri brigade, Major General John S. Bowen's division, Gates's men fought in the pivotal battle of Champion Hill on May 16. Green's brigade, with the 1st Cavalry on the left flank, drove the Federal line back for nearly a mile, but the Confederates in turn gave way to an enemy counterattack and retreated in defeat. The regiment lost 25 killed, 38 wounded, and 16 missing in the battle.

Following the repulse at Champion Hill, the Confederates established a defensive line on the east bank of Big Black River, with the 1st Cavalry on the extreme left. A Federal attack broke the rebel line on May 17, creating panic among the troops since only one bridge spanned the river. Denied a ready avenue of escape, many 1st Cavalry soldiers surrendered, while others swam to safety. The disaster at Big Black cost the regiment 1 soldier drowned, 7 wounded, and 128 taken prisoner, as well as the loss of the regimental colors. The remnant of the regiment retreated into Vicksburg and thereafter endured forty-seven days of siege operations. The 1st Cavalry initially served in reserve but entered the line on May 28 and subsequently manned revetments south of the Stockade Redan. The regiment assisted in repelling a Union attack on May 22 and engaged in sharpshooting and countermining for the duration of the siege.

When Vicksburg surrendered on July 4, casualties in the regiment included 17 killed, 23 wounded, and 4 dead from disease, leaving only 230 men to receive paroles. The 1st Cavalry parolees reported to Demopolis, Alabama, to await exchange. Several men took furloughs or deserted the regiment after Vicksburg capitulated; few of them ever returned. Owing to heavy battle losses, deaths by disease, and desertions, a reorganization of the Missouri Confederate regiments occurred at Demopolis. Per the provisions of Special Order No. 17, dated October 1, 1863, Headquarters, Paroled Prisoners, the 1st Cavalry Regiment consolidated with the 3rd Cavalry Battalion, forming the 1st & 3rd Cavalry Regiment (Dismounted), which Gates's men fought with until the war ended. About 1,125 men rode and marched with the 1st Cavalry during the war, and the regimental losses, including service in the consolidated regiment, amounted to 135 battle deaths, 153 lost to disease, 2 murdered, 1 drowned, and 3 killed accidentally. The collection of the Missouri State Museum at Jefferson City includes the original regimental flag captured at Big Black River on May 17, 1863. See the entry for the 1st & 3rd Cavalry Regiment (Dismounted) for the further service of the men of this regiment.

BIBLIOGRAPHY

Calkins, Homer, ed. "Elk Horn to Vicksburg: James Fauntleroy's Diary for the Year 1862." *Civil War History* 2 (March 1956): 7–44.

Farley, James W. *Forgotten Valor: The First Missouri Cavalry Regiment, C.S.A.* Independence: Two Trails, 1996.

Tucker, Phillip Thomas. "Colonel Elijah Gates: Heart and Soul of the Famous Missouri Brigade." *Confederate Veteran* (November–December 1993): 18–27.

"War Experiences of B. F. Garrett." *Fulton Daily Sun,* Fulton, Missouri, June 14, 1909.

1st Northeast Regiment (Porter's)

Colonel: Joseph Chrisman Porter

Lieutenant Colonel: William C. Blanton

Major: Elliott D. Major

Companies and Commanders:

Company A: (Lewis, Marion, Monroe, Shelby) James W. Porter

Company B: (Monroe, Ralls) Charles Powell

Company C: (Monroe, Schuyler) John Williams

Company D: (Lewis, Marion, Monroe, Schuyler, Shelby) Wurton F. Wills

Company E: (Schuyler) William Dunn

Company F: (Monroe, Ralls) Benjamin M. Ely

Company G: (Monroe) Thomas A. Sidner, executed by Federals October 18, 1862

Company H: (Schuyler, Scotland) James Leeper

Company I: (Lewis) Rufus M. Brown

Company K: (Adair, Marion, Schuyler) Elijah C. Arnold

Company L: (Audrain, Boone) Young Purcell

Company M: (Adair, Boone, Monroe) Henry C. Price

Company N: (Boone) Amos K. Hulett (Formerly in Poindexter's regiment)

Company O: (Audrain, Knox, Marion, Monroe) Robert Hager, killed August 6, 1862; James C. McDonald

Company P: (Adair, Audrain) Benjamin F. White

Company —: (Lewis) John N. Hicks

Major General Sterling Price sent Joseph C. Porter, a veteran colonel of the Missouri State Guard, to northeast Missouri in March 1862 to recruit a cavalry regiment for Confederate service. Arriving in Lewis County in June, Porter conducted low-key recruitment efforts while he stockpiled ammunition and supplies. He intended to recruit as many men as possible to take to the army in Arkansas; crossing the Missouri River in the enemy's presence posed the main obstacle to his plan. Porter initiated action on June 17 by striking near New Market, Marion County, and capturing 43 Union troops. He next raided Memphis, where he seized 100 needed muskets and ammunition. Three days later, his command fought its first major engagement at Vassar Hill after Porter enticed enemy cavalry into a well-prepared ambush. The bloody affair cost the Union troopers 83 killed and wounded, while the Confederates lost 9 killed and 10 wounded.

Porter's command attacked a company of the 3rd Iowa Cavalry at Florida on July 22, driving the Federals from the town with substantial losses. It defeated another detachment of the 3rd Iowa in a skirmish at Santa Fe the following day. On July 28, Porter engaged Colonel Odon Guitar's pursuing Union cavalry near Moore's Mill in Callaway County. Although outnumbered three to one and confronted by artillery, Porter's men fought desperately, even charging the enemy's cannons. Running low on ammunition after four hours of fighting, Porter's men abandoned the field with known losses of 6 killed and 21 wounded, while Guitar's command counted 11 dead and 43 wounded. Guitar did not pursue the Confederates, as he overestimated their strength in light of the resistance his troops faced.

After the fight at Moore's Mill, Porter moved northward, occupied Paris briefly, and then proceeded to Newark and captured 80 militiamen on August 2, at a cost of 8 killed and 22 wounded. The regiment formally organized and elected field officers on August 4 at a camp near Williamstown in Lewis County. At about the same time, Colonel Cyrus Franklin and his regiment joined Porter. Closely pressed by Union forces, Porter faced the dilemma of whether to ride for the Missouri River. Considering procurement of transportation across the river unlikely, he opted to fight so that boats might be acquired later. Porter initially intended to make his stand at Memphis but altered plans when he learned that Union troops had abandoned Kirksville to the Confederates. Porter's command arrived at Kirksville at midmorning on August 6, closely followed by Union forces under Colonel John McNeil. The Confederates had barely deployed for battle before the Federals opened the engagement with artillery fire directed at Porter's position. The Confederates initially made stubborn resistance, but with just half of them armed, Porter's men wilted before superior Federal firepower after two hours of fighting, at first in fairly good order, but then in a rush for safety across the Chariton River to the west. McNeil did not immediately pursue Porter's fleeing men as his exhausted troops and horses required rest. While no definitive statement of casualties for Porter's command exists, his losses greatly exceeded his opponent's. Porter suffered casualties of at least 50 killed, 100 wounded, and 50 captured at the battle, compared to losses in McNeil's command of 9 killed and 38 wounded. McNeil added to the Confederate death toll the day following by summarily executing 15 soldiers for alleged parole violations.

The Federal pursuit of Porter's command commenced on August 8. After crossing Walnut Creek, Porter left a detachment behind to deal with the enemy hounding his column. The Federals consequently rode into an ambush at See's Ford, suffering substantial casualties as they crossed the river. Porter disbanded his regiment on August 11, instructing his men to return home and move south as circumstances permitted. Porter had enough troops left to capture Palmyra on September 12. While taking Palmyra resulted in the freeing of 50 Confederate prisoners, and perhaps created a diversion that permitted some men to move south unmolested, Porter did not hold the town long.

An unfortunate incident occurred following the occupation of Palmyra, for some of Porter's men executed a captured Unionist civilian without the colonel's knowledge. General McNeil executed 10 more Confederate prisoners at Palmyra on October 18 in retaliation. Porter remained in northeast Missouri for another month, but in mid-October he and a number of his men crossed the Missouri River, headed for Arkansas. Porter's operations in northeast Missouri produced a goodly number of soldiers for the Confederates. His recruits infused Missouri units in the Trans-Mississippi Department with much-needed manpower. The number of men that served in Porter's regiment cannot be accurately determined, although over 1,700 appear on the company muster rolls. That number is certainly misleading, for the regiment's composition varied, and new companies joined Porter after he disbanded the regiment. It is doubtful that such a large number ever served at the same time. Casualty figures are uncertain owing to the nature of Porter's fast-paced, wide-ranging operations and the paucity of regimental records. Available casualty lists reveal 69 men lost in battle; 90 deaths by disease, mostly in Union prisons; 3 killed by accident; 1 murdered; and at least 27 executed by Federal troops. The latter figure surely sets the mark for any Confederate unit during the war. There is evidence that Confederate authorities planned to merge the 1st Northeast and 2nd Northeast regiments into an infantry regiment when the commands reached Arkansas, but that consolidation never occurred. See the entry for the 7th Infantry Regiment (Franklin's) for information in that regard.

BIBLIOGRAPHY

Cummings, G. R. "Joined Porter in Time for Battle." *Daily Express,* Kirksville, Missouri, August 6, 1912.

Hance, Charles Hewett. *Reminiscences of One Who Suffered in the Lost Cause.* Los Angeles: Privately printed, 1915.

Mudd, Joseph A. *With Porter in North Missouri: A Chapter in the History of the War between the States.* Iowa City: Camp Pope Bookshop, 1992.

Turner, C. C. "The Battle of Moore's Mill." *Columbia Herald,* Columbia, Missouri, March 19, 1897.

1st & 3rd Regiment Consolidated (Dismounted) (Gates's)

Colonel: Elijah P. Gates, wounded and captured November 30, 1864

Lieutenant Colonel: David Todd Samuel, killed September 27, 1864

Major: William C. Parker, killed November 30, 1864

Companies and Commanders

Company A: Joseph H. Neal, killed April 9, 1865 (Formerly Companies A and D, 1st Cavalry Regiment)

Company B: Logan Enyart, captured November 30, 1864 (Formerly Companies B and G, 1st Cavalry Regiment)

Company C: Davis Lanter (Formerly Companies F and C, 1st Cavalry Regiment)

Company D: John S. Holland, killed October 5, 1864 (Formerly Company E, 1st Cavalry Regiment)

Company E: John N. Archer, on detached service after February 15, 1864 (Formerly Companies H and I, 1st Cavalry Regiment)

Company F: Harris Wilkerson, captured November 30, 1864 (Formerly Company K, 1st Cavalry Regiment)

Company G: William C. Aldredge, captured November 30, 1864 (Formerly Companies A, D, and G, 3rd Cavalry Battalion)

Company H: Alexander F. Burns, captured November 30, 1864 (Formerly Company B, 3rd Cavalry Battalion)

Company I: James W. McSpadden, retired because of wounds July 1864 (Formerly Companies C and F, 3rd Cavalry Battalion)

Company K: Griffin Bayne, killed November 30, 1864 (Formerly Company H, 3rd Cavalry Battalion)

After the prisoner exchange following the surrender of Vicksburg, the 1st Cavalry Regiment and 3rd Cavalry Battalion consolidated and formed this regiment at Demopolis, Alabama, about October 1, 1863, under the provisions of Special Order No. 17, Headquarters, Paroled Prisoners. Heavy losses due to death and desertion prompted the consolidation. The unit became part of the 1st Missouri Brigade, which also included three similarly consolidated Missouri infantry regiments. The 1st & 3rd Cavalry mustered fewer than 400 men after the consolidation. The troops received new arms and accoutrements while at Demopolis and then moved to Meridian, Mississippi, and established winter quarters.

A two-month stay in Mississippi ended when the 1st & 3rd Regiment accompanied the 1st Missouri Brigade to Mobile, Alabama, on January 9, 1864. Rushed back to Mississippi in early February as the Confederates contended with Major General William T. Sherman's drive on Meridian, the regiment skirmished with Federal cavalry at Morton on February 10 before retreating. After more shifts in location, and duty corralling deserters in northern Alabama, the regiment faced the enemy in the Atlanta Campaign. At the beginning of the campaign, the 1st & 3rd Cavalry numbered some 350 officers and men and composed a part of Major General Samuel French's division. Exposed to artillery fire and skirmishing at Rome and Cassville as the Union army maneuvered southward, the 1st & 3rd Cavalry first experienced serious combat during late May and early June near New Hope Church, Georgia. On June 18, the Missourians fought at Latimer House north of Kennesaw Mountain before retreating to a line anchored on the mountain. In the Confederate line at Kennesaw the 1st & 3rd Regiment held a position on Pigeon Hill. The Federals assaulted the line on June 27 and penetrated the Confederate position, but the

Missourians drove them back with hard fighting. The regiment lost 7 killed and 32 wounded in the engagement.

Forced to evacuate the Kennesaw Mountain line, the Confederates withdrew toward Atlanta. The 1st & 3rd Cavalry fought at Smyrna on July 3 and at the Chattahoochee River two days later. The regiment next engaged in limited fighting along Peachtree Creek on July 18 before retreating into defensive works on the northwest side of Atlanta. For several weeks the regiment endured nearly constant enemy artillery and small-arms fire. On August 6, the regiment participated in an unsuccessful sortie against the Federal line near the Turner's Ferry Road. Finally, on September 1, the Confederates evacuated Atlanta, and the Missourians withdrew from their trenches. After leaving Atlanta, the regiment proceeded to a position near Lovejoy Station. On September 6, two companies of the regiment skirmished with the enemy near Jonesborough as the Atlanta Campaign concluded. The long campaign, extending from May 18 through September 6, resulted in casualties of 25 killed, 80 wounded, and 3 missing in the 1st & 3rd Regiment.

As General Sherman initiated his march through Georgia, General John B. Hood, commander of the Confederate Army of Tennessee, turned his army northward. On October 5, French's division, including the 1st Missouri Brigade, attacked the strong Federal position at Allatoona, Georgia. The 1st & 3rd Regiment occupied the extreme right of the brigade line as the attack began. Although the Confederates overran one redoubt, the defenders repulsed several attempts to capture the strong inner fort. Fearing the arrival of Union reinforcements, General French abandoned the attack and withdrew his troops. The engagement's casualty list included 10 dead, 48 wounded, and 2 missing from the 1st & 3rd Cavalry.

Next, the army moved into Tennessee. After a difficult march, the Army of Tennessee arrived at Franklin near noon on November 30. General Hood deployed his troops to attack the strong Federal breastworks; around 4:00 p.m. the rebel line marched forward. The 1st Missouri Brigade, aligned to the right of Major General Patrick R. Cleburne's division, numbered less than 700 men when it moved on the enemy. The 1st & 3rd Regiment held the brigade's extreme right flank. Confederate attempts to carry the Federal position resulted in a useless effusion of blood. The 1st & 3rd Cavalry struck the Union line near the Carter cotton gin, but artillery and massed infantry halted their attack at the outer walls of the

Federal works. Infantry clashes along the line degenerated into vicious mêlées of brutal hand-to-hand fighting across the head logs. The bloodletting finally ceased around 9:00 p.m., after five hours of desperate fighting; the victorious Federals moved on toward Nashville. Casualties for the 1st & 3rd Regiment at Franklin amounted to 35 killed, 33 wounded, another 22 wounded and captured, and 44 other prisoners, for a total loss of 134 officers and men, more than 60 percent of the regiment's strength. After burying their dead on the battlefield, the regimental survivors moved to join the army at Nashville on December 2.

Service at Nashville did not last long, for the 1st Missouri Brigade left the army on December 10 and marched to the Duck River to build fortifications near Johnsonville. Following the subsequent Confederate defeat at Nashville, the men of the 1st & 3rd Cavalry rejoined the army after it had retreated to Mississippi. Following an uneventful winter at Tupelo, Mississippi, the 1st Missouri Brigade joined troops defending Mobile, Alabama, on March 24, 1865, and became part of the garrison at Fort Blakely on the bay's eastern shore. A numerically superior Federal force overwhelmed the Confederates at Blakely on April 9, capturing it after a brief fight. The Federals sent the prisoners to Ship Island, Mississippi, where they endured some privation and mistreatment at the hands of their captors. The men of the 1st & 3rd Cavalry Regiment received paroles at Columbus and Jackson, Mississippi, in early May 1865.

BIBLIOGRAPHY

Farley, James W. *Forgotten Valor: The First Missouri Cavalry Regiment, C.S.A.* Independence: Two Trails, 1996.

Neese, W. C. "Scaling the Works at Franklin." *Confederate Veteran* 11 (1903): 274.

Noe, F. R. "Scattered Remnant of a Company." *Confederate Veteran* 11 (1903): 16.

2nd Regiment (McCulloch's) (Formerly the 4th Battalion)

Colonel: Robert McCulloch

Lieutenant Colonel: Robert A. McCulloch

Major: John J. Smith, resigned September 1, 1862; Robert A. McCulloch, promoted lieutenant colonel August 14, 1863; William H. Couzens

Companies and Commanders:

Company A: (Cooper, Moniteau) Robert A. McCulloch, promoted major January 1, 1863; Augustus L. Zollinger

Company B: (Bollinger, Stoddard) Solomon G. Kitchen, resigned October 16, 1862; John S. Thompson; resigned June 25, 1864; Thomas A. Bottom

Company C: (Bollinger, Stoddard, Wayne) David Reed, deserted June 1, 1863; Richard F. Lanning (Company consolidated with Company F)

Company D: (Dunklin) George W. Lindamoore, resigned September 3, 1862; George W. Mott, resigned February 2, 1864

Company E: (Madison, St. Francois, Ste. Genevieve, Washington) William H. Couzens, promoted major August 14, 1863; Francis J. Smith

Company F: (Bollinger, Madison, Stoddard, Wayne) Jesse R. Henson, resigned January 2, 1863; Richard F. Lanning

Company G: (Cooper) George B. Harper

Company H (1st): (St. Louis) John R. Champion, killed August 30, 1862 (Disbanded September 1, 1862)

Company H (2nd): (Marion, St. Louis) Robert H. Edmondson, resigned, 1862; Josiah Tippett

Company I: (Henry) Epaminondas M. Smith, resigned November 19, 1862; Robert Collins (Detached on or about March 18, 1862, as escort to Major General Sterling Price and sent to the Trans-Mississippi)

Company K: (Clay) Phineas M. Savery

This regiment bore the distinction of being the only Missouri cavalry regiment to serve mounted east of the Mississippi River. It had roots in the Missouri State Guard, for a majority of the troops had served in the 1st, 6th, or 8th divisions. The origins of the regiment can be traced to Special Order No. 66, Headquarters, Army of the West, dated April 26, 1862, at Memphis, Tennessee, which directed that five companies recruited in southeast Missouri (B–F) organize into a battalion. The day following, the battalion organized, but with eight companies rather than five. Thus, the original order had been modified, probably by the army's desire to incorporate unattached companies into larger units. The three additional companies added to the battalion (A, G, H [1st]), all fought at Pea Ridge, Arkansas, in March, two in an ad hoc regiment commanded by Colonel Robert McCulloch and the other as escort for Brigadier General Daniel M. Frost. The newly formed outfit officially became the 4th Battalion, although it was occasionally referred to as the 1st Battalion. Dismounted before crossing the Mississippi River, the companies regained their horses when the battalion organized shortly thereafter.

On May 5, the battalion mustered 444 troopers present while at Corinth, Mississippi. As Major General Henry W. Halleck's large Federal army inched toward Corinth, the 4th Battalion skirmished with the enemy advance almost daily until the Confederates abandoned the town at the end of the month. The battalion subsequently engaged the Federals in a sharp skirmish at Booneville on May 30. In June, a ninth company, formerly the escort for Brigadier General Martin E. Green, joined the battalion. On July 25, as an element of acting Brigadier General Frank C. Armstrong's brigade, the 4th Battalion participated in an attack on the Federal garrison at Courtland, Alabama, which resulted in the taking of 133 prisoners and destruction of a depot and bridge. The provisions of Special Order No. 5, Army of the West, dated July 2, 1862, directed formation of a regiment by adding two companies to the battalion, but that organization did not occur until August 17, at Guntown, Mississippi, and by then the merger of original companies C and F had reduced the battalion to eight companies once again. Oddly enough, the two companies added to create the 2nd Cavalry regiment, Edmondson's and Savery's, veteran companies of the Pea Ridge battle, continued to serve detached as escorts for general officers for some time thereafter.

In late August, the regiment accompanied Armstrong again as he raided into west Tennessee along the Mobile & Ohio Railroad. At Middleburg on August 30, the 2nd Cavalry helped drive the enemy into their works and killed the opposing commander, at a cost of 5 killed and 8 wounded. After skirmishing at Medon the next day, the Confederates began their return to Mississippi, when they unexpectedly encountered Federals near Denmark. In a prolonged engagement often known as the battle of Britton's Lane, the 2nd Cavalry made two mounted charges and one on foot against heavy Union rifle and artillery fire. While suffering significant casualties, Armstrong's troopers inflicted like losses on the enemy, captured their artillery, and then withdrew to Mississippi.

In mid-September, the regiment skirmished at Iuka for two days; when the Confederates retreated after the battle on September 19, the 2nd Cavalry formed part of an ambush that halted Union pursuit. The regiment fought at Corinth on October 3–4 and assisted in defending the Hatchie River crossing at Davis Bridge on the Confederate route of retreat. During late November and early December, the 2nd Cavalry skirmished often with the enemy between Holly Springs and Grenada in opposition to Major General Ulysses S. Grant's first overland advance on Vicksburg. The regiment rode into Holly Springs at the head of the column when Major General Earl Van Dorn surprised that important supply depot on December 20. The Missourians, fighting dismounted, captured nearly an entire Illinois regiment early in the engagement. They then occupied the town square, took more prisoners, and seized or destroyed a vast array of military supplies. Van Dorn's raid played a significant role in forcing Grant to postpone his advance against Vicksburg.

Beginning in February 1863, Colonel Robert McCulloch assumed command of a brigade, a position he held for the balance of the war; his cousin, Lieutenant Colonel Robert A. McCulloch became de facto regimental commander. Inactive in early 1863, in April the 2nd Cavalry opposed the Yazoo Expedition, another Union threat against Vicksburg. The regiment continuously scouted the Federal advance and kept Lieutenant General John C. Pemberton advised of enemy movements and progress. On April 5, a regimental patrol under Captain George W. Mott fired into a Union troop ship on the Tallahatchie River, disabling the boat and inflicting a number of casualties. As part of the cavalry of Brigadier General James R. Chalmers's district in northern Mississippi, the 2nd Cavalry helped prevent the enemy from crossing the Coldwater River on April 19, even though the Federals greatly outnumbered Chalmers's men.

Near Senatobia on May 23, the 2nd Regiment engaged a portion of Colonel Edward Hatch's Federal raiding force. The Missourians fought until nearly cut off by a separate part of Hatch's command, at which point they retreated, leaving 2 dead and several wounded on the field. A large Federal column overpowered the 2nd Cavalry at Quinn's Mill on June 16, and the regiment lost 1 killed and 5 taken prisoner before retiring. As part of General Chalmers's force once again, the 2nd Regiment engaged Union raiders at Salem on October 8. In his report of the fight, which cost the regiment 1 killed and 6 wounded, Chalmers alluded to the "gallantry . . . , which has ever distinguished the veterans of the Second Missouri." The regiment next accompanied Chalmers on a raid on the Federal garrison at Collierville, Tennessee, on October 11. After hard fighting, the Confederates withdrew to Mississippi, skirmishing at Byhalia and Wyatt's Ferry on the retreat. The 2nd Cavalry lost 6 killed, 11 wounded and 3 missing during the short campaign.

On November 3, the regiment rode with Chalmers when a second Confederate assault on Collierville failed. The regiment accompanied a large body of Confederate cavalry into Tennessee late in 1863 to provide a diversion for Major General Nathan Bedford Forrest's operations in the western part of the state. The Confederates encountered a formidable Union force near Moscow on December 4. A severe engagement followed in which the Union troops prevailed, driving the Confederates back to Mississippi in defeat.

Beginning in January 1864, the 2nd Cavalry began service in Forrest's cavalry corps. The 2nd Regiment participated in Forrest's rout of the Union army under Brigadier General William Sooy Smith at Okolona, Mississippi, on February 23; the Federals suffered heavy casualties and lost 6 artillery pieces and 33 flags. During the battle, Colonel McCulloch led a charge that probably prevented Forrest's capture. The ladies of Columbus, Mississippi, presented the regiment with a new flag on February 29. The regiment's next major engagement occurred on April 12, when Forrest made his controversial attack on the garrison at Fort Pillow, Tennessee. One of the first regiments to enter the enemy fortifications, the 2nd Cavalry lost 3 killed or mortally wounded and 13 other wounded in the battle.

In mid-July, the 2nd Regiment participated in operations against the Federals near Tupelo, Mississippi. Although in reserve on the first day, the regiment joined the fighting thereafter and participated in the pursuit as the enemy withdrew to Tennessee. The regiment's losses totaled at least 3 killed, 9 wounded, and 1 taken prisoner in two days of combat. A detachment of the 2nd Regiment participated in Forrest's raid on Memphis on August 21, as part of Colonel J. J. Neely's provisional brigade. Fighting in the southern part of the city, Federal infantry initially checked the brigade, but the Confederates rallied and drove the enemy to the area of the State Female College. Forrest withdrew his command after creating havoc among the Federal defenders for about six hours. The detachment of McCulloch's regiment lost 5 killed and 6 wounded, 2 of them mortally, during the raid.

In early September the 2nd Cavalry moved to Mobile, Alabama. For about four months the regiment scouted and patrolled in the Mobile and west Florida area and fought a few skirmishes. On February 9, 1865, the unit rejoined Forrest's cavalry command; it performed scout duty and rounded up deserters and stragglers in Mississippi before moving to Citronelle, Alabama. The regiment remained at that location until Lieutenant General Richard Taylor surrendered the department on May 5, 1865, thus ending the war for the 2nd Cavalry. Most troopers received paroles at Columbus, Mississippi. Approximately 900 soldiers served in the 2nd Cavalry Regiment during its years of service. Regimental casualties included 59 battle fatalities, 71 deaths by disease, 4 killed accidentally, 1 murdered, 1 slain in a personal dispute, and 1 executed by Federal authorities.

BIBLIOGRAPHY

Brand, William H. "The 2nd Missouri Cavalry." *Land We Love* 3 (August 1867): 273–82.

"Capt. Augustus L. Zollinger." *Confederate Veteran* 22 (1914): 327.

"Col. Robt. McCulloch, Venerable Veteran." *Confederate Veteran* 13 (1905): 35.

James Thornton Ellis Diary, 1863. Typescript. Missouri State Archives, Jefferson City, Missouri.

Ford, C. Y. "Fighting with Sabers." *Confederate Veteran* 30 (1922): 290.

———. "Pot Shot." *Confederate Veteran* 24 (1916): 167–68.

"H." "Second Missouri Cavalry." *Daily Missouri Republican,* St. Louis, Missouri, October 9, 1885.

———. "A Square Cavalry Fight." *Daily Missouri Republican,* St. Louis, Missouri, November 13, 1886.

Schmidt, Robert. *"Boys of the Best Families in the State": Company E, 2nd Missouri Cavalry.* Independence: Two Trails, 2003.

2nd Northeast Regiment (Franklin's)

Colonel: Cyrus F. Franklin

Lieutenant Colonel: Frisby H. McCullough, executed by Federal troops August 6, 1862

Major: Raphael Smith

Companies and Commanders:

Company B: Gabriel S. Kendrick

Company —: Richard B. Farr, died December 11, 1862

Company —: Joshua S. Hobbs

Company —: William H. Ousley

Company —: (Randolph) Delaney S. Washburn, executed by Federals September 26, 1862

Balance of regimental organization is unknown.

This short-lived regiment organized on July 25, 1862, at a place known as Camp Fabius, likely located on the North Fabius River in Lewis County, Missouri. After organizing, the regiment marched to Canton and occupied the town without loss, in the process capturing 125 weapons and other military supplies. Franklin's regiment then joined Colonel Joseph C. Porter's 1st Northeast Regiment in western Lewis County in early August, where it likely mustered into Confederate service. The Confederates could not remain immobile, for the Federals had pursued the elusive Porter for days, determined to bring him to battle.

The combined Confederate units moved to Kirksville and made a stand against the closely following enemy on August 6. Accounts differ regarding the role Franklin's men played in the battle at Kirksville. Some evidence suggests that Porter decided to defend Kirksville on Franklin's advice and that the regiment fought during the battle; other sources indicate that the 2nd Northeast remained in reserve and did not participate in the fight. It may or may not be significant that the piecemeal records show no losses for the regiment in the engagement. Following the Confederate defeat at Kirksville, the 2nd Northeast joined Porter in retreat.

The 2nd Northeast Regiment disbanded on August 11, during the retreat, for the purpose of facilitating movement of men across the

Missouri River and on to the Confederate army in Arkansas. Owing to incomplete records, it is impossible to determine the number of men that served in the regiment. A partial accounting of losses reveals that Federal authorities or state militia executed 6 men of the regiment, while another 8 died of disease in Union prisons. There is evidence that the Confederate hierarchy intended to consolidate the 1st Northeast and 2nd Northeast regiments into an infantry regiment once the commands reached Arkansas, but that consolidation never occurred. See the entry for the 7th Infantry Regiment (Franklin's) for information in that regard.

BIBLIOGRAPHY

Mudd, Joseph A. *With Porter in North Missouri: A Chapter in the History of the War between the States.* Iowa City: Camp Pope Bookshop, 1992.

James T. Wallace Diary. Southern Historical Collection, University of North Carolina, Chapel Hill, North Carolina.

3rd Regiment (Greene's)

Colonel: Colton Greene

Lieutenant Colonel: Leonidas C. Campbell, died November 19, 1863: Leonidas A. Campbell

Major: Leonidas A. Campbell, promoted lieutenant colonel December 30, 1863; James Surridge

Companies and Commanders:

Company A: (Christian, Greene, Webster) Alexander Don Brown

Company B: (Cape Girardeau, Iron, Madison, St. Francois) James Surridge, promoted major December 30, 1863; Charles N. Polk

Company C: (Reynolds, St. Francois, Washington) John Casey, resigned October 2, 1863; Frank Clark

Company D: (Webster, Wright) John C. Puryear

Company E: (Camden, Greene, Pulaski) Andrew J. Thompson

Company F: (Dent, Phelps) Howard S. Randall

Company G: (Cedar, Webster) Benjamin F. Crabtree

Company H: (Greene, Taney) James F. Wyatt, resigned March 12, 1863; Benjamin S. Johnson

Company I: (Dade, McDonald, Newton) William C. Clanton

Company K: (Ozark, Laclede) Thomas R. Sapp, died March 3, 1863; Joseph E. Trahin

On June 3, 1862, Brigadier General Martin E. Green, brigade commander in the Army of the West, urged his division commander, Major General Sterling Price, to grant authority to Colonel Colton Greene and Lieutenant Colonel Leonidas C. Campbell, then with the army, to recruit a regiment of partisan rangers in the Trans-Mississippi Department. Price apparently concurred with Green's solicitation, for both Greene and Campbell began raising cavalry companies in southern Missouri late that summer, the former with authority from the Confederate Secretary of War. The 3rd Cavalry Regiment mustered into service with ten companies on November 4 at Pocahontas, Arkansas. The appointment of the regimental field officers by Confederate authorities became a bone of contention with the company officers; they demanded an election, but their protest did not change the command structure. The regiment organized as regular cavalry rather than partisan rangers per the order of Major General Thomas C. Hindman, the department commander.

On November 7, part of the regiment accompanied Colonel John Q. Burbridge's Missouri cavalry brigade to attack a Union outpost near Clark's Mill in Douglas County, Missouri. After a short fight, the outnumbered enemy surrendered, resulting in the capture of 150 prisoners, 2 cannons, 200 stands of arms, a number of horses, stores valued at nearly $40,000, and destruction of the enemy fortification. The brigade next struck a Union supply train in Wright County, Missouri, on November 24, killing and wounding 28 enemy soldiers and taking 45 prisoners while burning supplies and a train of forty wagons. The regiment, along with Burbridge's battalion and the 8th Missouri Cavalry Regiment, became part of a newly organized brigade at Pocahontas in early December under the command of Colonel Moses J. White and subsequently Colonel Joseph C. Porter. A detail of the 3rd Regiment helped capture a Union forage party near Van Buren, Missouri, on December 28.

In early January 1863, a detachment accompanied the brigade, under the command of Porter, into southwest Missouri as part of Brigadier General John S. Marmaduke's raid into that area. Lieutenant Colonel Leonidas C. Campbell led the contingent of the 3rd Cavalry at the battle at Hartville on January 11. Porter's brigade rode into an ambush at Hartville and fought desperately until the Federals finally abandoned the field and retreated to Lebanon. The 3rd Regiment suffered losses of 6 killed or mortally wounded and 19 wounded in the battle. The regiment, with Colonel Greene leading the brigade because Porter had fallen mortally wounded at Hartville, participated in Marmaduke's raid into southeast Missouri in late April but never closely engaged the enemy. The 3rd Cavalry lost 3 killed and 6 wounded in the failed attack on Helena, Arkansas, on July 4. During the defense of Little Rock in late August and early September, the regiment fought at Brownsville, Bayou Metoe, Reed's Bridge, and Bayou Fourche with light casualties. In the assault on Pine Bluff on October 25, the 3rd Regiment attacked dismounted from the south. The Federals repulsed the Confederates after a sharp fight, with the 3rd Cavalry losing 3 killed and 7 wounded.

After a quiet winter camped in southern Arkansas, the 1864 spring campaign opened with the advance of Major General Frederick Steele's army from Little Rock toward Shreveport, Louisiana, as part of the Red River Campaign. The 3rd Regiment skirmished with the enemy from March 31 to April 15, as the Confederates fought a delaying action until Steele changed course and occupied Camden. On April 18, the 3rd Cavalry helped rout the enemy and capture a large forage train at Poison Spring. When Steele's army evacuated Camden and retreated toward Little Rock, the regiment joined in the pursuit. Marmaduke's Brigade, which included the 3rd Cavalry, took the field first at Jenkins's Ferry on April 30. The 3rd and 4th Regiments deployed in a swampy area to ascertain the Federal position. The regiments advanced at sunrise and soon engaged the enemy. After two hours of spirited fighting in rainy and foggy conditions, an Arkansas infantry brigade relieved the Missourians. Steele eventually escaped across the Saline River and moved on to Little Rock. The campaign against Steele's forces, including the engagements of Poison Spring and Jenkins's Ferry, had been costly for the 3rd Cavalry, as the regimental casualties amounted to at least 8 killed and 36 wounded.

In late May and early June, the regiment participated in actions against Federal shipping on the Mississippi River. Operating on the river's west bank in Chicot County, Arkansas, the Confederates sank several boats and burned, disabled, or captured others. The 3rd Cavalry occupied a part of the main line in the engagement at Ditch Bayou on June

6 as the badly outnumbered Confederates defeated a Union force in a battle of several hours' duration.

The regiment entered Missouri with Marmaduke's Brigade on September 20th as part of Major General Sterling Price's Missouri expedition and marched to Fort Davidson at Pilot Knob. When the brigade charged the fort on September 27, the 3rd Cavalry served in reserve behind the brigade line. When the main line faltered, Colonel Greene led his men around their irresolute comrades, rallied them on his right, and continued forward until the Federals repulsed the charge. The regiment lost 3 killed and 29 wounded in the assault.

Following the battle at Pilot Knob, the regiment skirmished at Leasburg, Union, and then at Hermann, where it scattered a militia force and captured a 6-pounder cannon. On October 9, the regiment skirmished with the pursuing enemy at Russellville and likewise fought at Boonville two days later. The 3rd Regiment held the right flank of the brigade line at Glasgow on October 15 and performed well in compelling the Union garrison to surrender, at a cost to the regiment of 4 killed and 27 wounded. At the crossing of the Little Blue River on October 21, the regiment fought against superior numbers; it acted alone until reinforcements arrived to drive the enemy. The 3rd Cavalry separated from the army on October 22 to guard the approach to Independence. Rejoining the brigade the day following, the regiment fought at Byram's Ford later that afternoon. A charge by the enemy at Mine Creek, Kansas, on October 25 routed the brigade, including the 3rd Regiment, which fled the field in considerable disorder. Colonel Greene rallied part of his regiment, and a few hundred other troops, at the Little Osage River and skirmished with the pursuing enemy until dark. The protracted Missouri expedition cost the regiment 19 killed, 110 wounded, and 29 missing.

The 3rd Cavalry retreated with the army through Indian Territory to Texas and then moved to Laynesport, Arkansas. The regiment remained in camps in southern Arkansas and northern Louisiana until the army surrendered in June 1865. While some evidence suggests that the 3rd and 4th Cavalry regiments consolidated before the surrender, the consolidation cannot be verified in the available records. Incomplete casualty reports reveal 44 troopers died in battle, 81 of disease, and 1 from an accident. Federal authorities executed 4.

Bibliography

Allardice, Bruce S. "Colton Greene." In *More Generals in Gray,* 105–6. Baton Rouge: Louisiana State University Press, 1995.

Furr, W. E. "Letter from an Old Timer." *Wright County Republican,* Hartville, Missouri, July 14 and August 12, 1924.

Colton Greene Papers. Memphis Public Library, Memphis, Tennessee.

Gullett, Capt. W. S. "Battle of Hartville, Mo." *Confederate Veteran* 29 (1921): 427–28.

John S. Marmaduke Correspondence. National Archives, Washington, D.C.

Polk, C. K. "General Price's Raid." *Iron County Register,* Ironton, Missouri, October 12, 1905.

4th Regiment (Burbridge's)

Colonel: John Quincy Burbridge

Lieutenant Colonel: John M. Wimer (battalion only), killed January 11, 1863; William I. Preston

Major: Dennis Smith, killed April 30, 1864; James W. Porter

Companies and Commanders:

Company A: (Stoddard) Joseph J. Miller, resigned because of wound October 2, 1863; James R. Jackson

Company B: (Stoddard) David G. Hicks

Company C: (Mississippi, Stoddard) William T. Lineback

Company D: (St. Louis) Dennis Smith, promoted major February 11, 1863; David Sappington

Company E: (Phelps, Pulaski, Texas, Wright) James O'Neill

Company F: (Audrain, Callaway, Ralls, Shelby) John W. Jacobs

Company G: (Boone, Lewis, Marion, Monroe, Shelby) James W. Porter, promoted major ca. 1864; Amos K. Hulett

Company H: (St. Louis) George Taylor

Company I (Old): (State of Arkansas) Lorenzo D. Bryant (Detached and transferred to the 8th Arkansas Cavalry Regiment as Company G)

Company I (New): (Camden, Dallas, Hickory, Morgan, Polk, Vernon) Leroy D. Roberts

Company K: (Clark, Ralls, Warren) Joseph C. Kent

Colonel John Q. Burbridge, a veteran Missouri State Guard colonel and subsequently commander of the 2nd Missouri Infantry Regiment, resigned his commission in the Army of the West on June 29, 1862, and returned to the Trans-Mississippi to recruit a regiment of partisan rangers in Missouri. He apparently acted with the authority of Major General Sterling Price. Burbridge faced considerable competition in recruiting in Missouri in the summer of 1862, but by September 27, he commanded six companies at Thomasville in Oregon County. Burbridge organized the recruits as regular cavalry since the department had ended recruitment of partisan rangers the previous July. The recruits organized as a regiment, but the command lacked sufficient companies for a regiment under Confederate law. Thus, Burbridge's unit, despite being called a regiment, actually constituted only a battalion. By early November, Burbridge commanded a small brigade consisting of his battalion, the 3rd Missouri Cavalry Regiment, and Captain Louis T. Brown's Arkansas battery (Newton Artillery).

This force attacked the Union outpost near Clark's Mill in Douglas County, Missouri, on November 7, procured its surrender after a short fight; captured 150 prisoners, 2 cannons, 200 stands of arms, a number of horses, and stores valued at nearly $40,000; and burned the enemy fortification before leaving the area. The brigade next struck in Wright County on November 24, destroying forty Federal supply wagons and inflicting substantial casualties on the enemy. In December, Burbridge's battalion joined a newly organized brigade that included the 3rd and 8th Missouri cavalry regiments and the Newton Artillery. Colonel Moses J. White commanded the brigade, but he soon relinquished leadership to Colonel Joseph C. Porter.

A detachment from the battalion, led by Lieutenant Colonel John M. Wimer, rode with Porter into southwest Missouri in January 1863 as part of Brigadier General John S. Marmaduke's raiding force. During the raid, the battalion fought at Hartville on January 11, where Wimer was killed and 9 men wounded. Pursuant to the provisions of Special Order No. 23, Headquarters, Trans-Mississippi Department, dated January 23, 1863, the battalion consolidated with Major William I. Preston's battalion to form a regiment on February 5. Special Order No. 41, same headquarters, dated February 11, recognized the consolidation and issued commissions to the field officers of the unit, which became 4th Cavalry Regiment. Before April 19, the 4th Cavalry, Colonel R. C. Newton's Arkansas cavalry regiment, and the Newton Artillery formed a new brigade, commanded by Burbridge, and joined Marmaduke's raid into southeast Missouri. The 4th Cavalry fought at Cape Girardeau on April 26, losing 7 men wounded, and then skirmished with enemy cavalry near Jackson the day following. It retreated with the army to Arkansas, skirmishing along the way, including a brisk fight at Chalk Bluff.

Upon returning to Arkansas, the 4th Cavalry performed outpost duty for several months in northeast Arkansas, scouting and reporting enemy movements north of their position, including in southeast Missouri. The regiment joined Marmaduke's Brigade, commanded by Colonel Colton Greene, on June 2 and remained in that organization for the balance of the war. The unit remained on outpost duty and missed the battle of Helena on July 4. The 4th Cavalry opposed the enemy advance on Little Rock, fighting at Brownsville, Reed's Bridge, Bayou Metoe, and Bayou Fourche, but suffered few losses as it often served in reserve. At Pine Bluff on October 25, the regiment attacked dismounted from south of town. In an uncoordinated assault, the Confederates suffered a repulse, with the 4th Cavalry losing 4 wounded.

The next significant combat for the regiment occurred in early spring 1864 in opposition to Major General Frederick Steele's advance from Little Rock to Shreveport, Louisiana, during the Red River Campaign. The 4th Cavalry fought at Elkin's Ferry, Prairie D'Ann, and near Camden as the Confederates delayed Steele's advance until he altered course and occupied Camden. At Poison Spring on April 18, the regiment participated in a charge that routed the enemy, resulting in the capture of a battery and numerous wagons and mule teams. The 4th Cavalry suffered 6 wounded in the fight. The regiment fought at Jenkins's Ferry on April 30, being among the first troops on the field. Sent forward with the 3rd Cavalry to develop the enemy's position, the 4th Regiment lost 1 killed and 12 wounded as it fought until relieved by an Arkansas infantry brigade.

In late May and early June, the regiment participated in operations against Union naval traffic on the Mississippi River, damaging, destroying, or capturing 13 enemy vessels of various types. On June 6, at Ditch Bayou, Arkansas, the 4th Cavalry brought on the engagement when its pickets encountered the Union advance, and also covered the Confederate withdrawal. The 4th Cavalry fought in most of the major engagements of Major General Sterling Price's Missouri expedition in the fall of 1864. At Pilot Knob, on September 27, the regiment occupied the extreme left of Marmaduke's Brigade when the Confederates charged Fort Davidson. Subjected to "galling and destructive" artillery and small-arms fire, once it debouched from Shepherd's Mountain to the floor of Arcadia Valley, the 4th Cavalry made little forward progress before the men sought shelter in a creek bed. The regiment suffered casualties of 7 killed and 28 wounded in less than twenty minutes of combat.

Following the disaster at Pilot Knob, the 4th Cavalry joined in the unsuccessful pursuit of the fleeing Union army and then moved with the brigade west along the south side of the Missouri River toward Jefferson City, skirmishing with the enemy, capturing arms and supplies, and destroying railroad facilities. The regiment skirmished at Boonville on October 11 as the army continued its westward march. The 4th Cavalry fought with the brigade at Glasgow on October 15; it lost 2 killed and 9 wounded before the Federal garrison surrendered after two hours of fighting. The brigade rejoined the main army and helped force a crossing of the Little Blue River on October 21. It next moved to Independence, fought as part of the rear guard on October 22, and then engaged the pursuing enemy at the Big Blue (Byram's Ford) the day following. The final engagement of the campaign for the 4th Cavalry occurred at Mine Creek, Kansas, on October 25. When a Federal charge struck the Confederate line, the 4th Cavalry broke and fled the field in disarray, having lost 13 killed, 27 wounded, and 34 taken prisoner.

After the Mine Creek debacle, the regiment accompanied the army on the demoralizing march through Indian Territory to Texas and then on to Arkansas. The casualties of the 4th Cavalry during the Missouri Expedition totaled 13 killed, 51 wounded, and over 50 taken prisoner. The regiment spent the balance of the war relatively inactive in camps in southern Arkansas and northwestern Louisiana. The troopers of the 4th Cavalry received paroles at Shreveport, Louisiana, on June 7, 1865. While some evidence suggests that the 3rd and 4th Cavalry regiments consolidated before the surrender, the parole records do not support such a combination. Regimental losses, doubtless short of the true numbers, included 38 killed in battle, 51 deaths by disease, 1 drowned, and 1 executed by Federal authorities. A regimental flag of this unit is housed in the collections of the Oklahoma Historical Society, Oklahoma City, Oklahoma.

BIBLIOGRAPHY

"Acts and Deeds of Colonel Burbridge's Regiments." Thomas L. Snead Papers. Missouri Historical Society, St. Louis, Missouri.

"F. M. Hope, 4th Missouri Cavalry." *Confederate Veteran* 33 (1925): 73.

"Henry C. Thurston." *Confederate Veteran* 9 (1901): 397.

Moore, M. M. "Corrections of Two Articles." *Confederate Veteran* 17 (1909): 550.

George Primrose. Letter to the editor. *Washington Telegraph,* Washington, Arkansas, November 16, 1863.

5th Regiment (Shelby's/Gordon's) (Referred to unofficially as the 1st Regiment in the Trans-Mississippi Department) "Lafayette County Cavalry"

Colonel: Joseph Orville Shelby, promoted to brigadier general December 15, 1863; Benjamin F. Gordon

Lieutenant Colonel: Benjamin F. Gordon, promoted colonel December 15, 1863; Yandell H. Blackwell

Major: George R. Kirtley, killed January 11, 1863; Yandell H. Blackwell; promoted lieutenant colonel December 15, 1863; George P. Gordon

Companies and Commanders:

Company A: (Lafayette) Joseph Orville Shelby, promoted colonel July 28, 1862; Yandell H. Blackwell, promoted major ca. January 1863; Charles G. Jones

Company B: (Lafayette) J. A. Boarman, resigned because of wound May 25, 1863; B. May Neale

Company C: (Lafayette) George P. Gordon; promoted major ca. December 1863; C. Columbus Catron

Company D (1st): (Lafayette, Saline) George R. Kirtley, promoted major September 12, 1862, John C. Clark, killed July 4, 1863; David R. Stallard. Company detached to serve as Marmaduke's Escort, May 15, 1863

Company D (2nd): George W. Evans. Formerly Company A, 10th Missouri Cavalry Regiment.

Company E: (Saline) James M. Garrett, mortally wounded on January 11, 1863; Robert C. Nunnelly, resigned September 9, 1863; Joseph P. Elliott

Company F: (Johnson, Lafayette) George S. Rathbun

Company G: (Lafayette) W. Scott Bullard

Company H: (Cooper, Lafayette, Saline) H. S. Titsworth, mortally wounded January 8, 1863; William R. Edwards, deserted ca. February 1864; William M. Moorman

Company I: (Lafayette) Benjamin F. Elliott, transferred December 1, 1862; Charles M. Turpin, killed January 11, 1863; William N. Thorp

Company K: (Bates, Cass) L. J. Crocker

The origins of this regiment can be traced to the "Lafayette County Mounted Rifles," a company Captain Joseph O. Shelby organized in 1861 for service in the 8th Division, Missouri State Guard. Shelby's company fought with credit in the Guard's battles from Carthage, Missouri, through Pea Ridge, Arkansas. The company then accompanied Major General Earl Van Dorn's Army of the West to the Cis-Mississippi as dismounted cavalry. In mid-1862 the company returned to Arkansas, where Shelby obtained authority to recruit a cavalry regiment from Major General Thomas C. Hindman, commander of the Trans-Mississippi Department. Shelby and his men rode northward for the Missouri River in late July. Arriving in Lafayette County about August 14, Shelby recruited sufficient men for a regiment in only four days. He led the recruits, many of them veterans of the Missouri State Guard, to Arkansas. On August 24 at Coon Creek in Jasper County, Missouri, elements of the 6th Kansas Cavalry Regiment struck Shelby's column. Shelby's men repulsed the enemy in a sharp fight and then proceeded southward unmolested. After a short time in northwest Arkansas, the troopers moved north again, and the regimental organization occurred at Camp Coffee in southern Newton County, Missouri, about September 12. The regiment, subsequently designated the

5th Cavalry, became part of a new cavalry brigade commanded by Shelby. Lieutenant Colonel Benjamin F. Gordon replaced Shelby as regimental commander.

On the morning of September 30, the 5th Cavalry rushed to Newtonia after Federals attacked that Confederate outpost. Gordon led the regiment to a position that flanked a charging enemy column, thereby blunting the Federal advance. The regiment experienced a full day of fighting, losing 3 killed and 7 wounded, before the Federals withdrew. Eventually forced from Missouri by a Union buildup around Newtonia, the Confederates retreated into northwest Arkansas. The 5th Regiment spent the next several weeks scouting and screening Confederate movements. On November 28, a Federal army attacked the Confederates as they foraged in the vicinity of Cane Hill, Arkansas. The outnumbered rebels waged a fighting retreat over several miles of mountainous terrain, deploying often to slow the Union pursuit. The running fight lasted several hours and resulted in the 5th Cavalry suffering 15 wounded. The regiment fought at Prairie Grove on December 7, generally on the right of Shelby's line and often in support of Captain Joseph Bledsoe's Missouri battery, the brigade's artillery complement. When the Confederates abandoned the field near midnight, the 5th Cavalry counted its losses as 1 killed and 7 wounded.

In early January 1863, the regiment accompanied Shelby's brigade as part of Brigadier General John S. Marmaduke's raid into southwest Missouri. The regiment participated in the attack on Springfield on January 8 and at Hartville three days later. The casualties for the regiment during the raid totaled 11 killed or mortally wounded, and 69 wounded. After a brief respite near Batesville, Arkansas, the 5th Regiment rode northward in Marmaduke's second raid, this time into southeast Missouri. Although there was skirmishing often during the ingress and egress from Missouri, the primary engagement occurred at Cape Girardeau on April 26. There, the regiment lost 4 killed and 11 wounded in a fight waged to extricate Colonel George W. Carter's Texas brigade from a dangerous position. On July 4, the regiment joined in the assault on Helena, Arkansas, by attacking "Battery A," a redoubt containing two artillery pieces atop Rightor Hill, on the Federal right flank. Shelby's brigade made no headway against the Union position but endured heavy artillery fire on its left flank before disengaging. The 5th Cavalry suffered casualties of 6 killed and 8 wounded in the attack.

The regiment opposed the Federal advance on Little Rock during late August and early September. Fighting at Brownsville, Bayou Metoe, and Bayou Fourche, the 5th Cavalry suffered minimal losses before the capital city fell to the enemy on September 10. In late September, a select few of the regiment, under Captain George P. Gordon, rode with Colonel Shelby on a raid into western Missouri. The raid lasted nearly a month, covered 1,500 miles, and resulted in the capture of many prisoners, the destruction of considerable enemy property, numerous skirmishes, and larger fights at Neosho and Marshall. It completely exhausted the long-riding Confederates. In April 1864 the 5th Regiment joined the forces that sought to delay Major General Frederick Steele's advance to Shreveport, Louisiana, during the Red River Campaign. The regiment engaged the enemy with Shelby's brigade near Spoonville, at Okolona, near Elkin's Ferry, and Prairie D'Ann, besides participating in several smaller skirmishes. On April 25, the regiment was part of the Confederate victory at Marks's Mill, which resulted in the capture of a large number of prisoners, 2 cannons, and many mule teams and wagons. Although in reserve when the fight began, the regiment joined a charge that routed the Federals and led to the capture of the artillery. The 5th Cavalry lost 3 killed, 9 wounded, and 2 missing in these extended operations.

In late May, Gordon's regiment marched with Shelby's brigade to northeast Arkansas to operate behind enemy lines. The brigade defeated several enemy detachments, as well as guerrilla outfits, before Shelby established himself in the White River valley and proceeded to interrupt river and railroad traffic. Shelby's men also recruited and conscripted hundreds of soldiers over the next few months. On June 24, the regiment helped capture and destroy the gunboat *Queen City* at Clarendon and fought in the subsequent engagement with three other gunboats later that day. The regiment next struck with the brigade at Ashley's Station and Jones's Hay Station near De Vall's Bluff on August 24. The rebels captured many prisoners in these actions and destroyed miles of the Memphis & Little Rock Railroad.

In mid-September, the 5th Cavalry joined in General Sterling Price's Missouri expedition. Entering Missouri with Shelby's brigade at Doniphan on September 19, the regiment proceeded to burn three railroad bridges on the St. Louis & Iron Mountain Railroad. That work accomplished, the regiment then destroyed several miles of railroad tracks. The 5th Cavalry headed west with the army thereafter, skirmished at various places, and acted as a decoy at Castle Rock on the Osage River, while the brigade forced a crossing elsewhere. The regiment skirmished hard with the enemy at Dixon's Plantation before rejoining the command near Jefferson City. The 5th Regiment accompanied the brigade to Sedalia on October 15, where it assisted in capturing 300 Union militiamen, along with arms and needed supplies. At Lexington on October 19, the 5th Cavalry led a charge that drove stubborn Federal defenders toward Independence. The regiment acted with Colonel Sidney D. Jackman's brigade of Shelby's division on October 22 as the Confederates forced a crossing of the Big Blue River before moving on to Westport. The 5th Cavalry deployed on the left of the line at Westport on October 23, a hard fight that saw the Confederates driven from the field after being outflanked. On October 25 the brigade moved to attack Fort Scott, Kansas, but turned about to save the army after the enemy routed two other divisions at Mine Creek. The 5th Regiment fought hard as the brigade delayed the pursing Federals by forming numerous temporary lines of defense until the pursuit ended for the day.

The last engagement of the expedition occurred on October 28, when Federals surprised the Confederate camp at Newtonia, Missouri. In a sharp but brief fight, in which part of the 5th Cavalry played a role, the Confederates repulsed the enemy with loss, and pursuit of the army ended. The army then proceeded through Arkansas and Indian Territory to Clarksville, Texas. During the Missouri expedition, the regimental losses totaled 20 killed or mortally wounded, 45 wounded, and 40 missing. The 5th Cavalry remained in Texas until June 2, 1865, when General Shelby disbanded his division. Some members of the regiment journeyed to Shreveport, Louisiana, to receive paroles, a few accompanied Shelby into voluntary exile in Mexico, and others simply went home or elsewhere. The regimental losses included 81 battle deaths, 53 men lost to disease, 2 killed by accident, and 1 executed by Federal authorities.

BIBLIOGRAPHY

Allardice, Bruce S. "Benjamin Franklin Gordon." In *More Generals in Gray*, 102–3. Baton Rouge: Louisiana State University Press, 1995.

"Col. Gordon's Regiment of Missouri Cavalry." In *History of Lafayette County, Missouri*, 380–82. St. Louis: Missouri Historical Co., 1881.

Coleman, R. B. "Brave Charles Snelling and His Fate." *Confederate Veteran* 1 (1893): 178.

———. "More of Scouting in Missouri and Arkansas." *Confederate Veteran* 19 (1911): 525–26.

———. "Various Small Fights in Missouri." *Confederate Veteran* 14 (1906): 120–21.

Edwards, John Newman. *Shelby and His Men; Or the War in the West.* Waverly: Joseph Shelby Memorial Association, 1993.

Rockwell, J. H. "A Rambling Reminiscence of Experiences during the Great War between the States." Unpublished typescript. Missouri State Archives, Jefferson City, Missouri.

Scott, T. A. G. "Battle of Marshall, Mo." *Confederate Veteran* 8 (1900): 58.

6th Regiment (Coffee's/Thompson's) "Southwest Cavalry"

Redesignated the 11th Regiment. See the entry for that regiment.

7th Regiment (Kitchen's) (Also known as the 10th Regiment)

Colonel: Solomon George Kitchen

Lieutenant Colonel: Solomon G. Kitchen, promoted colonel July 9, 1863; Jesse Ellison, resigned ca. January 1865

Major: Jesse Dooley (battalion only), dropped July 9, 1863; James A. Walker

Companies and Commanders:

Company A: (Dunklin) James Clark, deserted February 2, 1864; George Faulkner

Company B: (Stoddard) James A. Cooper

Company C: (Dunklin) H. S. B. Knight

Company D: (Bollinger, Stoddard) Jesse Ellison, promoted lieutenant colonel July 9, 1863

Company E: (Dunklin) W. H. Glenn

Company F: (Dunklin) Thomas St. Clair, killed October 26, 1862; John McWherter

Company G: (Dunklin) James Page, disposition not of record; William Wethers

Company H: (Dunklin, Stoddard) Andrew F. Jones, murdered ca. December 1862; Charles C. Williford

Company I: (Madison, Stoddard) Jesse R. Henson

Company K: (Greene County, Arkansas) Cullen H. Mobley, resigned October 26, 1863; Andrew Webb

This regiment originated as a battalion organized from remnants of eight companies of "Clark's Recruits" (see later) on April 9, 1863, near Scatterville, Arkansas. Recruited largely in southeast Missouri, many unit members had served in the 1st Division, Missouri State Guard. When the battalion organized, it contained only about 120 soldiers, who possessed merely 86 weapons. The battalion initially served as an independent unit, unattached to any brigade. Lt. Col. Kitchen led 100 of the men in a night attack on a Union camp near Chalk Bluff in Dunklin County, Missouri, on April 21. The Missourians inflicted 30 casualties, mostly prisoners, and captured weapons and equipment, with a loss of 2 killed and 2 wounded. By May 31, the battalion numbered over 300 troopers. It performed picket duty at Chalk Bluff and scouted into southeast Missouri as far north as Cape Girardeau County.

Assigned to Marmaduke's Missouri cavalry brigade on June 2, Kitchen's Battalion nonetheless remained on outpost duty in northeastern Arkansas. The battalion's strength continued to increase, as 560 troopers had enrolled by June 15, but arms remained a problem, for only 224 men possessed weapons. After two additional companies joined the battalion, Kitchen obtained authority to organize a regiment, which mustered into service on July 9 at Chalk Bluff, Arkansas. Originally known as the 10th Regiment, the Confederate War Department later designated the unit the 7th Missouri Cavalry Regiment. Captain John McWherter's scout party surprised a Federal supply train at Round Pond in Cape Girardeau County on August 16, killing and wounding 30, burning 65 wagons, and capturing horses and weapons. The 7th Cavalry performed duty in Little Rock during the Federal advance on the capital. When the Confederates evacuated the city on September 10, the regiment destroyed the pontoon bridges on the Arkansas River and then screened the infantry as it retreated through the city. The regiment also participated in the attack on Pine Bluff on October 25. During the engagement, Kitchen's mounted men protected the flanks of the brigade units that fought on foot. After the attack failed, the 7th Regiment covered the withdrawal, at one time sharply repelling an enemy charge on the rear of the column.

In early April 1864 the regiment fought with Marmaduke's brigade at Elkin's Ferry and Prairie D'Ann as it opposed the advance of Major General Frederick Steele's army into southern Arkansas as part of the Red River Campaign. The regiment performed guard duties and missed the battles of Poison Spring and Jenkins's Ferry. At the engagement at Ditch Bayou on June 6, the regiment participated in the Confederate victory and suffered 3 wounded. The attachment of Lieutenant Colonel J. F. Davies's Arkansas Cavalry Battalion augmented the regiment's strength at the beginning of Major General Sterling Price's expedition into Missouri in September. The combined unit guarded the division train at Pilot Knob on September 27 and thus did not join the fight.

The regiment skirmished with the enemy at Union on October 1, and eight days later, it checked a Federal charge at California that threatened the brigade rear. The 7th Cavalry assisted in capturing Glasgow and a large number of prisoners and weapons on October 15. A Federal attack stymied elements of Marmaduke's brigade at the crossing of the Little Blue River on October 21; a timely dismounted charge by the 7th Regiment stemmed the Federal advance and turned the tide of battle. The regiment fought the pursuing Federals at Independence for several hours on October 22 and at Byram's Ford a day later. A Federal charge collapsed the Confederate line at Mine Creek, Kansas, on October 25 and routed the troops, including the 7th Cavalry. The regiment suffered estimated losses of 6 killed, 12 wounded, and 57 taken prisoner in the fight that one regimental officer described as the "stampede on the prairie." For the entire Price raid, the casualties of the 7th Cavalry tallied 13 killed, 39 wounded and 69 taken prisoner. A report that 265 men deserted following the Mine Creek disaster is suspect. The allegation stemmed from a dubious source and appears to be based on the fact that Colonel Kitchen and many of his men left the army when the Confederates reached Arkansas. But General Price furloughed many units after the expedition, and since Price and Kitchen enjoyed a close relationship, it is unlikely that Kitchen left without Price's consent. About 70 men stayed with the main army and formed two companies that merged into the 8th Cavalry Regiment before February 28, 1865. Those soldiers received paroles at Shreveport, Louisiana on June 7, 1865, as members of Companies G and H of that regiment. The officers and men that accompanied Colonel Kitchen to northeast Arkansas took oaths at Jacksonport and Wittsburg, Arkansas, in late May and early June. Very incomplete regimental records reveal that 16 troopers died in battle, 73 succumbed to disease in camp or prison, 2 were murdered, and 1 was executed by Federal authorities.

BIBLIOGRAPHY

Civil War Journal of Jacob Bess. Missouri State Archives, Jefferson City, Missouri.

Draper, John Ballard. "William Curtis Ballard Diary, March 28–November 21, 1864." In *William Curtis Ballard—His Ancestors and Descendants,* 69–76. Austin: Privately printed, 1979.

Jesse Ellison Letters. W. L. Skaggs Collection. Arkansas History Center, Little Rock, Arkansas.

McGhee, James E. "Worth Remembering: Solomon G. Kitchen." *Daily Statesman,* Dexter, Missouri, February 26, 1976.

Stanton, Donal J., Goodwin F. Berquist, and Paul C. Bowers, eds. *The Civil War Reminiscences of General M. Jeff Thompson.* Dayton: Morningside Press, 1988.

8th Regiment (Jeffers's)

Colonel: William Lafayette Jeffers, taken prisoner October 25, 1864

Lieutenant Colonel: Samuel J. Ward

Major: James M. Parrott, died May 13, 1865

Companies and Commanders:

Company A: (Bollinger) John H. Suggs, mortally wounded June 6, 1864

Company B: (Cape Girardeau) John H. Cobb

Company C: (Cape Girardeau, Madison, Stoddard) Julian N. Giddings, resigned for disability February 27, 1863; Robert J. Brooks

Company D: (Cape Girardeau) Robert A. Hope, died March 12, 1863; William T. Thompson

Company E: (Mississippi, New Madrid) John N. Pritchard, killed September 27, 1864

Company F: (Cape Girardeau) William White Craig, killed September 27, 1864

Company G: (Cape Girardeau) Stephen J. Campbell

Company H: (Mississippi, Scott) Alexander Wright, resigned for disability August 1, 1863; William P. Powers

Company I: (New Madrid, Stoddard) Edward Phillips, taken prisoner April 7, 1864

Company K: (Cape Girardeau) Moses E. Cox

William L. Jeffers, a Mexican War and State Guard veteran, recruited this regiment in southeast Missouri during August–November 1862. It included over 300 soldiers that had served in the 1st and 2nd Cavalry Regiments, and 4th Infantry Regiment, 1st Division, Missouri State Guard. The recruits engaged the enemy several times before any formal organization. Jeffers's men nearly annihilated a small forage party near Bloomfield on July 30. The recruit force captured a Union militia company intact at Dallas (Marble Hill) on August 17, along with their weapons and horses, and accomplished a like feat at Appleton five days later. The command fought elements of the 12th Missouri State Militia Cavalry Regiment on August 24, on Crooked Creek in Bollinger County, defeating them with minimal losses. On September 11, Jeffers's command drove the Union troops from Bloomfield, resulting in the capture of 2 artillery pieces, 300 rifles, 3 tons of ammunition, and a large quantity of supplies, with a loss of 2 killed and 3 wounded.

Having recruited six companies, Jeffers organized a battalion in northern Dunklin County, Missouri, on October 4, 1862. The battalion attacked Commerce on October 19, capturing most of the militiamen, their horses, and weapons, without casualties. Four additional companies joined the battalion by December 6, and a regimental organization took place on Holcomb's Island in Dunklin County, resulting in the creation of the 8th Cavalry Regiment. Shortly thereafter, the regiment moved to Pocahontas, Arkansas, where it mustered into Confederate service on December 10 and joined a brigade commanded by Colonel Moses J. White.

A contingent of the regiment participated in a successful encounter with an enemy forage party near Van Buren, Missouri, on December 28, 1862. In early January 1863 a regimental detachment accompanied the brigade, then under the command of Colonel Joseph C. Porter, into southwest Missouri in conjunction with Brigadier General John S. Marmaduke's first raid into the state. The regiment fought at Hartville on January 11, where it lost 2 killed, 5 wounded, and 4 missing. The 8th Cavalry next participated in Marmaduke's raid into southeast Missouri in April but never closely engaged the enemy during the expedition. In June the regiment needed 300 additional horses to mount the entire command and possessed only 126 serviceable weapons.

The 8th Cavalry fought at Helena, Arkansas, on July 4 and had 1 killed and 1 missing in that Confederate defeat. During the defense of Little Rock in August and September, the regiment participated in fights at Brownsville, Bayou Metoe, and Bayou Fourche. In the latter engagement, on September 10, it helped capture two artillery pieces assigned to the 2nd Missouri Cavalry Regiment (Union). The regiment lost 2 killed and 8 wounded during the campaign. At Pine Bluff on October 25, the regiment fought dismounted on the right of the Confederate line and suffered losses of 2 killed and 3 wounded.

Only a company-sized unit commanded by Captain John H. Cobb participated in the engagements of the Camden Expedition in April 1864, including those at Elkins's Ferry, Prairie D'Ann, and Poison Spring. The balance of the regiment served in Louisiana during that time, where it skirmished with Federals advancing up the Red River on April 4 at Campti. It also scouted and served as escort for Major General John G. Walker's Texas infantry division during the Red River Campaign. The reunited 8th Cavalry led the pursuit of Major General Frederick Steele's army when the Federals evacuated Camden in late April and retreated to Little Rock. The pursuit involved nearly constant skirmishing with the enemy. Because of the regiment's low supply of ammunition, it played only a minor role in the battle of Jenkins's Ferry on April 30.

The regiment engaged in the operations against Federal shipping on the Mississippi River in Chicot County, Arkansas, in May and June 1864, and participated in the Confederate victory at Ditch Bayou on June 6. When Major General Sterling Price's expeditionary force reached Pocahontas, Arkansas, on September 19, 1864, en route to Missouri, the division commander detached the regiment for special service. The 8th Cavalry drove the enemy from Bloomfield, inflicted several casualties, captured supplies, and destroyed the fortifications at that outpost. It also captured a militia company and its arms and horses at Jackson two days later before rejoining the army. At the battle of Pilot Knob on September 27, Jeffers's men occupied a position on the left of Marmaduke's brigade during the charge on Fort Davidson. Exposed to a withering fire from the Union defenders, the regiment made no real headway against the enemy defenses and suffered estimated losses of 30 killed and wounded. After Pilot Knob, the 8th Cavalry skirmished at Leasburg, Union, Washington, and Hermann. Jeffers's men resisted the Federal advance at Boonville on October 11–12 and fought at Glasgow three days later when the rebels captured the Union garrison.

As Price's army moved west toward Kansas City, the 8th Cavalry engaged in hard fighting at the Little Blue and Independence, and on October 23 helped defend the crossing of the Big Blue River at Byram's Ford. One of the last units fighting after a Union cavalry charge shattered the Confederate line at Mine Creek, Kansas, on October 25, the regiment lost 9 killed, 21 wounded, and 16 taken prisoner in the engagement. After the disaster at Mine Creek, Price's defeated army retreated through Indian Territory to Texas and then on to Laynesport, Arkansas. During the Missouri raid the regiment reported 22 killed, 35 wounded, and 30 missing, but the casualties most certainly were higher, particularly among the wounded. The 8th Cavalry spent the balance of the war in camps in southern Arkansas or northern Louisiana. Near the end of hostilities, a small element of the 7th Missouri Cavalry merged into the regiment. Thus, when the troops accepted paroles at Shreveport, Louisiana, on June 7, 1865, companies A–F represented the original regiment, while companies G–H consisted primarily of veterans of the 7th Cavalry. About 250 of the original members of the regiment received paroles at Shreveport of approximately 1,050 who served in the 8th Cavalry during the war. Known regimental losses include 49 battle deaths, 86 deaths from disease, 2 drowned, 2 accidentally shot to death, 1 murdered, and 2 executed by Federal troops.

BIBLIOGRAPHY

Coker, James A. "Recollections of J. A. Coker." Unpublished manuscript. Thomas Ewing Family Papers, Library of Congress, Washington, D.C.

McGhee, James E. *Campaigning with Marmaduke: Narratives and Roster of the 8th Missouri Cavalry Regiment, C.S.A.* Independence: Two Trails, 2002.

———. "The Gallant Jeffers—A Soldier of Two Wars." *Cash-Book Journal,* Jackson, Missouri, October 12, 1994.

————. "A Most Disgraceful Thing": The Confederates Capture Bloomfield in 1862." *Blue and Grey Chronicle* 8 (December 2004): 12–13.

Nichols, Ray. "Eighth Missouri Cavalry." *Collage of Cape [Girardeau] County* 12 (September 1992): 1–7.

9th Regiment (Elliott's) (Formerly the 1st or 10th Battalion) "Elliott's Scouts"

Colonel: Benjamin Franklin Elliott

Lieutenant Colonel: Benjamin Franklin Elliott, promoted colonel ca. October 10, 1864; Washington McDaniel

Major: Benjamin Franklin Elliott, promoted lieutenant colonel ca. May 8, 1864; Washington McDaniel, promoted lieutenant colonel ca. October 10, 1864; Thomas H. Walton

Companies and Commanders:

Company A: (Lafayette, Polk) Washington McDaniel, promoted to major ca. May 8, 1864; Robert J. Tucker

Company B: (Saline) David Martin, killed November 28, 1862; Thomas H. Walton, promoted to major ca. October 10, 1864; W. B. Walker

Company C: (Cooper, Moniteau) William Mosby

Company D: (Boone, Randolph) David W. Davenport

Company E: (Lafayette, Pettis) William N. Thorp; disabled by wound ca. October 1864; William L. Patterson

Company F: (Cooper, Pettis, Saline) W. H. Greenwood

Company G: (Barry, Cass, Clay, Saline) John D. Holt

Company H: (Henry, Saline) Lucien M. Major, wounded and taken prisoner October 28, 1864

Company I: (Moniteau, Washington) Anderson Bowles

Company K: (Oregon, Shannon) Jacob B. Reaser

On November 19, 1862, Colonel Joseph O. Shelby, brigade commander, ordered Captain Benjamin F. Elliott, Company I, 5th Missouri Cavalry Regiment, to organize a company of "Guides and Spies." Men from various regimental companies transferred to the newly formed unit. The company, also referred to as "Elliott's Scouts," engaged the enemy initially at Cane Hill, Arkansas, on November 28. It deployed in several positions during a prolonged running battle that covered twelve miles and lost 3 killed and 7 wounded in close fighting. On December 1, 1862, Elliott acquired an additional company; he organized a battalion, technically a squadron, numbered the 1st Cavalry Battalion, although referred to at times as the 10th Cavalry Battalion. At Prairie Grove on December 7, Elliott's battalion, with other elements of Shelby's brigade, initiated the fight by charging the Federal cavalry advance, resulting in the capture of many prisoners and wagons. During the balance of that action, the battalion appears to have been only lightly engaged.

The men of Elliott's unit took the advance when Marmaduke's cavalry command raided southwest Missouri on December 31. At White Springs, Arkansas, on January 3, 1863, the battalion attacked a band of deserters and bushwhackers and inflicted heavy losses on them. When the command reached Springfield, Missouri, on January 8, Elliott's battalion first deployed on the Confederate right, where it skirmished until moved to support a section of Captain Joseph Bledsoe's battery that afternoon. When the raiders abandoned the attack on Springfield, the battalion covered the Confederate withdrawal. It subsequently moved with the command to Hartville, Missouri, where it fought on January 11. During the expedition, the battalion reported losses of 1 killed and 4 wounded. Part of the battalion moved north of Batesville, Arkansas, on February 10, for the purpose of rounding up deserters and stragglers. The detachment encountered an enemy scout party and, after a short fight, retreated to Batesville with the loss of 12 prisoners, 2 of whom the Federals executed.

At the engagement at Cape Girardeau, Missouri, on April 26 during Marmaduke's second Missouri raid, Elliott's men fought on the right flank of Shelby's brigade and helped repulse an enemy cavalry charge while losing 1 killed and 2 wounded. The battalion reported no casualties as a result of its participation in the Confederate defeat at Helena, Arkansas, on July 4. During the defense of Little Rock in August and early September, Elliott's battalion fought at Brownsville, Bayou Metoe, and Bayou Fourche, again without reported losses. When Shelby raided into Missouri in late September, 100 troopers of Elliott's battalion rode with the raiders. Early in the march, Elliott's men came upon 200 Federal irregulars near Caddo Gap, Arkansas, and killed and captured nearly half of them. Thereafter, Elliott's detachment participated in the other fights of the 1,500-mile raid and led the brigade through the Union lines after being nearly surrounded at Marshall, Missouri. Soldiers recruited during the raid joined the battalion, and by May 8, 1864, Elliott commanded seven companies and won promotion to lieutenant colonel.

The battalion opened the spring campaign opposing the advance of Major General Frederick Steele's army into southern Arkansas as part of the Red River Campaign. Elliott's men fought with Shelby's brigade in skirmishes at Okolona, Elkin's Ferry, Prairie D'Ann, and Prairie DeRohan in early April. Detached to guard a ford, the battalion did not join in the fight at Marks's Mill on April 25. Following the battle of Jenkins's Ferry, the battalion skirmished with Steele's rear guard to within 20 miles of Little Rock, capturing prisoners and property. The widespread operations against Steele in April and early May cost the battalion about 25 killed and wounded. In May, the battalion marched with the brigade to northeastern Arkansas to interrupt enemy communications and recruit for the army. Elliott's battalion scouted for the brigade, fought numerous skirmishes, and took part in the destruction of the gunboat *Queen City* at Clarendon on June 24.

The battalion's next significant action occurred in August, when Union outposts at Ashley's Station and Jones's Hay Station fell to the Confederates, along with prisoners and arms. In mid-September, Elliott's Battalion rode into Missouri with Shelby's brigade when Major General Sterling Price initiated his Missouri expedition. The battalion burned a railroad bridge at Irondale and then destroyed sections of the St. Louis & Iron Mountain Railroad. Elliott's men next joined the pursuit of Federals that escaped Fort Davidson after the battle of Pilot Knob. On October 5, when the brigade forced a crossing of the Osage River near Jefferson City, the battalion contributed largely to the success of the operation. While the army threatened Jefferson City, part of Elliott's battalion cut telegraph wires on the Missouri Pacific Railroad and captured several prisoners. Shelby's brigade occupied Boonville on October 10, and three recruit companies joined Elliott's Battalion, which increased it to a full regiment, subsequently known as the 9th Cavalry. The new regiment rode with the brigade toward Sedalia on October 12. Elliott's regiment led the charge into the town on October 15 and suffered a brief repulse, but reinforcements arrived, and

300 militiamen surrendered with all of their arms, equipment, and supplies. On October 19 the brigade encountered Union forces at Lexington but drove them toward Independence after a stubborn fight. Elliott's men played a leading role in this engagement. Shelby's brigade, dismounted, forced a crossing of the Little Blue River on October 21, and engaged in the decisive battle of Westport two days later. During that engagement, the 9th Cavalry formed on the brigade's right and fought all day. The regiment participated in the final Confederate charge of the battle, a failed effort that resulted in the army retreating southward before superior numbers. On October 25, Shelby's brigade moved to save the army after the Federals routed two divisions of Price's command at Mine Creek, Kansas. The brigade, including the 9th Cavalry, formed successive lines of defense to delay the Federal advance and succeeded in halting the pursuit temporarily. Elliott's regiment participated in the last fight of the expedition on October 28, when the Federals attacked the Confederate camp at Newtonia. Elliott led his men into the fray dismounted. After a sharp thirty-minute engagement, the enemy withdrew; the Confederates then continued their retreat into Arkansas. The reported losses for the 9th Cavalry during the Missouri expedition totaled 5 killed and 18 wounded.

After a grueling march through Indian Territory, the army finally reached Texas. Shelby's brigade, including the 9th Cavalry, essentially remained in Texas until Shelby disbanded his division on June 5, 1865, at Corsicana. Colonel Elliott and about 50 of his men followed General Shelby into voluntary exile in Mexico; some 230 others took paroles at Shreveport, Louisiana; and the balance simply went home or elsewhere. Approximately 525 troopers appear on the existing rolls of the 9th Cavalry. Because the records are inadequate, it is impossible to determine with any degree of certainty the regiment's overall losses. Fragmentary information garnered from various sources reveals 14 regimental troopers killed in battle, 12 deaths by disease, and 2 soldiers executed by Federal troops.

Bibliography

Bartels, Carolyn M. *Elliott's Scouts: 9th Missouri Cavalry Battalion* [*sic*]. Independence: Two Trails, 2005.

"Benjamin F. Elliott." In *History of Lafayette County, Missouri*, 379–80. St. Louis: National Historical Co., 1991.

Richard Higgins Benton Autobiography. Western Historical Manuscript Collection, University of Missouri, Columbia, Missouri.

Edwards, John Newman. *Shelby and His Men; Or the War in the West.*
Waverly: Joseph Shelby Memorial Association, 1993.

"Maj. Thomas Henry Walton." In *Portrait and Biographical Record of Clay,
Ray, Carroll, Chariton and Linn Counties, Missouri,* 624–29. Chicago:
Chapman Bros., 1893.

Marshall, Weed. "Fight to the Finish near Lake Village, Arkansas."
Confederate Veteran 19 (1911): 169.

10th Regiment (Lawther's/Barry's)
(Formerly MacDonald's Battalion, then 11th Battalion)

Colonel: Robert R. Lawther, resigned February 27, 1865;
William T. Barry

Lieutenant Colonel: Merritt L. Young, mortally wounded
October 21, 1864

Major: George W. C. Bennett, mortally wounded September 27,
1864; William T. Barry, promoted colonel March 12, 1865

Companies and Commanders:

Company A: (Cooper, Jackson) Charles Harrison, resigned ca.
March 31, 1863; John D. Brinker, resigned ca. 1865; George W.
Evans. (For reasons unknown, this company surrendered as
Company D [2nd], 5th Missouri Cavalry Regiment, at Shreveport,
Louisiana, June 15, 1865.)

Company B: (Boone, Howard, Ray) William H. Frazier, disabled by
wound January 8, 1863; Irving Brown

Company C: (Cedar, Clay, Greene, Holt) Lawson Moore, resigned
July 21, 1864

Company D: (Bates, Henry, St. Clair) Richard M. Hancock

Company E: (Cass, Henry, Johnson) James P. Rice, resigned
December 24, 1864; William A. White

Company F: (Cass, Cole, Jackson) James Porter, resigned May 23,
1864

Company G: (Henry, Johnson, Pettis) John C. Lee, disposition not
of record; William H. Sims

Company H: (Boone, Moniteau) William T. Barry, promoted major
ca. September 28, 1864; Albert Hornbeck, disabled by wound

October 25, 1864, and never assumed command; Charles L. Kretchmar

Company I: (Exchanged Vicksburg prisoners, very mixed) William H. McPike

Company K: (Exchanged Vicksburg prisoners, very mixed) Asbury Vandiver

On August 5, 1862, Major General Thomas C. Hindman, Trans-Mississippi Department commander, authorized Emmett MacDonald, a former officer of the Missouri State Guard and battery commander in Confederate service, to recruit a regiment of cavalry in Missouri. At the same time, he appointed MacDonald provost marshal of Missouri. MacDonald faced serious competition in recruiting in Missouri and did not enroll sufficient men to complete a regiment. By early November, MacDonald commanded the provost guard of Brigadier General John S. Marmaduke's cavalry division in northwest Arkansas. On November 9, Marmaduke sought authority to organize the provost guard as a regular cavalry battalion under MacDonald's command. Marmaduke's request won approval, and on November 16, MacDonald organized a battalion of five companies from the provost guard. Although often referred to as MacDonald's Missouri Cavalry Regiment, five companies did not meet the requirements of Confederate law to constitute a regiment; the unit legally constituted only a battalion.

The battalion initially engaged the enemy at Cane Hill, Arkansas, on November 28, 1862. Fighting close to Colonel Joseph O. Shelby's Missouri cavalry brigade, the battalion deployed in several positions as the Confederates contested Union attacks in order to protect a large forage train. During eight hours of fighting that stretched over 12 miles of mountainous terrain, the battalion lost 7 killed or mortally wounded, 16 wounded, and 3 missing of 200 troopers engaged in the fight. On December 7, at the battle of Prairie Grove, the battalion, under the command of Lieutenant Colonel Merritt L. Young while MacDonald led a small brigade, charged an enemy cavalry force and drove it some distance, capturing about 50 prisoners in the process. Following the initial action, the battalion deployed as dismounted skirmishers and then moved to protect the Confederate left flank and later the opposite flank. After a fight that lasted into the darkness, the Confederates abandoned the field to the Federals. MacDonald reported casualties of 3 killed and

2 wounded in the action. Before the end of the year, the battalion rode with Marmaduke's command on a raid into southwest Missouri.

On January 7, 1863, the battalion surprised a militia detachment quartered in a log fort at Lawrence Mill; the militia fled at the Confederate approach. MacDonald's men burned the fort and adjoining barracks and captured substantial supplies, including 300 Austrian muskets, which they buried because they had no means of transporting them. Moving northwest to Springfield, MacDonald's battalion joined the attack on that stronghold on January 8. Sent to the left of the Confederate line, the battalion fought among private residences, unable to move forward while casualties mounted in close fighting. After several hours of combat, Marmaduke withdrew his command to the east and moved toward Hartville. When the Confederates engaged the enemy at Hartville on January 11, the battalion performed picket duty and did minor skirmishing. Colonel MacDonald became separated from the battalion and fell mortally wounded while participating in a charge with another unit. During the raid, the battalion casualties amounted to 8 killed or mortally wounded and 18 wounded, with all losses occurring at Springfield except that of MacDonald.

An additional company (F) joined the battalion in late February. The battalion, commanded by Lieutenant Colonel Young after MacDonald's death, participated in Marmaduke's raid into southeast Missouri in April and deployed at the battle at Cape Girardeau but never closely engaged the enemy and suffered few losses. Two more companies (G and H) became part of the battalion in May and June. The unit, normally called Young's Battalion, although officially designated the 11th Battalion, fought at Helena, Arkansas, as part of Marmaduke's brigade on July 4, with minimal losses. The battalion participated in the engagements at Brownsville, Bayou Metoe, and Bayou Fourche during the defense of Little Rock in August and September. In the latter engagement, on September 10, it helped capture two enemy artillery pieces. Young's men fought dismounted on the left of the Confederate line at Pine Bluff on October 25 and suffered casualties of 1 killed and 7 wounded. On or about December 26, 1863, near Camden, Arkansas, the battalion's eight companies consolidated with the two companies of Lawther's Missouri Cavalry Squadron to form this regiment. Lawther's companies consisted in large part of Missourians paroled at Vicksburg the previous July. Like the battalion before it, the 10th Cavalry served in Marmaduke's brigade.

On January 19, 1864, the newly formed regiment, later reinforced by Lieutenant Colonel Benjamin F. Elliott's battalion, engaged a sizeable enemy force on the Pine Bluff Road in the vicinity of Branchville. Skirmishing continued into the next day until the Federals retired to Pine Bluff. The 10th Cavalry counted losses of 1 killed and 4 wounded in the regiment's first fight. Lawther's regiment next saw action against the army of Major General Frederick Steele as it pushed into southern Arkansas toward Shreveport, Louisiana, as part of the Red River Campaign. The 10th Cavalry skirmished with the Federals on March 31 on the road to Arkadelphia and fought again near the same place two days later. The regiment successfully attacked the enemy's flank on April 3. Rejoining the brigade on April 4, Lawther's troopers fought at Prairie D'Ann and Prairie DeRohan and skirmished heavily with the enemy for the better part of two days before the Federals occupied Camden. The regiment performed scout duty when the brigade engaged the enemy at Poison Spring and Jenkins's Ferry. The 10th Cavalry accompanied the brigade in late May to Chicot County, Arkansas, as the Confederates attacked, captured, and destroyed Union shipping on the Mississippi River over a period of several days. On June 6, the regiment played a minor role in the defeat of a Federal expeditionary force at Ditch Bayou. Detached from the brigade once again, the 10th Regiment crossed the Arkansas River in small boats and assaulted an enemy fortification on June 22. The fort's defenders repulsed the regiment after a sharp fight. Lawther's regiment accompanied Marmaduke's brigade into Missouri at the start of Major General Sterling Price's Missouri expedition. On September 27, the 10th Cavalry joined in the brigade's dismounted charge on Fort Davidson at Pilot Knob. The fort's defenders quickly repulsed the Confederate attack with a withering mixture of small-arms and cannon fire, inflicting losses of 4 killed and 26 wounded on the 10th Regiment.

Following the Pilot Knob defeat, the regiment skirmished at Leasburg, Union, and Washington as the army moved west roughly parallel to the Missouri River. After a sharp skirmish at Boonville on October 11, the 10th Cavalry crossed the Missouri with the brigade and attacked Glasgow four days later. During that engagement, the regiment remained mounted while the rest of the brigade fought on foot; it deployed on the north and west outskirts of Glasgow to prevent the garrison's escape. After a hard fight, some 800 Federal troops surrendered, and Marmaduke's brigade returned to the south side of the river. On October 21, the 10th Regiment made an ill-advised assault on a Union position while crossing the Little Blue River. The Federals summarily repulsed the attack and stampeded the regiment, which suffered losses of 1 killed, 13 wounded, and 6 missing, before reinforcements arrived to drive the enemy. Moving further west thereafter, the 10th Cavalry fought at Independence on October 22 and at Byram's Ford on the Big Blue River the day following. At Mine Creek, Kansas, on October 25 the regiment fired one volley before charging Federals broke the Confederate line and scattered the rebel soldiers. At the Mine Creek debacle the 10th Regiment suffered estimated losses of 9 killed, 21 wounded, and 65 taken prisoner. After the army left Missouri, the regiment endured the long and trying retreat through the Indian Territory to Texas, and then on to Arkansas. Regimental casualties for the entire Missouri Expedition tallied 16 killed, 74 wounded, and 73 taken prisoner.

The 10th Cavalry spent the balance of the war in southern Arkansas and northern Louisiana. It appears the regiment disbanded before the surrender, for less than 100 regimental members received paroles at Shreveport, Louisiana, in June 1865. Approximately 890 men served in the 10th Cavalry during its relatively short existence. The regiment's overall personnel losses cannot be determined because of the paucity of available records.

BIBLIOGRAPHY

Joel M. Bolton Memoir. Western Historical Manuscript Collection, University of Missouri, Columbia, Missouri.

Luttrell, Henry C. "Battle of Lake River." *Daily Missouri Republican,* St. Louis, Missouri, February 19, 1887.

———. "Battle of Pilot Knob." *Daily Missouri Republican,* St. Louis, Missouri, October 24, 1885.

———. "A Confederate Trooper's Diary." *Daily Missouri Republican,* St. Louis, Missouri, February 6, 1886.

———. "A Dash for a Train." *Daily Missouri Republican,* St. Louis, Missouri, December 19, 1885.

———. "Fight on a Sand-Bar." *Daily Missouri Republican,* St. Louis, Missouri, May 15, 1886.

———. "Marmaduke's Brigade and the Tinclads." *Daily Missouri Republican,* St. Louis, Missouri, January 29, 1887.

———. "Price's Great Raid." *Daily Missouri Republican,* St. Louis, Missouri, February 27, 1886; March 6, 13, and 20, 1886.

———. "Reminiscence of the 10th Missouri Cavalry." *Daily Missouri Republican,* St. Louis, Missouri, May 7, 1887.

———. "Same Old Sand-Bar," *Daily Missouri Republican,* St. Louis, Missouri, July 17, 1886.

———. "Young's Battalion at Pine Bluff." *Daily Missouri Republican,* St. Louis, Missouri, November 13, 1886.

"Robert R. Lawther." In *Memorial and Biographical History of Dallas County, Texas,* 754. Chicago: Lewis, 1976.

11th Regiment (Coffee's/Thompson's/Smith's/Hooper's) (Formerly the 6th Regiment and referred to unofficially as the 3rd Regiment in the Trans-Mississippi Department) "Southwest Cavalry"

Colonel: John Trousdale Coffee, relieved of command ca. October 22, 1862; Gideon W. Thompson, appointed November 9, 1862, not elected December 3, 1863; Moses W. Smith, mortally wounded October 28, 1864; James C. Hooper

Lieutenant Colonel: James C. Hooper, promoted to colonel ca. 1865; Jeremiah C. Cravens

Major: Charles H. Nichols, relieved of command ca. October 22, 1862; Moses W. Smith, promoted to colonel December 3, 1863; Jeremiah C. Cravens, promoted to lieutenant colonel ca. 1865; Tilman H. Lea

Companies and Commanders

Company A: (Dade) Tilman H. Lea, promoted major ca. 1865

Company B: (Newton) John C. Toney

Company C: (Cedar, Newton, Polk, St. Clair) Charles M. Henry, resigned December 30, 1862; G. L. Noland, disposition not of record; W. P. Norman

Company D: (Boone, Buchanan, Monroe, Randolph) George R. McMahan, deserted January 11, 1863; David A. Williams, transferred ca. October 17, 1864

Company E: (Cedar, Vernon) J. H. Groff, resigned May 24, 1863; James M. Blanton

Company F: (Cedar, Dade) Isham J. West

Company G: (Newton, Vernon) Henry D. Stengel

Company H: (Cooper, Dade, Lawrence) N. R. Berry, cashiered
April 18, 1863; E. A. Dickey

Company I: (Dade, Greene) John T. Crisp

Company K: (Buchanan, Macon, Randolph) Jeremiah C. Cravens,
promoted to major December 3, 1863; Henry Burt

Colonel John T. Coffee, an officer of the 8th Division, Missouri State
Guard, recruited this regiment for the Guard in the summer of 1862; by
the end of July, he had nearly 300 men under arms. To complete the regiment, Coffee moved into Missouri in early August in conjunction with
John C. Tracy's Confederate recruit command. The joint column reached
Vernon County, successfully skirmished with the enemy near Montevallo,
and then continued northward. Coffee and Tracy camped near Lone Jack
in Jackson County during the evening of August 15; elements of the 7th
Missouri State Militia Cavalry Regiment surprised and dispersed the rebels.
The day following, Confederate recruit commands in the area prevailed
in a bloody encounter with Union troops that lasted some five hours at
Lone Jack. Coffee's scattered command, finally regrouped, appeared at
Lone Jack as the battle ended but took no significant part in the action.
Following the fight at Lone Jack, all of the recruit commands rapidly
marched to Arkansas to avoid a growing Federal concentration in the area.
Coffee's regiment numbered about 800 troopers when it reached Arkansas.
Reluctant to give up the freedom he felt its State Guard status provided
and fearful that the regiment would be dismounted, Coffee resisted con-
verting to Confederate service. He finally relented to pressure from Major
General Thomas C. Hindman, and the regiment mustered into the
Confederate army about September 12 at Camp Coffee in Newton County,
Missouri. Subsequently designated the 6th Cavalry, the regiment joined
Colonel Joseph O. Shelby's newly created brigade.

The regiment remained in reserve during the battle of Newtonia on
September 30, although a small detachment saw some action. Hindman
ordered Coffee arrested for drunkenness and deprived him of command
in late October; Colonel Gideon W. Thompson replaced Coffee on
November 9. The regiment participated in the running fight at Cane Hill,
Arkansas, on November 28, losing 1 killed and 8 wounded. At Prairie Grove
on December 7, the regiment fought dismounted with Shelby's brigade
on the right of the Confederate line. Although two companies refused to

enter the fight, the 6th Cavalry lost 4 killed and 17 wounded in the battle, the most in the brigade.

In January 1863 the regiment accompanied the brigade into southwest Missouri as part of Brigadier General John S. Marmaduke's raiding force. The 6th Cavalry fought dismounted on the right of the brigade line at Springfield on January 8 and saw action at Hartville on January 11. Again, two companies stayed out of the fight; as a result, their company commanders were charged before a courts-martial. Regimental losses incurred during the raid amounted to 3 killed, 22 wounded, and 8 missing, with a large number of desertions. During Marmaduke's raid into southeast Missouri in late April, the 6th Cavalry fought with the brigade at Cape Girardeau on April 26 and in skirmishes on the retreat to Arkansas, with reported casualties of 6 wounded and 10 missing. On July 4 the regiment engaged in the assault on Fort Rightor at Helena, Arkansas. After enduring a hail of artillery fire, the brigade withdrew, but not before the 6th Regiment lost 1 killed, 17 wounded, and 1 missing.

Thompson's regiment next participated in the defense of Little Rock in late August and early September. The regiment fought with minimal losses at Brownsville, Bayou Metoe, and Bayou Fourche before the capital fell to the enemy on September 10. When Shelby raided Missouri in late September, his force included 200 men of the 6th Cavalry under the command of Lieutenant Colonel James C. Hooper. En route to Missouri, Hooper's detachment engaged the 2nd Arkansas Infantry Regiment (Union) 12 miles south of the Arkansas River and inflicted considerable damage on the Federals. At Neosho, Missouri, on October 3, the 6th Regiment helped capture 300 Union militiamen and their weapons. Continuing on a northward course, the raiders overwhelmed several militia units and destroyed fortifications and railroad bridges as they found them. On October 10, Hooper's men skirmished with a pursuing Union cavalry near Boonville. Three days later, at Marshall, the men of the 6th Cavalry anchored the Confederate left until Shelby led his troopers through a gap in the Federal line in retreat to Arkansas. Although details are lacking in the records, the 6th Regiment reorganized about December 3, the consequences of which included the replacement of Colonel Thompson with Moses W. Smith and redesignation of the regiment as the 11th Cavalry. The reorganization probably resulted from battle losses and the large number of desertions.

The next significant combat for the regiment occurred during the advance of Major General Frederick Steele's Union army into southern Arkansas in April 1864 as part of the Red River Campaign. On April 2, Shelby's brigade, including the 11th Regiment, struck the enemy's rear on the Arkadelphia Road and drove it into retreat. The day following, the brigade fought the Federals near Okolona in a tremendous hailstorm. Skirmishing continued for several days; the Federals drove the rebels back on Prairie D'Ann and then to Prairie DeRohan. The 11th Cavalry's casualties during these operations tallied 5 killed, 9 wounded, and 10 missing. The regiment fought at Marks's Mill on April 25, the last battle of the campaign, which resulted in the capture of a Federal wagon train along with 6 pieces of artillery and 1,100 prisoners. On May 9 the regiment accompanied the brigade to northeast Arkansas for the purpose of interfering with Federal movements in the White River valley and recruiting for the army. Over the next several weeks the 11th Cavalry participated in several small fights, the most significant being the capture and destruction of the Federal gunboat *Queen City* at Clarendon on June 24. The regiment played only a minor role in the actions at Ashley's Station and Jones's Hay Station in August.

The 11th Cavalry destroyed a section of the St. Louis & Iron Mountain Railroad as its first assignment during Major General Sterling Price's Missouri expedition in mid-September. The regiment also took part in the pursuit of Federals that escaped Fort Davidson in the night after the battle at Pilot Knob on September 27. As the army moved west toward Jefferson City, the 11th Cavalry joined in destroying railroad tracks and bridges en route. After forcing a crossing of the Osage River, the brigade marched on the capital city, but General Price declined to attack and moved westward. The 11th Regiment skirmished at Sedalia when the brigade captured that post on October 15. Hard fighting occurred with the enemy near Lexington on October 19, and the brigade fought dismounted when forcing a crossing of the Little Blue River two days later. On October 22, the Union forces retreated to Westport when pressed by the rebels; the next day the Confederates fought a numerically superior enemy there in a slugfest that lasted several hours. The 11th Cavalry anchored the left center of the brigade line at Westport until the Confederates made a fighting withdrawal. The regiment likewise participated in the desperate fighting of October 25, when Shelby's division delayed the enemy advance following the Confederate disaster at Mine Creek, Kansas. On October 28, the brigade engaged the enemy at Newtonia in the last battle of the Price raid. Colonel Smith led his dismounted troops into the fight and fell mortally wounded as the battle ended. The regimental casualties for the Price raid totaled 9 killed, 39 wounded, and 20 missing.

After Newtonia, the army retreated to Arkansas and then trekked across Indian Territory, hungry and exhausted, to Clarksville, Texas. The 11th Regiment remained with the brigade at different locations in Texas until Shelby disbanded his division at Corsicana on June 5, 1865. Some few troopers of the regiment followed Shelby in exile to Mexico; approximately 230 received paroles at Shreveport, Louisiana, in early June; and others simply went their separate ways. Known regimental losses include 42 killed in action, 70 deaths by disease, and 2 executed by Federal authorities.

Bibliography

Edwards, John Newman. *Shelby and His Men; Or the War in the West.* Waverly: Joseph Shelby Memorial Association, 1993.

Fowler, Mrs. W. T. "A Missouri Boy's Experiences." *Confederate Veteran* 40 (1932): 432–35.

Hulston, John K., and James W. Goodrich. "John Trousdale Coffee: Lawyer, Politician, Confederate." *Missouri Historical Review* 77 (April 1983): 272–95.

"Jeremiah C. Cravens." *Confederate Veteran* 7 (1899): 175.

Snuffer, Owen M. "About the Battle of Lone Jack." *Osceola Sun,* Osceola, Missouri, November 12 and 19, 1885; December 3, 1885.

12th Regiment (Hays's/Jeans's/Shanks's) (Referred to unofficially as the 2nd Regiment in the Trans-Mississippi Department) "Jackson County Cavalry"

Colonel: Upton Hays, killed ca. September 13, 1862; Beal Green Jeans, resigned before August 20, 1863; David Shanks, wounded and made prisoner October 6, 1864.

Lieutenant Colonel: Beal Green Jeans, promoted to colonel September 18, 1862; Charles A. Gilkey, mortally wounded August 14, 1863; David Shanks, promoted to colonel August 20, 1863; William H. Erwin

Major: Charles A. Gilkey, promoted to lieutenant colonel September 13, 1862; David Shanks, promoted to lieutenant colonel June 20, 1863; Harvey J. Vivien

Companies and Commanders:

Company A: (Cass, Jackson) Samuel Bowman, mortally wounded January 8, 1863; Robert H. Adams

Company B: (Clay, Cooper, Jackson, Ray) Jacob T. Burkholder, deserted on January 25, 1863; Harvey J. Vivien, promoted to major December 3, 1863; John H. Groom, killed in Missouri, 1864

Company C: (Chariton, Jackson, Lafayette) Francis M. Davis, disposition not of record; George B. Webb, mortally wounded October 22, 1864

Company D: (Clay, Jackson) James L. Tucker, made prisoner November 4, 1864

Company E: (Carroll, Cass, Howard, Jackson, Lafayette, Saline) John Jarratte, disposition not of record; Maurice M. Langhorne. Company served as Shelby's Escort Company from the fall of 1862.

Company F: (Chariton, Clay, Platte) Henry M. Woodsmall, disabled by wound April 26, 1863; Salem H. Ford

Company G: (Cass, Jackson, Johnson) James W. Franklin

Company H: (Carroll, Jackson) John Webb

Company I: (Jackson, Johnson, Lafayette, Platte, Saline) James B. Simpson

Company K: (Cass, Jackson, Lafayette, Saline) Peter Snook, resigned May 26, 1863; R. M. Nace

Upton Hays, formerly colonel in the 8th Division, Missouri State Guard, recruited this regiment primarily in Jackson County, Missouri, in July and August 1862. The recruits experienced combat before any formal organization occurred, fighting hard battles at Independence on August 11 and at Lone Jack five days later, both Confederate victories. Following the latter engagement, Hays led the troops to Arkansas in an exhausting forced march that barely eluded the pursuing enemy. After a short period in northern Arkansas, Hays's command moved to Newton County, Missouri. The regiment mustered into Confederate service on or about

September 12 at Camp Coffee in Newton County; it joined Colonel Joseph O. Shelby's newly formed brigade. Although sometimes referred to as the 2nd Regiment, the Confederate War Department officially designated it the 12th Regiment. Hays lost his life in a skirmish near Newtonia shortly after the regiment completed its organization; Beal G. Jeans succeeded Hays as regimental commander.

At Newtonia, on September 30, the 12th Cavalry rode to the front as the fighting began and initially provided support for Captain Sylvanus Howell's Texas Battery. Soon directed to attack the Federal left with a Texas regiment, the units were driven back in disorder as they came under heavy Union artillery fire. The regiment then fought behind a stone fence until the Federals retreated at dark. The 12th Cavalry lost 2 men wounded and 1 missing in the fighting. After the battle of Newtonia, the Confederates withdrew to Arkansas because of a heavy Union concentration in their front. Union forces under Brigadier General James G. Blunt attacked the brigade while it escorted a forage train near Cane Hill on November 28. For twelve miles, the outnumbered Confederates deployed repeatedly to delay the Federals and save the train. After escaping enemy pursuit, the 12th Cavalry reported casualties of 2 killed and 8 wounded. The regiment joined the brigade on the right of the Confederate line at Prairie Grove on December 7, losing 1 killed and 5 wounded as it fought dismounted against infantry.

The 12th Regiment, under the command of Lieutenant Colonel Charles A. Gilkey, rode into Missouri with the brigade when Brigadier General John S. Marmaduke undertook a raid into southwest Missouri in January 1863. At Springfield on January 8, the regiment fought dismounted in the vain attack on the fortifications; three days later, it engaged the enemy at Hartville. The raid proved costly for the 12th Cavalry, as losses included 12 killed, 46 wounded, and 14 missing. After a period of recuperation in northeastern Arkansas, the 12th Cavalry moved into southeast Missouri with Shelby's brigade in connection with Marmaduke's second raid into the state. On April 26 the brigade fought at Cape Girardeau to help a Texas cavalry brigade withdraw from a tenuous position; it then skirmished with the enemy several times as the Confederates withdrew southward to Arkansas. During the course of the raid, the 12th Regiment suffered casualties of 1 killed, 11 wounded, and 3 missing. The regiment participated in the battle at Helena, Arkansas, on July 4, where the attack against that Union stronghold went awry, and lost 3 killed and 9 wounded before the assault ended. From mid-August until September 10, the brigade engaged the enemy at Brownsville, Bayou Metoe, and Bayou Fourche in an unsuccessful effort to prevent the fall of Little Rock. The regiment reported minimal losses for the campaign.

In late August, David Shanks assumed regimental command as the replacement for Beal G. Jeans, who resigned his commission. Shanks led 200 members of the 12th Cavalry as select brigade members rode to Missouri in late September as participants in Shelby's raid into the western part of the state. Riding into Missouri at a hard pace, the raiders captured Neosho on October 3 and then moved on to overcome militia units at Greenfield, Stockton, Humansville, Warsaw, Cole Camp, and Tipton. In addition to capturing prisoners, horses, and weapons, the raiders cut telegraph lines and destroyed fortifications and bridges. After a brief sojourn at Boonville, the Confederates moved west as Union forces threatened the column. On October 13 the raiders fought the enemy at Marshall. Shanks's detachment served as the Confederate rear guard at Salt Fork Creek. After fighting an hour, the Federals outflanked the position, and when Shelby abandoned the field, Shanks led his men to the northeast and then headed south to Arkansas. The Confederates arrived in Arkansas safely after a brutal ride that completely exhausted men and horses alike.

The 12th Cavalry next participated in serious combat in the spring of 1864, when the brigade opposed the advance of Major General Frederick Steele's army into southern Arkansas as part of the Red River Campaign. The regiment fought near Arkadelphia, Okolona, Prairie D'Ann, and Prairie DeRohan as the Confederates delayed Steele's progress. During these extended operations, the 12th Regiment suffered losses of 3 killed, 19 wounded, and 3 missing. The regiment took part in the Confederate victory at Marks's Mill on April 25, where the rebels captured a Union wagon train, 2 artillery pieces, and a large number of prisoners. The 12th Cavalry lost 3 killed and 15 wounded in the engagement. At the end of May, the regiment operated with the brigade behind enemy lines in the White River valley of northeast Arkansas. The 12th Cavalry joined in several fights over the next several weeks, including the capture of the gunboat *Queen City* at Clarendon on June 24. The brigade also recruited and conscripted men into the Confederate army during the summer months. In August, the regiment played a role in actions at Ashley's Station and Jones's Hay Station on the Memphis & Little Rock Railroad, which resulted in the capture of many enemy prisoners, weapons, and supplies. On September 19, the 12th Cavalry, under the command of Lieutenant Colonel William H. Ervin because Colonel Shanks had taken command of Shelby's brigade, rode into southeast Missouri as part of Major General Sterling Price's Missouri expedition. The brigade initially destroyed sections of the St. Louis & Iron Mountain Railroad and then pursued the Union escapees from Fort Davidson to Leasburg on September 28. Thereafter, the brigade pushed through various towns along the Missouri River, capturing prisoners and seizing weapons and supplies.

After forcing a crossing of the Osage River, the brigade threatened Jefferson City, but General Price declined to attack the fortifications there, and the army moved west to California. On October 15 the brigade overwhelmed the militia defending Sedalia, capturing 200 prisoners and their weapons, and destroying their fort. After fighting the enemy near Lexington on October 19, the brigade crossed the Little Blue River dismounted two days later and struck the right flank of the Yankee defenders, driving them from the field. On the day following, the brigade pushed the enemy back to Westport on the Kansas-Missouri line. The 12th Cavalry occupied the right center of the brigade line on October 23, when the Confederates fought at Westport, the largest engagement of the expedition. The brigade charged and countercharged until outflanked on the right, which resulted in the Confederates making a fighting withdrawal from the battleground. The 12th Regiment next fought on October 25 in opposition to aggressive Federals that had routed two Confederate divisions at Mine Creek, Kansas. The brigade regiments deployed and redeployed in a successful rear guard action that slowed and finally stopped the Federal pursuit that day. The 12th Cavalry participated in the last fight of the expedition at Newtonia on October 28. Fighting dismounted, the brigade drove the Federals back, and later that evening continued the retreat into Arkansas. The 12th Cavalry, assigned to monitor enemy movements, kept watch until 8:00 a.m. the next morning, when it followed the army south, the last Confederate unit on the field. During the Missouri expedition, the regiment reported losses of 9 killed or mortally wounded, 18 wounded, and 15 missing.

After a torturous march through Indian Territory, the brigade finally reached Clarksville, Texas. The 12th Cavalry remained with the brigade at different locations in Texas until General Shelby disbanded his division on June 5, 1865, at Corsicana. Several troopers accepted paroles at Shreveport, Louisiana; some followed Shelby into exile in Mexico; and others simply dispersed. Approximately 950 men served in the regiment during the war, and known losses include 55 men killed in battle, 31 deaths by disease, and 1 executed by Federal authorities.

BIBLIOGRAPHY

"Col. David Shanks." *Confederate Veteran* 22 (1914): 123.

Courtney, W. J. "The Battle of Hartville." *Confederate Veteran* 29 (1921): 357–58.

Edwards, John Newman. *Shelby and His Men; Or the War in the West.* Waverly: Joseph Shelby Memorial Association, 1993.

Ford, S. H. "Recruiting in North Missouri." *Confederate Veteran* 19 (1911): 335.

Kritzer, John S. "Captured Guns at Lone Jack." *Confederate Veteran* 24 (1916): 184.

"Reminiscences of Salem H. Ford." Typescript. State Historical Society of Missouri Library, Columbia, Missouri.

Vivian, Harvey J. "Personal Reminiscences of Major H. J. Vivian of the Last Day of the Battle of Westport." In *Gettysburg of the West: The Battle of Westport, October 21–23, 1864,* edited by Fred L. Gee, 37–38. Independence: Two Trails, 1996.

13th Regiment (Wood's) (Formerly the 14th Battalion)

Colonel: Robert Clifton Wood

Lieutenant Colonel: Richard J. Wickersham

Major: William T. Payne

Companies and Commanders:

Company A: (Saline, Webster, Wright) Richard J. Wickersham, promoted to lieutenant colonel ca. December 1864; Warren S. Briscoe

Company B: (Callaway, Greene, Ralls, St. Louis, Shelby) James C. Buckner

Company C: (Chariton, Christian, Henry, Texas) William Woodson, disposition not of record; William Allen

Company D: (Camden, Wright) James Cummins, wounded and taken prisoner October 23, 1864

Company E: (Marion) William T. Payne, promoted to major ca. December 1864; Robert S. Owsley

Company F: (Cass, Moniteau) William Mankin, wounded and taken prisoner October 25, 1864

Company G: (Cooper, Moniteau) Francis M. Claybrook

Company H: (Cole, Saline, St. Louis) Thomas B. Selby

Company I: (Lafayette, Pettis) T. Leslie Smith

Company K: (Callaway, Cole, Henry, Saline) Presley Wilkerson

Robert C. Wood served Major General Sterling Price as an aide de camp when the general assumed division command at Little Rock, Arkansas, on April 1, 1863. Wood did not long perform staff duty, for on April 6, General Order No. 6, District of Arkansas, ordered sixteen troopers of Price's escort company transferred to "Captain Wood's light artillery company," which is the first mention found of the organization that eventually became the 13th Cavalry Regiment. Wood subsequently reported to Brigadier General John S. Marmaduke on May 9 that he commanded a "cavalry and light artillery" unit that consisted of 2 officers and 24 men that manned four Williams' Rapid-Fire Guns. The provisions of Special Order No. 62, Headquarters, District of Arkansas, dated June 12, 1863, granted Wood authority to organize one or more companies of cavalry; he immediately began recruiting. Union scouts in Fulton County on August 3 estimated Wood's command at 150 men and 4 pieces of "flying" artillery.

District headquarters directed Wood's mixed unit to report to Marmaduke for duty on September 28 but rescinded the order the same day after Wood insisted that his troops required further discipline to be efficient. At that time, Wood commanded a battalion of six companies numbering some 275 men near Arkadelphia. On October 25 the battalion participated in the Confederate attack on Pine Bluff, fighting with Colonel Archibald Dobbins's Arkansas cavalry brigade. The battalion attacked from the west and lost 1 killed and 1 wounded before the Federals repulsed the assault. Sometime after November 1, two companies recruited in Missouri by James T. Cearnal during Colonel Joseph O. Shelby's late raid into the state joined the battalion. According to a strength report filed on November 10, Wood's battalion consisted of eight mounted companies numbering about 400 men, with no mention of an artillery complement in the unit. The disposition of the four artillery pieces is not recorded. The battalion appears on the returns of Marmaduke's division as an independent unit, unattached to any brigade, through December 31, 1863.

During early 1864, Wood's Battalion generally operated near General Price's headquarters. When Price assumed command of the Confederate cavalry resisting the advance of Major General Frederick Steele's army into southern Arkansas during the Red River Campaign, the battalion accompanied him. The battalion skirmished with the enemy on several occasions, especially with scouting parties, after Steele occupied Camden. On April 18, the battalion took part in the attack on a large Union forage train near Poison Spring. It dismounted and deployed on the extreme right of Marmaduke's brigade, which also had dismounted. Sent forward when the Federal line gave way, Marmaduke quickly recalled the battalion and ordered the men to prepare the captured wagons for movement. The battalion next participated in the pursuit of Steele's army after the general evacuated Camden and marched toward Little Rock. The unit skirmished with the enemy's rear guard until the Federals reached the Saline River. During the battle of Jenkins's Ferry on April 30, Wood's troopers remained in reserve. For most of the summer of 1864, the battalion performed outpost duty at Princeton, 60 miles south of Little Rock.

When General Price initiated his expedition into Missouri that fall, Wood's Battalion joined Marmaduke's brigade, then under the command of Brigadier General John B. Clark Jr. The battalion stormed the ramparts of Fort Davidson with the brigade at Pilot Knob on September 27 and lost about 30 men killed and wounded in the failed assault. The following morning, Wood's men joined the pursuit of Federals that escaped the fort during the night. On September 30, the battalion, along with the 4th Cavalry Regiment, burned the depot at Cuba and destroyed a mile of railroad track. Returning to the brigade, the battalion burned a railroad bridge over the Meramec River and then marched on to Union and Washington. Near Hermann, the battalion loaded onto boxcars and started for Jefferson City, the state capital. Before traveling far, scouts discovered the track ahead had been destroyed, so the men burned the train and remounted. After essentially bypassing Jefferson City, the battalion moved west to California and then on to Marshall. At the latter place, four recruit companies joined the battalion to increase the command to a regiment, but the recruits moved ahead with the unarmed men, while the battalion returned to operate with the brigade. The brigade engaged the enemy at Lexington, fought hard at the Little Blue on October 21, and at Independence the day following. On October 23, the brigade made a determined stand at Byram's Ford on the Big Blue River, but the Federals eventually drove it in retreat. A Federal cavalry charge routed the battalion, along with other Confederate units, at Mine Creek, Kansas, on October 25. It suffered casualties in that debacle of 5 killed, 17 wounded, and 50 taken prisoner. Thereafter, the battalion made the long and demoralizing trek through Indian Territory to Texas, and then moved to Laynesport, Arkansas. The battalion's total losses during the expedition are unknown. One battalion veteran later claimed that only 52 of the 400 men that began the raid in September remained after the battle of Mine Creek, but this is certainly an exaggeration.

Just when the battalion organized as the 13th Cavalry Regiment cannot be determined from the existing records. In all likelihood, no formal organization occurred until the army reached Texas, or perhaps Arkansas. It appears that some companies consolidated, for the eight existing companies, and the four added during the expedition, were reduced to ten in the final organization. The troopers of the 13th Cavalry performed outpost and picket duty in Arkansas after returning from Missouri and received paroles at Shreveport, Louisiana, on June 8, 1865. Some 670 men appear on the rolls of the 13th Cavalry Regiment during its term of service. Very incomplete casualty reports show 12 soldiers killed in action and another 55 lost to disease

BIBLIOGRAPHY

"John Coats Was a Confederate Hero." *Nevada Herald,* Nevada, Missouri, July 3, 1955.

Eli Bass McHenry to Edgar Taylor McHenry, October 1, 1909. Typescript letter. Missouri State Archives, Jefferson City, Missouri.

"R. J. Wickersham." In *History of Laclede, Camden, Dallas, Webster, Wright, Texas, Pulaski, Phelps, and Dent Counties, Missouri,* 762–63. Chicago: Goodspeed Publishing Co., 1889.

"Reminiscences of James H. Campbell's Experiences in the Civil War." Typescript. Fort Davidson Historic Site Collections, Pilot Knob, Missouri.

Paul F. Thornton Letters. W. L. Skaggs Collection. Arkansas History Commission, Little Rock, Arkansas.

Trans-Mississippi Order and Letter Book, Brigadier-General John S. Marmaduke. Transcribed by Carolyn M. Bartels. Independence: Two Trails, 2000.

15th Regiment (Reeves's)

Colonel: Timothy J. Reeves

Lieutenant Colonel: Benjamin A. Johnson

Major: James L. Sexton

Companies and Commanders:

Company A: (Ripley) Henry C. Sloan

Company B: (Ripley) Daniel P. Patterson

Company C: (Bollinger, Wayne) David Reed

Company D: (Carter, Shannon) John C. Smart

Company E: (State of Arkansas) John C. Mitchell

Company F: (Oregon, Ripley) James M. Phelps

Company G: (Butler, Wayne) Richard H. Lehr

Company H: (Carter, Oregon, Shannon) Webb Conner

Company I: (Carter, Oregon, Ripley, Wayne) George W. Greenwood

Company K: (State of Arkansas) 1st Lieutenant Thomas McCarley

Company L: (Ripley) 1st Lieutenant O. H. Cline

Company M: (Butler, Jefferson, Madison, St. Francois) Samuel Anthony

Company N: (Iron, Reynolds, Shannon) Jesse R. Pratt

Timothy Reeves, a former officer of the 1st Division, Missouri State Guard, commanded a Confederate company known as the "Independent Missouri Scouts" through much of 1862–63. After returning from service east of the Mississippi River, Reeves's company operated on the Arkansas-Missouri border; it did good service reporting enemy movements and occasionally engaging Union scouts and patrols. As early as July 1863 Reeves sought permission to increase his unit, as he reported his command had grown too large for a company. Although no record has been found that he received authority to increase his organization, by September, Reeves had begun recruiting in southern Missouri. The recruiting effort enjoyed some success, for by December 11, Reeves had 300 men camped near Cherokee Bay, Arkansas. At a date uncertain, but before June 7, 1864, Reeves organized a battalion and received promotion to major. On June 7, Brigadier General Joseph O. Shelby, then organizing troops in northeast Arkansas, instructed Reeves to recruit his command as much as possible. The combined efforts of Shelby and others, including Reeves, resulted in the organization of several new Confederate units by enforcing the conscript law, gathering recruits, and incorporating independent companies into larger units. Reeves soon commanded enough men to form a regiment. The regiment, subsequently denominated the 15th Cavalry, mustered into Confederate service about July 20 at Pocahontas, Arkansas, and numbered perhaps 500 men. Apparently, only half of the troopers of the 15th Cavalry possessed weapons. The regiment became part of Colonel Thomas H. McCray's mostly Arkansas brigade in mid-September, just before the beginning of Major General Sterling Price's expedition into Missouri.

At the battle of Pilot Knob on September 27, McCray's Brigade, including the 15th Cavalry, attacked the Federal stronghold at Fort Davidson from the southeast. Enemy artillery and small-arms fire quickly repulsed the attempt, and the men sought shelter in a creek bed. The brigade took little part in the fight thereafter, except for sharpshooting from the relative safety of the creek bed. The 15th Cavalry reported 2 men wounded, one mortally, in the failed assault. Following the battle at Pilot Knob, Reeves and his regiment won lasting notoriety by summarily executing a Union officer and five of his men on October 3 for perceived wrongs against southerners in southeast Missouri. The regiment's activities during the balance of the expedition are not well documented.

Undoubtedly, the 15th Cavalry participated in some skirmishing as the army advanced across Missouri. The regiment fought at Westport on October 23, deployed with the brigade along the Harrisonville Road perpendicular to the right of the main Confederate line along Brush Creek. After the Federals broke Brigadier General John S. Marmaduke's line at Byram's Ford, east of the brigade's position, McCray's units and other elements of Brigadier General James F. Fagan's division resisted the Federals until finally overwhelmed and driven from the field. On October 25, McCray's brigade held a position south of Mine Creek, Kansas, when the Confederates suffered a disastrous defeat. Being south of the creek, the 15th Regiment avoided the high casualties suffered by Confederate units on the north side, recording losses of 3 wounded and 3 taken prisoner. The Mine Creek disaster ended the fighting for the 15th Cavalry during the expedition. Although Colonel McCray filed no report of the losses of his brigade during the expedition, it appears that the casualties of the 15th Cavalry totaled 1 mortally wounded, 5 wounded, and 12 missing.

On November 3 General Price furloughed McCray's Brigade to northeast Arkansas to round up stragglers and deserters. Price intended for the furloughed units to rejoin the army in southern Arkansas by early December, but that did not occur. Once back in northeast Arkansas, the 15th Cavalry enjoyed a relatively quiet time, although skirmishes with enemy patrols occurred occasionally. On June 5, 1865, the regiment surrendered and received parole at Jacksonport, Arkansas. It seems likely that companies L–N, probably independent or newly formed units, joined the regiment not long before the surrender. The enrollment and casualties of the 15th Cavalry cannot be determined with any certainty due to the fragmentary nature of the regimental records.

BIBLIOGRAPHY

Collins, Andy. "To the Victor Belongs the Spoils." *Missouri Historical Review* 80 (January 1986): 176–95.

Ross, Kirby. "The Burning of Doniphan." *North and South* 6 (November 2003): 76–84.

Speer, Lonnie R. "It's Me You Want." In *War of Vengeance: Acts of Retaliation against Civil War POWs,* 1–13. Harrisburg: Stackpole Books, 2002.

Wehmer, Lou. "Profile: Colonel Timothy Reeves, CSA." *Ripley County Heritage* 9 (Spring 2000): 20–23.

Coffee's Regiment

Colonel: John Trousdale Coffee

Lieutenant Colonel: John T. Crisp

Major: M. J. B. Young

Companies and Commanders:

Company A: —— Kelley, disposition not of record; Henry M. Woodsmall

Company B: —— Fulkerson

Company C: Thomas J. Shaw, disposition not of record; John W. Cypert

Company D: —— Dark

Company G: O. B. Smith

Company —: —— Jackway

Balance of organization is unknown.

Around June 1, 1864, General Edmund Kirby Smith, commander of the Trans-Mississippi Department, authorized John T. Coffee, a former regimental commander in the Missouri State Guard and later the 6th Missouri Cavalry Regiment, to recruit a regiment of cavalry. Coffee had until September 1 to complete the regimental organization. He had been recruiting exiled Missourians and unattached Arkansans in northeast Arkansas since May; Brigadier General Joseph O. Shelby, conscripting and recruiting in that area, reported on May 31 that Coffee would soon fill his regiment. Garnering recruits must have been more difficult than Shelby believed, for Coffee did not complete the organization of a regiment until about August 10 near Searcy. Coffee's regiment contained a small number of mostly unarmed men.

Assigned to Colonel Sidney D. Jackman's newly formed brigade, the regiment participated in the actions at Ashley's Station and Jones's Hay Station in August. In mid-September, Coffee's regiment entered southeast Missouri with the brigade as part of the Army of Missouri, the force Major General Sterling Price created for his expedition into the state. Most of the regiment joined the brigade in destroying railroad tracks north of Pilot Knob, while Captain Thomas J. Shaw's company marched to attack

Farmington. That company, along with a detachment from a different regiment, captured a company of militiamen at Farmington after burning them out of the local courthouse. Coffee also sent recruiters throughout the area. For reasons not recorded, Price detached the regiment from Jackman's brigade on October 4 and ordered Coffee to report to headquarters. Thereafter, probably in late October, Coffee's regiment joined Colonel Charles H. Tyler's recruit brigade, a command of largely unarmed troops, doubtless indicating the shortage of weapons in Coffee's unit.

Tyler's newly organized brigade guarded the army's large wagon train and saw little combat until October 23 at Hickman Mills, when the brigade deployed with Brigadier General William L. Cabell's Arkansas brigade to make the force defending the train appear formidable. The ruse worked, for when Union Brigadier General John McNeil saw the large number of Confederates positioned to defend the wagons, he canceled his attack. Coffee's Regiment also participated in an unlikely action on October 25 following the defeat of two Confederate divisions at Mine Creek, Kansas. Fearing the loss of his train, General Price ordered Tyler's brigade to charge a pursuing Union force. The mostly unarmed brigade's charge temporarily halted the pursuit and allowed the wagon train to continue southward unmolested. Coffee's regiment suffered losses of 3 killed and 7 wounded in the action. The regimental troopers saw no additional fighting during the raid, for the army soon retreated into Arkansas and on to Texas. After the army reached Clarksville, Texas, the regiment likely disbanded, as no parole records for the unit have been located. No regimental muster rolls are known to exist.

BIBLIOGRAPHY

Halliburton, J. W. "That Charge." *Confederate Veteran* 28 (1920): 264.

Hulston John K., and James W. Goodrich. "John Trousdale Coffee: Lawyer, Politician, Confederate." *Missouri Historical Review* 77 (April 1983): 272–95.

Roberts, O. M. "M. J. B. Young." In *Texas,* by Roberts, 711–12. Vol. 15 of *Confederate Military History,* edited by Clement A. Evans. Expanded Edition. Atlanta: Confederate Publishing Co., 1899.

Winns, R. M. "Scouting in Arkansas and Missouri." *Confederate Veteran* 21 (1913): 538–39.

Freeman's Regiment

Colonel: Thomas Roe Freeman

Lieutenant Colonel: Joseph B. Love

Major: Michael V. B. Shaver

Companies and Commanders:

Company A: Richard A. Powell

Company B: A. K. Cook

Company C: L. B. Brown

Company D: T. Y. Huddleston

Company E: (Johnson) James E. Sexton

Company F: Christopher C. Cook

Company G: Benjamin F. Austin

Company H: (Oregon) William A. Orchard

Company I: J. M. Copeland

Company K: W. R. Lawson

Thomas R. Freeman, former regimental commander in the 7th Division, Missouri State Guard, recruited a number of companies that operated on the Arkansas-Missouri border by mid-1863. Although the date of organization is unknown, Freeman organized these companies into a cavalry battalion, possibly denominated the 12th Battalion. Often probing into south-central Missouri from a base near Mammoth Spring, Arkansas, Freeman's battalion attacked Union outposts, scouting parties, and supply trains during the late summer and early fall with mixed results. The battalion attracted the enemy's interest, for Union commanders often reported Freeman's presumed location and movements and dispatched numerous expeditions to search for the command. Near the end of 1863, Freeman moved his men to the vicinity of Batesville, Arkansas.

On January 23, 1864, Federals attacked Freeman's camp, killed and wounded 20 of his men, and captured nearly 50, along with wagons and camp equipage. New companies soon joined Freeman's outfit, and on January 26, 1864, the battalion reorganized as a regiment near Batesville. The regiment continued to operate independently, unattached to any brigade. Although usually called a "guerrilla" or "bushwhacker" by Union forces, Freeman in fact attempted to enforce discipline in his ranks, at one time issuing orders threatening to shoot soldiers that robbed civilians. Freeman's men attacked a Union scouting party northwest of Batesville on February 20. They badly defeated the outnumbered enemy, which lost 14 killed and wounded, plus 24 taken prisoner. After a few weeks of inactivity, Freeman joined other Confederates on April 1 in attacking a Federal force at Fitzhugh's Wood, a few miles north of Augusta. After a series of ineffective charges against disciplined infantry, the Confederates broke off contact after suffering the loss of 25 killed and 70 wounded, including Freeman among the latter. The regiment likewise unsuccessfully attacked Jacksonport on April 20. When Brigadier General Joseph O. Shelby arrived in northeast Arkansas in May to push recruitment and conscription, he ordered Freeman to move his regiment to Powhatan; in mid-June he instructed Freeman to report at Jacksonport with all his armed men.

The next serious action for the regiment occurred during Major General Sterling Price's Missouri expedition in September. When Price organized his army at Pocahontas, Arkansas, in mid-September, he created a brigade for Freeman that included his own regiment, Fristoe's Missouri Cavalry Regiment, and Ford's Arkansas Cavalry Battalion; Price assigned the brigade to Brigadier General John S. Marmaduke's Missouri Cavalry Division. Freeman's regiment initially fought at Pilot Knob, Missouri, on September 27, when it made an unsuccessful charge against Union troops defending Fort Davidson. The regiment thereafter accompanied the brigade as the army moved north toward the Missouri River and then turned west. The exact role the regiment played in the army's march across Missouri is not recorded, although Colonel Freeman personally shot some of his men along the way for plundering civilians.

The regiment fought at Independence on October 21 and at the Big Blue River (Byram's Ford) two days later. Freeman's regiment performed poorly at Mine Creek, Kansas, on October 25, as it quickly gave way to a Federal charge with but little resistance. In the regiment's defense, Brigadier General John B. Clark Jr., who commanded the division following General Marmaduke's capture, noted that Freeman's brigade, being "mostly unarmed," did not perform as well as the other brigades. During the course of the expedition, the regiment reported losses of 13 killed, 20 wounded, 27 taken prisoner, and 75 missing. After the army retreated into Arkansas, Price furloughed Freeman's brigade at Maysville on October 30 to proceed to northeast Arkansas to round up stragglers and deserters. Price also ordered the regiment, numbering only 250 troopers at the time, to report to Camden by December 15. Despite Price's order, the regiment never again left northeast Arkansas, where it remained relatively inactive for the balance of hostilities. The troops of Freeman's regiment surrendered and received paroles at Jacksonport, Arkansas, in early June 1865. Incomplete records prohibit any meaningful statement of numbers and losses for the regiment during its short term of service.

BIBLIOGRAPHY

"A Captain in Freeman's Missouri Cavalry." *Confederate Veteran* 14 (1906): 179–80.

Ogilvie, Craig. "The Long Way Back to the Ozarks." *Ozarks Mountaineer* (September/October 2005): 14–16, 48.

Sevier, Mildred C. "Thomas Roe Freeman, 1829–1898." In *Coppedge/Freeman and Next of Kin,* 283–85. Claremore, Oklahoma: Privately printed, 1983.

Fristoe's Regiment

Colonel: Edward T. Fristoe

Lieutenant Colonel: Jesse H. Tracy

Major: Matthew G. Norman

Companies and Commanders:

Company A: (State of Arkansas) N. H. Tracy

Company B: (State of Arkansas) William J. Smith

Company C: (State of Arkansas) R. W. Miner

Company D: (State of Arkansas) —— Copler

Company E: (State of Arkansas) M. H. Wolf

Company F: (State of Arkansas) David C. Meadows, died February 11, 1865, as prisoner; S. M. Elliott

Company G: (Oregon) John J. Sitton, wounded and made prisoner October 23, 1864

Company H: (Oregon) James B. Old

Company I: (Oregon) Thomas J. Weaver, killed in October 1864

Company K: (Oregon) Jesse Orchard

Company L: (Oregon) Samuel W. Greer

Companies recruited by Jesse H. Tracy in Arkansas and Matthew G. Norman in southern Missouri formed the nucleus of this regiment. Elements of the regiment saw initial combat in northern Arkansas on March 1 and 2, 1864, when Tracy's men skirmished with a company of the 6th Missouri State Militia Cavalry Regiment near Buffalo City and Bennett's Bayou on the White River. By May 11, Tracy had joined Colonel Sidney D. Jackman's command in the vicinity of Pocahontas. A month later, Tracy raided in Douglas and Ozark Counties in southwestern Missouri with unknown results. Matthew G. Norman, a former company commander in the 4th Missouri Infantry Regiment, returned to Oregon County, Missouri, from the Cis-Mississippi and organized a cavalry outfit sometimes referred to as the 17th battalion. On July 5, at Hubble Hollow in Fulton County, Arkansas, the commands of Tracy and Norman united to form this regiment with 830 men. Edward T. Fristoe, a graduate of the Virginia Military Institute and an experienced officer, took command.

After muster, Fristoe's regiment often operated in conjunction with Colonel Thomas R. Freeman's Missouri cavalry regiment. When Major General Sterling Price began his expedition into Missouri in mid-September, Fristoe's regiment, mustering 530 men, became part of Freeman's newly formed brigade in Brigadier General John S. Marmaduke's division. It appears that only the armed troops participated in the raid. The regiment had a mixed performance during the Missouri expedition, in large part because it lacked good weapons and included mostly raw troops. At the battle of Pilot Knob on September 27, Freeman's brigade deployed on the north side of Fort Davidson, the Federal stronghold. After three other brigades charged the fort dismounted and the fort's defenders bloodily repulsed them, Freeman led a number of his men, doubtless including some from Fristoe's Regiment, in an ineffective mounted charge that Federal artillery fire easily dispersed. The activities of the regiment for the balance of the raid are not well documented. The regiment reportedly fought well at Independence on October 21 and at the Big Blue River two days later, suffering several casualties in the latter fight. But on October

25, at the battle of Mine Creek, Kansas, Freeman's brigade held the center of the Confederate line and gave way to a Federal charge without firing a shot, which contributed substantially to the collapse of the line.

Mine Creek effectively ended the regiment's combat career. Fristoe reported regimental casualties of 11 killed, 40 wounded, 20 taken prisoner, and 45 missing for the raid, but only 175 troopers apparently remained with the unit when the operation terminated. After Price's broken army reached safe haven in Arkansas, he furloughed Freeman's brigade to the northeastern part of the state to rest and collect deserters and stragglers. While the record is not particularly clear, it appears that Fristoe's regiment disbanded before the close of hostilities. It is certain that Major Norman attempted to surrender five companies under his command in Oregon County, Missouri, on May 28, 1865, but the Federals declined to accept them since he had orders from his superior to report to Jacksonport, Arkansas, to surrender. Many troopers of the regiment thereafter received paroles at Jacksonport about June 5, 1865. The known losses of the regiment amounted to 14 killed or mortally wounded and 16 deaths by disease.

Bibliography

"Col. Jesse H. Tracey." *Confederate Veteran* 23 (1915): 420.

"Edward T. Fristoe." In *Appleton's Cyclopedia of American Biography,* edited by James Grant Wilson and John Fisher, 552. New York: D. Appleton & Co., 1890.

"Matthew George Norman." In *A Reminiscent History of the Ozark Region,* 703–4. Independence: BLN Library Services, 1976.

Hodge's Regiment

Colonel: Eli Hodge

Lieutenant Colonel: John L. Merrick

Major: Thomas Todd

Companies and Commanders:

Company —: —— Annaburg, killed October 29, 1864

Company —: —— Arnold

Company —: —— Kimball

Company —: (Carroll) John L. Merrick

Company —: (Boone) —— Onan
Company —: John Redd
Company —: (Callaway) W. Milton Scholl
Company —: (Callaway) Isaac N. Sitton
Company —: (Boone) Thomas Todd
Company —: (Carroll) J. H. Withers

Before Major General Sterling Price's expedition into Missouri in September 1864, Brigadier General Joseph O. Shelby sent sixty men in advance of the army to recruit. Eli Hodge, adjutant of the 11th Missouri Cavalry Regiment and a prewar resident of Boone County, proceeded to that county and began recruiting there and in the surrounding area. By October, he had enlisted six companies north of the Missouri River, consisting of 485 largely unarmed recruits, and moved to join Price's army. His command crossed the Missouri at Brunswick and camped at Waverly in Lafayette County. At Waverly, four additional companies joined the command, in consequence of which Hodge organized a regiment with himself as commander. Learning that Price had already passed through the area, Hodge's command, with only a third of the troops armed, rode south to find Price. On October 29, 1864, Federal cavalry, primarily the 2nd Arkansas Cavalry Regiment, attacked Hodge's command at Upshaw's Farm in Barry County, Missouri. The attack quickly scattered the Missourians, who made little resistance since they lacked weapons. The Federal commander estimated Hodge's regiment suffered casualties of 50 killed, an unknown number wounded, and 37 taken prisoner. Those who escaped the disaster hurriedly continued the journey southward. The regiment drastically decreased in number because of sickness and desertions during the trying and dangerous movement from the Missouri River to Texas. On reaching Texas in November, the remnant of the regiment, numbering less than 300 troopers, disbanded. The recruits formed four new companies and consolidated with David A. Williams's Missouri cavalry battalion to create a regiment commanded by Williams. No muster rolls of the companies of Hodge's regiment are known to exist, only partial prisoner of war and parole records.

Bibliography

"Battle History Forgotten." *Kansas City Star,* Kansas City, Missouri, April 17, 1908.

"Col. Eli Hodge." *Confederate Veteran* 33 (1925): 186.

Eli Hodge Letters. W. L. Skaggs Collection. Arkansas History Commission, Little Rock, Arkansas.

Hunter's Regiment

Colonel: DeWitt Clinton Hunter

Lieutenant Colonel: Richard K. Murrell, disposition unknown: Daniel N. Fulbright

Major: William Yountz, mortally wounded October 23, 1864; Casper Headrick

Companies and Commanders:

Company A: (Dent) Casper Headrick, promoted to major ca. December 1864; R. L. Wells

Company —: John Cecil

Company —: —— Dixon

Company —: —— English

Company —: —— Gillett

Company —: John S. Herriford

Company —: Francis M. Hill

Company —: Charles R. Jackman

Company —: George T. Maddox

Balance of organizational composition is unknown.

This regiment formally organized in August 1864 and should not be confused with an earlier cavalry regiment Hunter commanded in 1862. Major General Thomas C. Hindman dismounted the earlier organization, which eventually became the 11th Missouri Infantry Regiment. Hunter resigned his commission in the infantry on February 4, 1863, and began recruiting a new cavalry command in southwest Missouri. By the end of April, he led a body of men that he styled a regiment at Fayetteville, Arkansas, although he commanded too few troops to constitute a legitimate regimental organization. In May, Hunter had some 100 men with him at Pineville, Missouri, and shortly thereafter, he continued his recruiting in

Cedar County. Union forces often pursued his command, but Hunter usually avoided engaging the enemy. Little is known of Hunter's activities during the summer of 1863; he presumably continued recruiting. By early fall, he commanded a battalion-sized unit with an aggregate strength of approximately 300 largely unarmed troopers.

Colonel Joseph O. Shelby initiated a raid into western Missouri from Arkadelphia, Arkansas, on September 21. Hunter joined Shelby with 200 of his men at McKissick Springs on October 1. Crossing into Missouri the day following, Shelby elected to strike Neosho, which was then defended by a contingent of Union militia. The Confederates completely surrounded the courthouse in which the Unionists had taken refuge. Hunter's command moved on the enemy from the south, and after a brief exchange of fire, including two rounds of artillery shot into the courthouse by the Confederates, some 300 militiamen surrendered. The fast moving column then swept on northward, captured several detachments of militia at various locales, destroyed railroad tracks and bridges, and gathered arms and supplies along the way. By October 11, the Confederates occupied Boonville on the Missouri River but soon abandoned the town as superior Union forces approached from the east.

The Union troops brought the raiders to bay at Marshall on October 13. Shelby attacked an enemy command already occupying Marshall, with Hunter's cavalry placed on the right of the rebel line. Unable to breach the Union line in their front and pressed by the enemy in the rear, the Confederates finally disengaged, with Shelby leading one element to the west while Hunter led another to the east before veering south. Hunter rejoined Shelby in Arkansas on October 20 after a long and precarious ride. Hunter's command spent the winter months relatively inactive in northwest Arkansas. As the spring campaign of 1864 opened, Hunter's unit moved to the vicinity of Camden, where it joined Shelby's brigade. Hunter's command operated with the brigade as the Confederates fought to delay Major General Frederick Steele's advance into southern Arkansas as one pincer of the Red River Campaign. No special mention is made of Hunter's command during the campaign. It participated in the battle of Marks's Mill on April 25, losing 3 wounded and 4 missing in action. The unit remained small in number, as Hunter and Major Jesse F. Pickler's battalions combined numbered only about 200 men present for duty on a field return of Shelby's brigade dated May 3.

Hunter's cavalry next marched with Shelby to northeastern Arkansas, when the general moved there to recruit and interrupt Federal communications. While in that area, Hunter attempted to increase his unit to full strength. On August 10, Shelby ordered some newly recruited companies to report to Hunter to fill his ranks. At least three companies joined Hunter's command as a result of Shelby's order. The regiment organized at or near Batesville and became part of a newly formed brigade commanded by Colonel Sidney D. Jackman. On August 24, Jackman, with some 500 men from various regiments of his brigade, moved toward Ashley's Station. Jackman detached Hunter's small element to guard a road intersection while the remainder of Jackman's men proceeded to Ashley's Station but arrived too late to participate in the fight. The Confederates then attacked a Union outpost at Jones's Hay Station on the Memphis & Little Rock Railroad. Hunter's men joined in the fighting, which resulted in the capture of some 400 prisoners and much-needed supplies. A Federal relief force from DeVall's Bluff soon struck the Confederates, and Hunter's detachment fought for an hour before receiving orders to leave the field.

Hunter's regiment accompanied the brigade into southeast Missouri as part of Major General Sterling Price's Missouri expedition in mid-September. Initially, the regiment skirmished some but avoided major combat, and spent time destroying sections of the southwest branch of the Pacific Railroad. Hunter's regiment engaged the militia at Union on October 2 and a few days later pursued the enemy from the Osage River to the outskirts of Jefferson City. On October 12, the regiment fought with a superior Union cavalry force for over an hour on the Boonville-Tipton road. Three days later, Jackman took 500 men of the brigade, probably including some of Hunter's men, and crossed the Missouri River to join in the assault on Glasgow, which resulted in the capture of about 800 prisoners and their weapons. At the crossing of the Little Blue River on October 21, Hunter's regiment pressed forward dismounted to attack the enemy, but the Union defenders retreated before the regiment engaged them. On October 22, the regiment held its ground against a Federal force advancing from Westport and then drove the Federals in retreat. During the battle of Westport the day following, Hunter's command fought on the right center of the Confederate line south of Brush Creek. After three hours of fierce fighting, Jackman's brigade moved to support Brigadier General James F. Fagan's Arkansas division, then pressed by Union forces from the east. Jackman dismounted his regiments and held back the numerically superior enemy long enough to remount his men and leave the field of battle.

On October 25, Hunter's regiment constituted part of the rear guard that fought pursuing Federals to a standstill following the defeat of two Confederate divisions at Mine Creek, Kansas. While present at the fight at Newtonia on October 28, the regiment never became closely engaged. Price furloughed Hunter's regiment on October 30, after the army reached relative safety in Arkansas. The regiment numbered only about 325 troopers at the time. Neither Jackman nor Hunter reported regimental losses for the Missouri expedition. Hunter's regiment eventually regrouped and moved to join the army at Bonham, Texas. Near the end of the war, the regimental members received 30-day furloughs and never came together again. There are no regimental rolls in existence, and the records of the unit's losses are fragmentary at best.

BIBLIOGRAPHY

"DeWitt Clinton Hunter." In *History of Vernon County, Missouri*, 646–47. St. Louis: Brown & Co., 1877.

Maddox, George T. *Hard Trials and Tribulations of an Old Confederate Soldier.* Springfield: Oak Hills, 1997.

Murrell, Richard K. "Letters from Hunter's Missouri Cavalry." *Blue and Grey Chronicle* 9 (June 2006): 5–8.

Jackman's Regiment

Colonel: Sidney Drake Jackman, assigned to duty as brigadier general by General Edmund Kirby Smith, May 16, 1865, but never confirmed by the Confederate Senate

Lieutenant Colonel: Charles H. Nichols

Major: George W. Newton

Companies and Commanders

Company G: George W. Newton, promoted to major ca. June 1864; John M. Simmons

Company H: J. F. Scott

Company —: J. L. Campbell

Company —: Elijah B. Dowell

Company — Fountain King

Company —: Francis M. Lowry

Company —: —— Rollins

Company —: ——Rusk

Company —: James F. Sugg

Company —: Rowland Wilson

This regiment mustered into the Confederate army in the spring of 1864 and should not be confused with the regiment Jackman commanded in 1862. Major General Thomas C. Hindman dismounted the earlier organization, which eventually became the 16th Infantry Regiment. Not desiring an infantry command, Jackman resigned his commission about October 23, 1862, and proceeded to Missouri with authority from Hindman to recruit a mounted regiment for the Confederacy. He lingered in Missouri for a year, recruiting and harassing Union forces; in late October 1863, he led recruits to Major General Sterling Price in southern Arkansas. Jackman's activities until the following spring are unknown. He joined Brigadier General Joseph O. Shelby's command in northeast Arkansas in the spring of 1864, for on May 18, Shelby granted Jackman authority to recruit one or more regiments of cavalry. Shelby ordered Jackman to report with his men to Jacksonport on June 16; Jackman had organized a full regiment of cavalry by June 22, although only a third of his troops had weapons. In July, Jackman's regiment operated along the Memphis & Little Rock Railroad; on one occasion, the regiment attacked a Union detachment, killing 10 of the enemy, taking 23 prisoners, and destroying about a mile of track. In mid-August, Jackman assumed command of a newly formed brigade in the Batesville vicinity, and Lieutenant Colonel Charles H. Nichols thereafter led the regiment in that brigade. Part of the regiment moved with the brigade to attack Ashley's Station on the Memphis & Little Rock Railroad on August 23 but arrived as the Federals surrendered and did no fighting. Later that day, the regiment joined in a dismounted charge against Federal defenders at Jones's Hay Station. The enemy made little resistance, resulting in the Confederates' capturing 400 prisoners, weapons, supplies, and a flag. Jackman's regiment next engaged a Federal relief force that approached from DeVall's Bluff. The Confederates directed heavy fire at the enemy for an hour until ordered to retreat from the field.

The regiment saw little further action until the brigade rode into Missouri in September as part of Major General Sterling Price's expedition. Crossing the Missouri line on September 19, the regiment, still poorly armed, moved with Jackman's brigade, in Shelby's division, to Potosi in Washington County. On September 28, the regiment participated in the failed attempt to capture or destroy the Federal garrison that escaped Fort Davidson in the aftermath of the battle of Pilot Knob. It destroyed segments of the Pacific Railroad on September 30 and October 1. The regiment then accompanied the brigade to the outskirts of Jefferson City, skirmishing with the Federals en route. After moving on to Boonville, where it arrived on October 10, the regiment took a position on the Tipton road south of Boonville to guard against an attack from that direction. On October 12, Federals attacked the brigade, and the regiment fought for over an hour before driving the enemy in retreat. Per Shelby's orders, Jackman selected 500 men of his command to act in concert with a brigade under Brigadier General John B. Clark Jr. in assaulting Glasgow, north of the Missouri River. Fighting on the left of the Confederate line, Jackman's troops helped overwhelm the Federal garrison on October 15, resulting in the capture of 800 prisoners and a large cache of weapons and supplies. On October 21, Jackman's regiment charged enemy troops disputing the crossing of the Little Blue River and helped break the Federal line. The day following, the regiment encountered the enemy near Westport, drove them from their position, and captured a 24-pounder brass howitzer, a caisson, and several wagons.

The regiment deployed on the Confederate left at Westport on October 23 as the contending armies charged back and forth along Brush Creek for three hours. Around noon, Jackman's brigade received orders to move to the support of Brigadier General James F. Fagan's division, then threatened by a Federal force from east of the Confederate position. The brigade, including Jackman's regiment, fought dismounted until the enemy withdrew long enough to allow the troopers to remount and execute a fighting retreat. The regiment joined Shelby's brigade on October 25 as the Confederates contended with exultant Federals who had routed two Confederate divisions at Mine Creek, Kansas. After a running fight that covered a considerable distance, the enemy temporarily broke off contact. Although present at the battle of Newtonia on October 28, Jackman's regiment supported Captain Richard A. Collins's battery and did not become closely engaged in that brief fight. Jackman did not report regimental losses for the expedition. On October 30, after the army retreated into Arkansas, Jackman's regiment, still under the command of Lieutenant Colonel Nichols, left the army on furlough with orders to report back to Camden, Arkansas, in mid-December. Although specific evidence is lacking, it appears the regiment did rejoin the army at some point. Further, the regiment doubtless disbanded near the end of the war, probably in Texas with the remainder of Shelby's division. Only a few of the regimental troopers received paroles at Shreveport, Louisiana, in early June 1865. No complete regimental muster rolls exist, and reliable unit losses cannot be ascertained.

BIBLIOGRAPHY

"Colonel Sidney Jackman." *Confederate Veteran* 19 (1911): 436.

Maddox, George T. *Hard Trials and Tribulations of an Old Confederate Soldier.* Springfield: Oak Hills, 1997.

Musser, Richard H. "Sketch of Col. S. D. Jackman." *Daily Missouri Republican,* St. Louis, Missouri, August 28, 1886.

Norton, Richard L., ed. *Behind Enemy Lines: The Memoirs and Writings of Brigadier General Sidney Drake Jackman.* Springfield: Oak Hills, 1997.

Lawther's Temporary Dismounted Regiment

Commander: Robert R. Lawther

The provisions of Special Order No. 125, Headquarters, District of Arkansas, dated August 1, 1863, created this unit and prescribed its name. The order directed that dismounted cavalrymen from the regiments of Brigadier General John S. Marmaduke's Missouri cavalry division be assigned to the unit until they acquired horses. Men from the same regiment composed separate companies. When a trooper procured a horse, he went back to his original unit, keeping the regimental composition in a constant state of flux. Robert R. Lawther, formerly major of the 1st

Missouri Cavalry Regiment, commanded the unit. While the regiment camped at Bayou Metoe in late August, Brigadier General Mosby M. Parsons, commanding a Missouri infantry brigade, sent recruiters to the camp to procure soldiers for his infantry and artillery units. Lawther refused to permit recruiting, for he had assurances from Major General Sterling Price, district commander, that his men would not be forced into other branches of service. Subsequently, Parsons ordered Lawther to furnish a detail to man a battery, which Lawther also declined to provide. Parsons placed Lawther under arrest and sent Captain Joseph M. Kelley, his brigade inspector, to the regiment's camp, where Kelley summarily ordered Lawther's officers to designate men to fill the detail. The officers refused to do so, and Kelley immediately arrested them. Kelley then had the 9th Missouri Sharpshooter Battalion and a company of the 10th Missouri Infantry Regiment brought to the camp and forced the detail. Lawther and the other arrested officers reported to the post commander at Little Rock the next morning as ordered. Lawther learned that Parsons had no authority to take men from his command. Lawther and his officers obtained release from arrest and returned to the regiment. Whether the forced detail for the artillery returned to the regiment is not of record.

On September 30, the unit moved to Arkadelphia to perform guard duty. The command, numbering some 160 officers and men, then moved to Camden on October 12, where it served as a reserve. On November 7, Lawther turned over temporary command of the regiment to Captain Henry A. Peabody. The regiment does not appear in the records after November 15, 1863, while still at Camden, and presumably disbanded shortly thereafter.

Bibliography

Correspondence of General John S. Marmaduke. National Archives, Washington, D.C.

Trans-Mississippi Order and Letter Book, Brigadier-General John S. Marmaduke. Transcribed by Carolyn M. Bartels. Independence: Two Trails, 2000.

Perkins's Regiment
(Reorganized as Perkins's Infantry Battalion)

Colonel: Caleb J. Perkins

Lieutenant Colonel: Quinton Peacher

Major: Thomas B. Patton

Companies and Commanders:

Company A: (Howard, Monroe, Randolph) Frank Davis

Company B: (Randolph) Nicholas G. Matlock

Company C: (Audrain, Boone, Cooper) George W. Bryson

Company D: (Audrain, Callaway) Alexander Day

Company E: (Boone, Howard) Thomas W. Todd, killed October 1864

Company F: (Boone, Howard) George W. Rowland

Company G: (Howard, Randolph) Isham Powell

Company —: (Saline) —— Chinn

Company —: (Monroe) Elliott D. Major

Company —: (Randolph) Samuel Powell

This regiment gathered north of the Missouri River in the late summer and early fall of 1864 in anticipation of Major General Sterling Price's expedition into the state. Although often described by Union authorities as guerrillas, the companies formally organized for regular cavalry service. At least two of the companies participated in the capture of a militia company at Paris on October 15. Poorly armed but well mounted, the regiment moved to join Price's army as it approached Boonville, crossing the river at Glasgow and Rocheport. The regiment mustered into Confederate service in Jackson County about October 20 as the army pushed the enemy toward Kansas City. Caleb J. Perkins, previously an officer in the Missouri State Guard, commanded the unit. Price assigned the regiment to Colonel Charles H. Tyler's partially armed brigade, which guarded the army's large supply train. Brigadier General John McNeil's Union brigade threatened the train on October 23; Tyler's units deployed with elements of Brigadier General James F. Fagan's

CAVALRY

125

Arkansas division to present the appearance of a large force and to hopefully prevent an attack. The ploy worked, as McNeil deemed the force guarding the train too formidable and canceled his assault.

Perkins's regiment first experienced combat on October 25, when the men of the regiment, most of them unarmed, participated in an unlikely charge against the pursuing Federals. The charge succeeded in temporarily stalling the pursuit, which permitted the army's train to move out of harm's way. The regiment lost 5 killed and 13 wounded in the short fight. Perkins's regiment retreated into Arkansas with Tyler's brigade and then made the long and exhausting trek through Indian Territory to Clarksville, Texas, where it arrived in late November. In early January 1865, Tyler's brigade, including Perkins's regiment, moved to Fulton, Arkansas, where many cavalry units converted to infantry service. Perkins's regiment reorganized there as an infantry battalion of six companies on January 21. The reorganization involved the consolidation of companies that had been reduced by death and desertion, resulting in a battalion containing about 420 men. Perkins's battalion joined the 1st Brigade, Brigadier General Mosby M. Parsons's Missouri infantry division, north of Fulton on the Red River. The battalion spent the next two months camped near Camden, Arkansas. In late March it moved to a camp south of Shreveport, Louisiana, where it drilled and performed routine guard duty. The men of the battalion received paroles at Shreveport on June 7 and that same day boarded the steamers *Countess* and *Maria Denning* for transportation to Missouri. Known losses of Perkins's command numbered 6 killed in action and 6 deaths by disease.

BIBLIOGRAPHY

Baker, Dr. J. H. P. "Memories of the War." *Press-Spectator,* Salisbury, Missouri, August 13—October 8, 1915.

"Capt. Samuel Powell." *Confederate Veteran* 16 (1908): 650.

Confederate Organizations, Officers, and Posts, 1861—1865, Missouri Units. Springfield: Ozark Genealogical Society, 1988.

Rickman, Daniel T. "Events in the Trans-Mississippi Department." *Confederate Veteran* 21 (1913): 71.

Poindexter's Regiment

Colonel: John A. Poindexter

Lieutenant Colonel: Harvey G. McKinney

Major: John Hudson

Companies and Commanders:

Company H: (Ralls, Shelby) Fairbanks Larabee

Company K: (Randolph) Nicholas G. Matlock

Company —: (Carroll, Howard) Robert Austin

Company —: (Carroll, Howard) Logan H. Ballew

Company —: (Boone) Mastin G. Corlew

Company —: —— Davenport

Company —: (Randolph) Asa T. Force

Company —: (Boone) Amos K. Hulett (Transferred to 1st Northeast Cavalry Regiment)

Company —: (Carroll, Howard) William G. Mirick

Company —: (Boone) Robert H. Sweeney

In April 1862, in the aftermath of the Confederate defeat at Pea Ridge, Arkansas, John A. Poindexter, a regimental commander in the Missouri State Guard, crossed the Mississippi River to Memphis, Tennessee, with the Army of the West. He remained with the army only a short time, for Major General Sterling Price sent him to Missouri to recruit a regiment in June. Before the end of that month, Poindexter reached Randolph County, where he mounted a discreet recruiting campaign. He enjoyed considerable success, for ten companies organized in Randolph and surrounding counties reported to Poindexter near Keytesville in late July. Poindexter intended to cross the Missouri River at Waverly once he organized the regiment and then move south to Arkansas and the Confederate army. He eventually camped near Glasgow, where on August 8 he organized the companies into a regiment of about 800 poorly armed men. The plan to move south of the Missouri soon went awry, for on the day he organized the regiment, Colonel Odon Guitar, 9th Missouri State Militia Regiment, led a column from Glasgow with the intention of destroying

Poindexter's command. As Poindexter moved his troops west toward Waverly, Guitar pursued him relentlessly for three days, often skirmishing with the Confederate rear guard but unable to overtake the main column. Near sunset on August 11, Guitar's advance discovered the Confederates in the process of crossing the Grand River at Compton's Ferry. Pushing his artillery forward, Guitar opened on Poindexter's disjointed command. The artillery fire created panic in the Confederate ranks, and the neophyte soldiers fled after offering but feeble resistance. The Union colonel estimated Confederate losses at 250 killed, wounded, and captured, and recovered some 100 weapons left by the retreating rebels. Despite the damage inflicted on Poindexter's command, Guitar persisted in his pursuit.

Poindexter moved rapidly north to Utica, apparently intent on joining Colonel Joseph C. Porter's command, but he encountered another Union force commanded by Brigadier General Benjamin C. Loan. The rebel commander immediately turned about and headed southwest. Having continued the pursuit, Guitar's command struck the Confederates again at Yellow Creek in Chariton County and nearly destroyed Poindexter's column. In serious danger of being totally surrounded, and facing potential annihilation, Poindexter disbanded his regiment on or about August 15, 1862. Remnants of the regiment sought to make it to Arkansas, and some troopers succeeded in doing so, traveling in companies, squads, and individually, but the enemy captured many as they traveled south. Confederate authorities dismounted Poindexter's men after they joined the army and placed them in various infantry commands. A substantial number joined the regiment that subsequently became the 9th Infantry (Clark's). While the total losses of the regiment cannot be determined because the records are incomplete, 68 of Poindexter's soldiers died in prison, while Union authorities executed 2 others.

BIBLIOGRAPHY

Atwater, Gloria. "Colonel John A. Poindexter: Third Division. Missouri State Guard and Confederate Guerrilla." *Old'N Newsletter* (October/November/December 2000).

Confederate Organizations, Officers and Posts, 1861–1865, Missouri Units. Springfield: Ozarks Genealogical Society, 1988.

Searcy's Regiment (Reorganized as Searcy's Sharpshooter Battalion, or 1st Sharpshooter Battalion)

Colonel: James Jasper Searcy

Lieutenant Colonel: John C. Moore

Major: Amos F. Cake

Companies and Commanders:

Company A: (Boone, Callaway) William B. Strode

Company B: (Boone, Monroe) Abel M. Johnson

Company C: (Chariton, Cole, Randolph) William E. Warden

Company D: (Chariton) Berry Owens

Company E: (Audrain, Boone, Howard) William H. Todd

Company F: (Howard) Joel H. Greene

Company —: (Chariton) James Kennedy

Company —:—— Chorn

Company —: —— Cone

Company —: ——Stow

Recruited primarily north of the Missouri River in the late summer and early fall of 1864, the companies that constituted this regiment secretly organized in anticipation of the arrival of Major General Sterling Price's army during his expedition into the state. After crossing to the south side of the river at Rocheport, the companies formed a cavalry regiment of some 600 troopers on about October 20 as the army approached Kansas City. James J. Searcy, a graduate of the Virginia Military Institute and an experienced officer with service in the Missouri State Guard and 9th Missouri Infantry Regiment, assumed command. The regiment joined the mostly unarmed brigade of Colonel Charles H. Tyler, which organized at about the same time as the regiment. Tyler's brigade guarded the large wagon train that accompanied the army. On October 23, Brigadier General John McNeil's Union brigade threatened the train. To present a bold front and stave off an attack on the wagons, Tyler's men deployed in line with elements of Brigadier General James F. Fagan's Arkansas division. Believing the force guarding the train too formidable to overcome, McNeil canceled his attack. Searcy's regiment experienced its only combat on October 25, when it participated in a charge against pursuing Federals and succeeded in delaying the pursuit enough to permit the army's wagon train to move to safety. The regiment lost 3 killed and 4 wounded in the brief encounter. Searcy's regiment retreated from Missouri into Arkansas with Tyler's brigade and then undertook the trying march through Indian Territory to Clarksville, Texas, where it arrived in late November.

In early January 1865, the brigade moved to Fulton, Arkansas, and established a camp. Confederate authorities dismounted Tyler's brigade, including Searcy's regiment, at Fulton on January 7. The regiment then reorganized as a sharpshooter battalion of six companies on January 21, while still at Fulton. The reorganization involved the consolidation of companies that had been reduced in strength by death and desertion, and resulted in a battalion numbering about 425 men. The battalion then joined the 1st Brigade, Brigadier General Mosby M. Parsons's Missouri infantry division, above Fulton on the Red River. The battalion spent the winter months in quarters near Camden, Arkansas, and in late March moved to a camp south of Shreveport, Louisiana, where it drilled and performed guard duty. The men of the battalion received paroles at Shreveport on June 7 and that same day boarded the steamboat *Countess* for shipment to Missouri. Known losses of Searcy's unit numbered 3 killed in action and 5 deaths by disease.

BIBLIOGRAPHY

"Capt. James Kennedy." *Confederate Veteran* 36 (1928): 25.

"Charge of Unarmed Men." *Confederate Veteran* 36 (1920): 25.

Joseph Cooley Autobiography. Typescript. Missouri State Archives, Jefferson City, Missouri.

Halliburton, J. W. "That Charge." *Confederate Veteran* 28 (1920): 264.

"R. F. Crews Recounts Personal Recollections of the Battle of Westport." *Daily Tribune,* Columbia, Missouri, December 14 and 21, 1923.

Slayback's Regiment

Colonel: Alonzo William Slayback

Lieutenant Colonel: Caleb W. Dorsey

Major: John H. Guthrie

Companies and Commanders:

Company A: (Cape Girardeau, Mississippi, Scott, St. Charles) John H. Guthrie, promoted major ca. February 1865; James H. Fugate

Company B: (Cape Girardeau, Carroll, Platte) William J. Howard

Company C: (Lincoln, Pike) Benjamin F. Meade

Company D: (Cooper, Moniteau, Texas) James M. Cowden

Company E: (Lincoln) William Dorsey

Company F: (Chariton, Cooper) Milton Cross

Company G: (Randolph, Ray) A. T. Prewitt

Company H: (Saline) John Guthrie

Company I: (Moniteau, Morgan) Peter Narns

Company K: (Benton, Moniteau, Morgan) Joel Ivey

This unit remains an enigma, as no source fully delineates its origins or final disposition. Alonzo W. Slayback recruited the regiment during Major General Sterling Price's expedition into Missouri in the fall of 1864. Brigadier General Joseph O. Shelby authorized Slayback, a former regimental commander in the Missouri State Guard and a member of Brigadier General John S. Marmaduke's staff in Confederate service, to raise a regiment on August 14, 1864. Slayback began recruiting when Price's army entered southeast Missouri in mid-September. He initially accompanied elements of Marmaduke's brigade into the state and subsequently joined Marmaduke's column with a command likely consisting of two small companies at Bollinger's Mill (now Zalma) on September 23. Slayback's men participated in a brief mounted charge on Fort Davidson at the battle of Pilot Knob on September 27, with minimal losses. His recruits became part of Shelby's brigade in that general's division at Union on October 2. Brigadier General M. Jeff Thompson, who commanded Shelby's brigade during much of the raid, consistently referred to Slayback's unit as a "battalion." It is evident that Slayback continued to recruit as the army moved through Missouri; his command probably totaled at least six companies before the expedition ended in late October.

The battalion participated in the attack on Sedalia on October 15 and acted as provost guard after the enemy surrendered. On October 19 the battalion joined the brigade in attacking the Federals near Lexington. Operating on the left of the line, Slayback's men quickly drove the enemy in their front in retreat. Thompson cited the battalion for its "courage and steadiness" in making the fight. The battalion next helped force a crossing of the Little Blue River on October 21. The day following, the brigade crossed the Big Blue River and pressed on to Westport. On October 23, the battalion, near the center of the Confederate formation, took part in a charge that temporarily broke the Federal line as the battle of Westport raged along Brush Creek. Shortly afterward, the brigade pulled back and shifted to defend against a heavy Union assault on its right flank. Slayback's men fought all afternoon in a hotly contested delaying action as the brigade repeatedly formed new lines to stem the enemy pursuit. Finally evading the enemy after an all-day fight, the brigade joined the main army in moving toward Arkansas. Two days later, on October 25, Slayback's battalion engaged in another delaying action as Shelby's entire division temporarily stymied the Federal pursuit after two other Confederate divisions had been shattered at the battle of Mine Creek, Kansas. The battalion's final action occurred at Newtonia on October 28, the last engagement of the expedition, where the troopers fought dismounted and helped repulse a Union attack before retreating into Arkansas. Slayback did not report battalion casualties incurred during the expedition.

After the army reached the relative safety of Arkansas, Price furloughed Slayback's battalion to recuperate from the exhausting expedition. By mid-December the battalion reported to the army in Texas, at which time the strength of the unit totaled merely 300 men. Sometime thereafter, most likely in February 1865, the battalion consolidated with recruit companies brought out of northeast Missouri by Caleb W. Dorsey and formed this regiment. One source indicates that the military authorities issued lances to the regiment since so few soldiers possessed firearms, but that claim is likely apocryphal. The regiment appears to have disbanded before the surrender, as remnants of eight companies received paroles at Shreveport, Louisiana, on June 14, while two companies with ties to southeast Missouri accepted paroles at Wittsburg, Arkansas, at about the same time. Losses of the command cannot be established due to the lack of regimental records.

BIBLIOGRAPHY

"Alonzo W. Slayback." In *The United States Biographical Dictionary and Portrait Gallery of Eminent and Self-Made Men,* 116–18. Missouri Volume. Kansas City: United States Biographical Pub. Co., 1878.

"Capt. I. C. Cruzzen." *Confederate Veteran* 26 (1918): 215.

John H. Gutherie File. Union Provost Marshal Files of Papers Relating to Two or More Civilians. Roll 61. National Archives, Washington, D. C.

A. W. Slayback to M. Jeff Thompson, December 8, 1867. M. Jeff Thompson Collection. Howard-Tilton Library, Tulane University, New Orleans, Louisiana.

Stanton, Donal J., Goodwin F. Berquist, and Paul C. Bowers, eds. *The Civil War Reminiscences of General M. Jeff Thompson.* Dayton: Morningside Press, 1988.

Williams's Regiment "Williams's Rangers"

Colonel: David Alexander Williams

Lieutenant Colonel: Eli Hodge

Major: John L. Merrick

Companies and Commanders

Company A: (Carroll, St. Charles) Unknown

Company B: (Callaway, Montgomery) W. Milton Scholl

Company C: (Audrain, Callaway) Daniel H. McIntyre

Company D: (Carroll) J. H. Withers

Company E: (Carroll, Chariton, Randolph) J. M. Cottingham

Company F: (Moniteau, Saline) Unknown

Company G: (Boone, Callaway, Chariton) Isaac N. Sitton

Company H: (Carroll, Randolph) David H. Hammons

Company I: (Carroll, Chariton, Cooper) R. E. Williams

Company K: (Boone, Callaway) John H. H. Maxwell

During Major General Sterling Price's expedition into Missouri in the fall of 1864, Captain David A. Williams, 6th Cavalry Regiment, commanded Brigadier General Joseph O. Shelby's advance. After reaching Boonville on October 10, Shelby dispatched Williams north of the Missouri River to recruit; in a few days he had raised sufficient men in Carroll and surrounding counties to organize a battalion. On October 15, Williams approached Carrollton, the county seat, and demanded surrender of the Union militia defending the town. The militia commander initially refused the Confederate ultimatum but agreed to terms after Williams met him under a flag of truce; the garrison of 300 militiamen then stacked arms and yielded to the rebels. Unfortunately, the recruits quickly looted some stores and stole other private property.

Williams's battalion crossed the Missouri River at Glasgow and reported to the army near Independence on October 20. It joined Shelby's brigade, then commanded by Brigadier General M. Jeff Thompson. The battalion, comparatively well armed with the weapons captured at Carrollton, participated in the battle of Westport on October 23. During that engagement, the battalion supported Captain Richard A. Collins's Missouri battery and performed well on the field. After a Union assault on the Confederate right flank drove them from their position, Williams's battalion fought with the brigade to slow the enemy pursuit. On October 25, the battalion formed part of the brigade line when Shelby's men saved the army from destruction following the rout of two other Confederate divisions at Mine Creek, Kansas. Three days later, Williams's battalion fought dismounted when Major General James G. Blunt's command attacked the army at Newtonia. After a brief but hotly contested engagement, the Confederates repulsed Blunt and then continued their retreat into Arkansas. Generals Shelby and Thompson complimented the battalion's fighting prowess after the army reached Texas. The unit's losses during these engagements are not recorded. Shelby reassigned Williams's battalion to Colonel Sidney D. Jackman's brigade after the army left Missouri. Jackman applauded the care and attention Williams showed his command during the difficult march through Indian Territory to Clarksville, Texas.

After the army arrived in Texas, but at a date and location not recorded, Williams's battalion and remnants of Colonel Eli Hodge's badly depleted recruit command merged to form this regiment. Many members of the new organization took paroles at Shreveport, Louisiana, in early June 1865; some followed General Shelby to Mexico in exile; and others simply dispersed.

Bibliography

Baker, Dr. J. H. P. "Memories of the War." *Press-Spectator,* Salisbury, Missouri, August 13–October 8, 1915.

Cloyd, W. W. "Experiences of W. W. Cloyd with the Army of General Sterling Price in the Great American Civil War." In *Genealogy of the Cloyd, Bayse and Tapp Families,* by A. D. Cloyd, 179–81. Columbus: Champlin Press, 1912.

"David A. Williams." In *Memorial and Biographical History of Dallas County, Texas,* 409. Chicago: Lewis, 1976.

History of Carroll County, Missouri. St. Louis: National Historical Co., 1881.

Watts, Hamp B. *The Babe of the Company.* Springfield: Oak Hills, 1996.

B. BATTALIONS

1st Battalion (Elliott's) (Also known as the 10th Battalion)

Increased to 9th Regiment. See the entry for that regiment.

1st Battalion, 1st Indian Brigade
(Livingston's/Pickler's/Piercy's) "Cherokee Spikes"

Major: Thomas R. Livingston, killed July 11, 1863; Jesse F. Pickler, killed July 28, 1864; Andrew J. Piercy

Companies and Commanders

(ca. May 1864 until battalion disbanded):

Company A: David V. Rusk

Company B: William Robinson

Company C: Lafayette (or Lewis) F. Roberts

Company D: Matthew R. Johnson

This battalion evolved from a company recruited in the spring of 1862 in Jasper County by Thomas R. Livingston, a former cavalry officer in the Missouri State Guard. Livingston recruited the company under the provisions of the Partisan Ranger Act passed by the Confederate Congress in April. While the exact date of the company's formation is unknown, correspondence indicates it occurred before May 4. Livingston scouted for Colonel Stand Watie, commander of the 1st Cherokee Cavalry Regiment, in the vicinity of Granby, Missouri, in late May. On May 31, the company joined parts of Watie's and Colonel John T. Coffee's units in stampeding a detachment of the 14th Missouri State Militia Cavalry Regiment near Neosho. Thereafter, Livingston recruited two additional companies to create a battalion that purportedly became part of a regiment organized in June by Colonel James J. Clarkson. Significantly, the battalion continued operations with Watie in Indian Territory. Any alleged association the battalion had with Clarkson's regiment ended when Union troops captured

Clarkson at Locust Grove on July 3, resulting in the dispersal of his regiment.

Apparently, none of Livingston's men participated in the Locust Grove defeat. A month later, Livingston's battalion, increased by the addition of a company formerly of Clarkson's outfit under Captain Matthew R. Johnson, returned to southwest Missouri and briefly occupied Neosho. On September 19 the battalion cooperated with the 31st Texas Cavalry Regiment in attacking the 2nd Indian Home Guard Regiment on Spring River in Jasper County. While the Confederates were initially successful in driving the enemy from their camp, the Union troops quickly rallied, and the Confederates withdrew after four hours of fighting, having suffered relatively heavy casualties. Following the engagement at Spring River, the battalion performed scout duty in southwest Missouri for Major General Thomas C. Hindman's corps, then organizing in northwest Arkansas. In late October, Brigadier General James G. Blunt's command attacked and scattered Livingston's men and other Confederate units near Old Fort Wayne in Indian Territory.

Livingston subsequently operated in the Indian Territory, northwest Arkansas, and southwest Missouri during the winter and spring of 1862–63. During this period, the battalion conducted numerous operations, primarily in Jasper County, with mixed results. The 3rd Indian Home Guard Regiment routed the battalion with substantial losses in mid-January 1863, near Maysville, Arkansas. Returning to Missouri, Livingston successfully attacked Granby on March 3 and skirmished with elements of the 6th Kansas Cavalry two days later before retiring into Indian Territory. On May 14, Livingston's men encountered a Missouri militia regiment near Neosho and inflicted heavy casualties while pursuing the militiamen over three miles. Near Rader's Farm, in Jasper County, the battalion attacked a Union forage party on May 18, killed 17 of the Union troops, and captured wagons and supplies; it later engaged another enemy force and drove it with considerable loss. At Stockton, on July 11, Livingston's men suffered a deadly repulse when they attacked militia occupying the local courthouse. Livingston and 3 of his men fell mortally wounded in the action, while an additional 15 wounded retreated with the battalion. Following Livingston's death, Jesse F. Pickler assumed command of the battalion.

At least part of the battalion participated in Colonel Joseph O. Shelby's October 1863 raid into western Missouri. The battalion's role in the raid is not documented, but it apparently rode with Colonel John T. Coffee's command. The Federals captured Pickler and some of his men encamped at Carthage during the retreat from Missouri. Pickler obtained a quick release from captivity, for in mid-December he and the battalion established winter quarters at the camp of Brigadier General Douglas H. Cooper in Indian Territory. In May 1864 the battalion, with merely 100 men present, joined Shelby's brigade, at least temporarily. Shelby, by then a general officer, directed Pickler to recruit in northwest Arkansas and to report the results of his efforts within forty days. Pickler may have been recruiting when Unions scouts noted him operating in Newton County, Missouri, with 250 men in early June. On July 27, the battalion engaged in a hard fight in Benton County, Arkansas, with the 1st Arkansas Cavalry Regiment (Union); the Arkansans defeated the battalion and killed Pickler. Command of the battalion then passed to Major Andrew J. Piercy, a Virginia Military Institute graduate.

Although General Shelby expected the battalion to join the army for Major General Sterling Price's expedition into Missouri in September 1864, it failed to participate in that undertaking. Instead, the battalion raided southwest Missouri during that time and participated in an attack on Marmaton, Kansas, on October 23. In that rather infamous incident, the raiders burned several buildings, including private homes, and executed 6 discharged Union soldiers. The battalion also captured a wagon train of Arkansas refugees escorted by a detail of the 6th Kansas Cavalry Regiment near Cow Creek, Kansas, the same day, killing 3 soldiers and 13 civilians. The battalion spent the balance of the war in Indian Territory, where it disbanded near Fort Washita at a date unknown. A partial muster roll, dated March 1865, which lists only the battalion officers, is the only official personnel record for this unit known to exist. The unit is often designated as the "1st Cavalry Battalion, 1st Indian Brigade," but any official assignment as such is unlikely.

BIBLIOGRAPHY

Livingston, John C., Jr. *Such a Foe as Livingston: The Campaign of Confederate Major Thomas R. Livingston's First Missouri Cavalry Battalion of Southwest Missouri.* Wyandotte: Gregath, 2004.

Schrantz, Ward L. *Jasper County, Missouri, in the Civil War.* Carthage: Carthage Kiwanis Club, 1992.

———. "The Life and Death of Civil War Guerrilla Tom Livingston." *Ozarks Mountaineer* 48 (April/May 2000): 32–34.

3rd Battalion (Dismounted) (Campbell's/Samuel's) (Also known as the 5th and 6th Battalion)

Lieutenant Colonel: Leonidas C. Campbell, transferred to Trans-Mississippi Department ca. June, resigned August 12, 1862; David Todd Samuel, killed September 27, 1864

Major: David Todd Samuel, promoted lieutenant colonel, June 11, 1862; Thomas J. McQuiddy, deserted September 15, 1862

Companies and Commanders:

Company A: (Miller, Moniteau) John Inglish, dropped May 8, 1862; William C. Aldredge

Company B: (Nodaway, Worth) Thomas J. McQuiddy, promoted major June 11, 1862; Alexander F. Burns (Formerly Company G)

Company C: (Greene, Polk) Leonidas C. Campbell, promoted lieutenant colonel May 15, 1862; James W. McSpadden, retired ca. June 1864 (Formerly Company B)

Company D (1st): (Greene) Jonas W. Graves, did not seek election when company merged into Company F (2nd) on June 15, 1862

Company D (2nd): (Andrew, Platte) David Todd Samuel, promoted major May 15, 1862; Lewis Furnish (Formerly Company C)

Company E: (Greene, Laclede, Miller) James H. C. Branham, resigned May 8, 1862; Felix Lotspeich, resigned April 23, 1863; William H. Evington

Company F (1st): (Greene, Webster) Alexander D. Brown, did not seek election when company merged into Company F (2nd) on June 15, 1862

Company F (2nd): (Cass, Greene, Webster) Thomas A. Graves, killed October 3, 1862; William H. Glenn, prisoner of war May 17, 1863

Company G: (Exchanged prisoners, very mixed) Henry C. Price, sent on recruiting duty ca. June 1863 but deserted instead (Disbanded at consolidation with 1st Missouri Cavalry Regiment)

Company H: (Exchanged prisoners, very mixed) John G. Payton, killed July 1863; Griffin Bayne, killed November 30, 1864

The genesis of this battalion occurred at Springfield, Missouri, in early 1862, when seven companies of mounted recruits from the ranks of the 5th, 7th, and 8th Divisions of the Missouri State Guard mustered into Confederate service. Initially, the companies did not belong to the same organization. While companies A, B, D (1st), and D (2nd) served in [Major General Sterling] "Price's Body Guard Battalion," commanded by Lieutenant Colonel James T. Cearnal, the remaining three companies acted independently of each other for several weeks. The companies participated in some skirmishing during the retreat of Price's army from Springfield into northwest Arkansas in mid-February. When the Confederate Army of the West, under the command of Major General Earl Van Dorn, advanced on the Union position near Pea Ridge, Arkansas, on March 6, Cearnal's battalion joined the 1st Missouri Cavalry Regiment in attacking Federal soldiers fleeing Bentonville and drove them into retreat. The following morning, the battalion encountered enemy pickets near Elkhorn Tavern, which soon brought on a general engagement. Quickly reinforced by infantry of the 1st Missouri Brigade, Cearnal's men fought dismounted near the tavern until ordered to the left flank of the army, where it helped push the enemy back for nearly a mile. On the second day of the battle, the battalion guarded roads to prevent an enemy flank attack and did no fighting.

The remaining three companies that eventually constituted the 3rd Cavalry Battalion (C, E, and F) apparently served in Colonel Colton Greene's 3rd Missouri Brigade at the battle, with all companies except Captain Leonidas C. Campbell's fighting dismounted. The 3rd Brigade spent the first day of the engagement deployed with the 1st Missouri Brigade near Elkhorn Tavern, generally on the left of the line, and advanced with the brigade as the enemy grudgingly retreated to a new battle line near sunset. Early the next day, the 3rd Brigade fell back to the vicinity of Elkhorn Tavern after the Federals launched a heavy artillery barrage, soon followed by an infantry assault. The brigade joined the army in retreat as the Confederates, low on ammunition and overcome by a rejuvenated Federal army, yielded the field to the enemy. The aggregate losses of the seven companies engaged at Pea Ridge numbered at least 5 killed, 8 wounded, and 12 missing. The Army of the West retreated from Pea Ridge to Frog Bayou near Van Buren and recuperated there until ordered to Memphis, Tennessee. After an arduous trip across Arkansas in bad weather and on worse roads, the army arrived at Des Arc.

Before embarking for Memphis around April 14, General Van Dorn dismounted all cavalry units. The companies that later formed the 3rd Battalion reluctantly gave up their horses, which they left in Arkansas with 50 soldiers detailed as herdsmen. After arrival in Memphis, the companies occupied camps scattered about the city. On April 25, a dismounted cavalry battalion formed from companies C, E, and F (1st), under the command of Major Leonidas C. Campbell. A reorganization of the Army of the West occurred at Corinth, Mississippi, in mid-May, and four companies, A, B, D (1st), and D (2nd) of Cearnal's Battalion joined Campbell's unit. The newly formed battalion, designated the 3rd Cavalry Battalion although sometimes also known as the 5th or 6th Battalion, remained dismounted and drilled as infantry as part of Brigadier General Martin E. Greene's brigade. As the enemy advanced against Corinth, the battalion deployed at Farmington on May 9 but never became closely engaged. After the army evacuated Corinth in late May, the battalion occupied different camps in Mississippi and continued to train for its unwanted infantry role. Lieutenant Colonel Campbell crossed the Mississippi River in June to recruit a cavalry unit for service in that theater; D. Todd Samuel replaced him as battalion commander. About the same time, the battalion reorganized again, and companies D (1st) and F (1st) merged to form F (2nd). In the engagement of Iuka on September 19, the battalion remained in reserve and suffered no casualties.

The battalion's first significant battle test occurred October 3–4 at Corinth. On the first day, the battalion assisted in driving the Federals from two defensive positions into a third, while on the day following, it participated in a charge on Battery Powell. The Confederates carried Battery Powell at a terrible cost, only to be pushed out of the position by tremendous artillery crossfire and a Federal countercharge. By the time the 3rd Battalion left the field, its losses totaled 12 killed, 62 wounded, and 26 missing. General Price attempted to remount the battalion in November, but Van Dorn rejected the proposal. The battalion spent the winter months of 1862–63 in camp performing routine duty. The 3rd Battalion played a significant role in the Vicksburg Campaign but saw no close fighting until the battle of Champion Hill on May 16. As part of Green's brigade, the battalion participated in an attack that drove the Federals in retreat. Fighting on the extreme right flank of the brigade, the battalion charged forward as the Confederates shattered the center of the Federal line. The attack lost momentum when unsupported on the right, and then the

Confederates confronted a counterattack that sent them reeling in defeat. During the withdrawal, 64 men became separated from the battalion and eventually joined General Joseph E. Johnston's Army of Relief near Jackson, but most of the unit, under Captain Felix Lotspeich, retreated with the brigade. The defeat at Champion Hill, the pivotal battle of the Vicksburg Campaign, resulted in battalion losses of 9 killed, 15 wounded, and 15 missing.

After retreating from Champion Hill, the Missourians occupied a defensive line east of the Big Black River. Union troops breached the line on May 17, forcing the army to rapidly retreat into Vicksburg. The Federals captured at least 17 battalion soldiers at the Big Black debacle, while 1 fell wounded. Although briefly held in reserve inside the Vicksburg fortifications, the 3rd Battalion contingent soon joined the firing line and manned ramparts south of the Stockade Redan, where it remained for the balance of the siege. The battalion constantly skirmished with the enemy, performed countermining, and assisted in repulsing a determined enemy attack on May 22. After forty-seven days of siege, the Vicksburg garrison surrendered on July 4. Some 120 members of the 3rd battalion received paroles. The losses of the battalion during the long ordeal amounted to 4 killed, 18 wounded, and 4 deaths by disease.

Following the surrender, members of the 3rd Battalion reported to a parole camp at Demopolis, Alabama. Around August 1, two companies of exchanged prisoners who had served primarily in Missouri units in the Trans-Mississippi Department joined the battalion. Also, the part of the battalion that joined General Johnston after the Champion Hill disaster returned. Because of heavy losses due to combat, disease, and desertion, a reorganization of the Missouri Confederate units occurred at Demopolis. Per the provisions of Special Order No. 17, dated October 1, 1863, Headquarters, Paroled Prisoners, the 3rd Battalion consolidated with the 1st Cavalry Regiment, forming the 1st & 3rd Cavalry Regiment (Dismounted), which fought as a consolidated unit until the war ended. Approximately 665 soldiers actively campaigned with the 3rd Battalion during the war, including the period of consolidation with the 1st Cavalry Regiment; of that number, 91 died in battle, 56 died of disease, and 1 was murdered. See the entry for the 1st & 3rd Cavalry Regiment (Dismounted) for the further service of the men of this battalion.

Bibliography

Thomas Graves Collection. Mississippi State Archives, Jackson, Mississippi.

Neese, W. C. "Scaling the Works at Franklin." *Confederate Veteran* 11 (1903): 274.

Noe, F. R. "Scattered Remnant of a Company" *Confederate Veteran* 11 (1903): 16.

4th Battalion (McCulloch's)

Increased to 2nd Regiment. See the entry for that regiment.

10th Battalion (Elliott's) (Also known as 1st Battalion)

Increased to 9th Regiment. See the entry for that regiment.

11th Battalion (Young's)

Increased to 10th Regiment. See the entry for that regiment.

12th Battalion (Freeman's)

Increased to Freeman's Regiment. See the entry for that regiment.

14th Battalion (Wood's)

Increased to 13th Regiment. See the entry for that regiment.

17th Battalion (Norman's)

A designation, apparently unofficial, sometimes used for the five companies recruited by Major Matthew G. Norman in 1864, which subsequently became part of Fristoe's Regiment. These companies had no known combat record separate from Fristoe's Regiment. See the entry for Fristoe's Regiment for the service of the men of this battalion.

Clardy's Battalion

Major: Martin Linn Clardy

Companies and Commanders:

Company A: (Reynolds) Elijah D. Brawley

Company B: (St. Francois, Ste. Genevieve) Robert Blackwell Holmes

Company C: (Madison, Reynolds) William Bumbaugh

Company D: Robert B. Halwell

Company E: (Reynolds) Lucian N. Farris

This battalion's organization and service is extremely obscure. Paltry records suggest that the companies organized in the fall of 1864, during Major General Sterling Price's Missouri Expedition. Certainly, that is true of Farris's Company, which formed in Reynolds County following the battle of Pilot Knob of September 27. The southeast Missouri counties of Madison, Reynolds, St. Francois, and Ste. Genevieve furnished most troops for the unit; several of them had previously served in the 1st Division, Missouri State Guard, or in other Confederate outfits. The command, as a very loosely organized unit, may have participated in some engagements of Price's Missouri raid. But that service cannot be definitely established and is very doubtful, since part of the battalion operated in St. Francois County in October, after Price's army left the area.

Apparently, Major Richard C. Berryman initially commanded the battalion, or elements of it at least. The Federals considered the unit guerrillas because of its activities, which included some general plundering and horse stealing. On October 6, part of the 6th Missouri Volunteer Cavalry Regiment attacked a camp of 300 men under Berryman and the noted guerrilla Samuel S. Hildebrand on Big River in St. Francois County; the rebels suffered considerable losses in a short engagement. Martin L. Clardy, who may have served in the battalion, appears to have been elected commander of a more formally organized unit in January 1865, near Newport, Arkansas. After Brigadier General M. Jeff Thompson assumed command of northeast Arkansas in mid-March, he noted that he had to "rely on them [Clardy's battalion] for all actual service." Although Thompson did not note the nature of that service, it doubtless entailed scouting, courier service, and picket and guard duty. In mid-May, Company B performed provost marshal duty at Jonesboro, Arkansas, and at Thompson's direction executed a Confederate soldier for stealing. The men of the battalion, about 120 in number, received paroles at Wittsburg and Jacksonport, Arkansas, on May 25 and June 5, 1865, respectively. The parole lists are the only records of the battalion known to exist.

BIBLIOGRAPHY

Ponder, Jerry, and Victor Ponder. *Confederate Surrender and Parole, Jacksonport and Wittsburg, Arkansas, May and June, 1865.* Doniphan: Ponder Books, 1995.

Schmidt, Bob. *Veterans and Events in the Civil War in Southeast Missouri.* French Village: Privately printed, 2000.

Stanton, Donal J., Goodwin F. Berquist, and Paul C. Bowers, eds. *The Civil War Reminiscences of General M. Jeff Thompson.* Dayton: Morningside Press, 1988.

Davies's Cavalry Battalion

An Arkansas organization sometimes credited to Missouri. It served attached to the 7th Cavalry Regiment during the Price Expedition of 1864.

BIBLIOGRAPHY

Confederate Organizations, Officers and Posts, 1861–1865, Missouri Units. Springfield: Ozarks Genealogical Society, 1988.

Ford's Cavalry Battalion

An Arkansas organization sometimes credited to Missouri. The battalion contained some Missourians, especially in Company C.

Bibliography

Confederate Organizations, Officers and Posts, 1861–1865, Missouri Units.
Springfield: Ozarks Genealogical Society, 1988.

MacDonald's Battalion

Increased to the 10th Regiment. See the entry for that regiment.

Preston's Battalion

Major: William I. Preston

Companies and Commanders:

Company A: (Stoddard) Joseph J. Miller
Company B: (Stoddard) William T. Lineback
Company C: (Stoddard) David G. Hicks

As early as December 1861, William I. Preston, a graduate of the Virginia Military Institute and former aide to Brigadier General M. Jeff Thompson, Missouri State Guard, sought permission to raise "one or more" companies of cavalry for Confederate service. In seeking authority to recruit, he advised Major General Leonidas Polk that the men he sought to enlist had "horses, and double barrel shot-guns," and were "more or less familiar with South Eastern Missouri and ready for service." No reply from Polk has been located. Nothing apparently occurred in connection with Preston's recruiting efforts until late spring 1862, when he gathered three companies near Bloomfield, Missouri, and organized them into a battalion. Little is known of the service of the battalion. The records suggest that the advance of Brigadier General John W. Davidson's command scattered Company A at Jonesboro, Arkansas, on July 18, 1862. Elements of the battalion helped Captain William L. Jeffers's recruits capture Bloomfield on September 11, 1862, seizing 2 cannons, 400 muskets, and a large cache of other military supplies. Because of some irregularity in the original organization, the battalion remustered into Confederate service on about October 1, in

Stoddard County. The battalion likely served with Colonels John Q. Burbridge and Colton Greene in some of their actions on the Arkansas-Missouri border in the fall of 1862. Troopers of the battalion participated in a successful skirmish with the enemy near Van Buren, Missouri, on December 28, 1862. On January 23, 1863, Special Order No. 23, Trans-Mississippi Department, directed the battalion to consolidate with Burbridge's cavalry battalion to form a regiment. The consolidated organization became the 4th Missouri Cavalry Regiment, commanded by Burbridge, with Preston as his executive officer. Preston's battalion mustered as companies A, B, and C of the new regiment with the original captains, and the battalion ceased to exist as a separate organization thereafter. See the entry for the 4th Cavalry Regiment for the further service of the men of this battalion.

Bibliography

Confederate Organizations, Officers and Posts, 1861–1865, Missouri Units. Springfield: Ozarks Genealogical Society, 1988.

William I. Preston to Major General L. Polk, December 2, 1861. William I. Preston Envelope, Compiled Service Records, Roll 188, National Archives, Washington, D.C.

Trans-Mississippi Order and Letter Book, Brigadier-General John S. Marmaduke. Transcribed by Carolyn M. Bartels. Independence: Two Trails, 2000.

Reeves's Battalion

Increased to the 15th Regiment. See the entry for that regiment.

Schnable's Battalion

Lieutenant Colonel: John A. Schnable

Major: B. H. Clark, disposition not of record; Jesse Mooney

Companies and Commanders:

Company A: G. B. Thompson

Company B: J. R. Dowd, disposition not of record; J. B. David

Company F: John P. Norvell

Company G: William Chapman

Company H: W. B. Weast

Company —: Thomas B. Goforth

Company —: Benjamin Ivey

Company —: James J. Weast

In early June 1864, John A. Schnable, a former Missouri State Guard colonel who often commanded unattached units during the war, began recruiting in northeast Arkansas, most likely under authority granted by Brigadier General Joseph O. Shelby. On June 15, Shelby ordered Schnable to prepare his armed men for a forward movement. Shortly thereafter, Schnable's recruits moved to the vicinity of Batesville, Arkansas. On August 10, Shelby ordered four recruit companies to report to Schnable so that his unit could be organized in accordance with law. Presumably, the battalion formally organized at that time with eight companies.

The battalion participated in the capture of 400 Federals at Jones's Hay Station by Shelby's command on August 24. When the army organized for Major General Sterling Price's expedition into Missouri, Schnable's Battalion, with only a third of the men armed, became part of Colonel Sidney D. Jackman's brigade, Shelby's division. Schnable's men destroyed sections of the St. Louis & Iron Mountain Railroad after the army entered Missouri. The battalion participated in the pursuit of the Federals that evacuated Fort Davidson following the battle at Pilot Knob on September 27 and then destroyed sections of the southwest branch of the Pacific Railroad.

On October 8 the battalion performed picket duty near the Union fortifications at Jefferson City. Federals attacked Schnable's command, which repulsed two charges and then in turn charged and drove the enemy back momentarily. Soon, the Federals outflanked the battalion, which withdrew with the loss of 4 killed and 14 wounded. As the army proceeded west from Jefferson City, Schnable's battalion skirmished with the enemy on the Tipton road south of Boonville on October 12. The battalion fought dismounted on October 21 as the Confederates breached the enemy line at the Little Blue River. On the day following, Schnable's unit participated in a charge that routed the enemy and resulted in the capture of a 24-pounder howitzer, its caisson, and teams. The battalion engaged in the battle at Westport on October 23, fighting beside Shelby's brigade, and reinforced Brigadier General James F. Fagan's division when the charging enemy threatened to overwhelm the Arkansans. During the retreat from Westport, the battalion fought in several rear-guard actions, and a detail assisted in burning the burdensome Confederate wagon train. Schnable's battalion participated in the fight at Newtonia on October 28, the last engagement of the expedition.

After the army reached relative safety in Arkansas, Price furloughed Schnable's battalion. Over the next few months, the battalion lingered in the area of Yellville, Arkansas, comparatively inactive. As the war wound down, Schnable offered to surrender his command to the Federals at Yellville in late May 1865. The Federals agreed to receive the surrender but then revoked the arrangement for reasons that remain unclear. The majority of the battalion troopers surrendered at Jacksonport, Arkansas, on June 5 as part of Brigadier General M. Jeff Thompson's command in northeast Arkansas. Over 200 men refused to report to Jacksonville and received paroles at Yellville at a date not of record.

BIBLIOGRAPHY

R. L. Hurst Letters. W. L. Skaggs Collection. Arkansas History Commission, Little Rock, Arkansas.

Schnable-Fenix Correspondence Regarding Surrender of Confederate Troops. William Fenix Probate File. Dallas County Courthouse, Buffalo, Missouri.

Shaw's Battalion

Major: W. M. Shaw

Companies and Commanders

Company A: Unknown

Company B: Samuel Irvin

Balance of organization, if any, is unknown.

This battalion, recruited during Major General Sterling Price's expedition into Missouri in the fall of 1864, is very obscure. The unit may have consisted of only two companies, and if this is so, it legally constituted a squadron rather than a battalion, but the available records generally refer to it as a battalion. During the course of the raid, Colonel Sidney D. Jackman made the sole reference to the battalion, and that concerned its participation in the fight at Newtonia, Missouri, on October 28, the last engagement of the raid. Therefore, the battalion apparently served with his brigade in Brigadier General Joseph O. Shelby's division as the army prepared to exit Missouri. The battalion may have been recruited in southwest Missouri. Shaw's battalion apparently did not accompany the army to Texas. It may well have been furloughed, for Company B surrendered at Wittsburg, Arkansas, on May 25, 1865. No rolls of the battalion are known to exist. The only unit members identified are the few soldiers that appear on parole or prisoner of war lists.

BIBLIOGRAPHY

Confederate Organizations, Officers and Posts, 1861–1865, Missouri Units. Springfield: Ozarks Genealogical Society, 1988.

Ponder, Jerry, and Victor Ponder. *Confederate Surrender and Parole, Jacksonport and Wittsburg, Arkansas, May and June 1865.* Doniphan: Ponder Books, 1995.

Snider's Battalion (Also known as the Northeast Battalion or 1st Northeast Battalion)

Major: Henry Snider

Companies and Commanders:

Company A: (Callaway) David W. Craig

Company B: Harrison Brown

Company C: Andrew W. Frame

Company D: (Lincoln) Westly Penny, killed July 28, 1862; Moses Beck, killed August 28, 1862, Edward H. Knight

Company E: (Boone, Callaway) George R. Brooks

Company —: (Adair) ——Barnard

Company —: (Marion) Braxton Pollard

This battalion appears to have been organized in early August 1862 in the counties of northeast Missouri, probably in conjunction with the organization of the 1st Northeast Regiment. Elements of the battalion participated in the battle at Moore's Mill on July 28, with unknown losses. The battalion fought in the engagement at Kirksville on August 6, where it lost 5 killed in action and an unknown number of wounded. It retreated from Kirksville with Colonel Joseph C. Porter's command and thereafter apparently operated more or less independently. On August 28, Snider led some 150 men of the battalion against the militia garrison at Ashley, hoping to capture weapons stored there. After fighting for about an hour with little success, the Confederates broke off the attack, having suffered losses of 3 killed and 2 wounded. It is possible that some companies of Porter's 1st Northeast Regiment transferred to the battalion, or simply acted in conjunction with it, as a few of them are identified as operating with Snider in September. Two militia commands attacked the battalion on Sandy Creek in Monroe County on September 18. Forewarned of the approach of the enemy, the Confederates offered only slight resistance before retreating with 2 killed and the loss of much of their camp equipage.

Like other units recruited in northeast Missouri in the summer of 1862, the battalion disbanded at a date unknown to more readily move through enemy lines to the army in Arkansas. Several members of the battalion subsequently served in the 9th Missouri Infantry Regiment (Clark's). Approximately 510 men served in the battalion during its short existence, and known losses of the unit include 11 killed in battle, 4 executed by Federal authorities, and 1 death by disease.

BIBLIOGRAPHY

Ball, George W. "The Ashley Fight." *Bowling Green Times,* Bowling Green, Missouri, January 23, 1919.

Fagg, T. J. C. "The Battle of Ashley." *Bowling Green Times,* Bowling Green, Missouri, October 31, 1918.

"Henry G. Snider." In *History of Vernon County, Missouri,* 871–72. St. Louis: Brown & Co., 1887.

Minor, Samuel O. "Reminiscences." *Press-Journal,* Louisiana, Missouri, August 4, 1931.

C. Squadrons

Dorsey's Squadron

Commander: Captain Caleb Dorsey

Companies and Commanders:

Company A: Caleb Dorsey
Company B: William T. Barry

This squadron formed on November 10, 1862, near Yellville, Arkansas, from veterans of the Missouri State Guard returned from service in Mississippi with Brigadier General Mosby Monroe Parsons's command. Initially, the unit operated independently, doing scout, courier, and escort duties along the front of Major General Thomas C. Hindman's embryonic corps. The squadron subsequently became part of Brigadier General Daniel M. Frost's brigade, but when the brigade transferred to Little Rock in January 1863, the squadron remained on duty in northwest Arkansas. On February 2, Dorsey's unit skirmished with a Union scout party near Ozark, Arkansas, and lost 3 wounded, while inflicting casualties of 4 killed and 17 wounded on the enemy. Thereafter, Dorsey led his squadron in Brigadier General William L. Cabell's assault on Fayetteville, Arkansas, on April 18. Although the Federals repulsed the Confederate attack after more than three hours of spirited fighting, Cabell credited Dorsey's troopers with making a "dashing charge" that helped drive the enemy into their defensive works. The squadron apparently disbanded at a date not of record in 1863, for Captain Barry's company subsequently became part of the 11th Cavalry Battalion (Young's) as Company H, while the further service of Dorsey's company, if any, is unknown. Dorsey attempted to recruit a cavalry regiment during the fall of 1864, but that organization had no connection to this squadron. No muster rolls or casualty reports for this unit have been found.

BIBLIOGRAPHY

Joel M. Bolton Memoir. Western Historical Manuscript Collection, University of Missouri, Columbia, Missouri.

Correspondence of John S. Marmaduke. National Archives, Washington, D. C.

Samuel McDaniel Memoir. Unpublished typescript. Richard C. Peterson
Private Collection, Memphis, Tennessee.

Eli Bass McHenry to Edgar McHenry, October 1, 1909. Missouri State
Archives, Jefferson City, Missouri.

*Trans-Mississippi Order and Letter Book, Brigadier-General John S.
Marmaduke*. Transcribed by Carolyn M. Bartels. Independence:
Two Trails, 2000.

Hulett's Squadron "Hulett Horse"

Commander: Captain Amos K. Hulett

Companies and Commanders

Company A: (Boone) Amos K. Hulett
Company B: Unknown

Little is known about this particular squadron, as it does not appear in the war records or on any known list of Missouri Confederate units. References to the battalion occur in service records of men paroled at Monroe, Louisiana, on June 10, 1865, and in some postwar correspondence. The evidence suggests that this squadron formed following the return of the army from Major General Sterling Price's Missouri Expedition in late 1864 and included men detailed from the different regiments of Brigadier General John S. Marmaduke's Missouri cavalry brigade. Some references describe the unit as an escort command; thus, it may have been a temporary escort for a general officer. Indeed, one source indicates that the battalion served as escort for Colonel Colton Greene, who often commanded Marmaduke's brigade. A soldier's recollection relates that the squadron acted as the "advance" for Marmaduke's brigade. The squadron may well have performed both functions. In the spring of 1865, date unknown, some thirty men of the squadron moved to Hamburg, Arkansas, to arrest deserters and end their depredations against civilians. After successfully performing that assignment, the detail returned to the brigade camp at Homer, Louisiana. Nothing further has been discovered regarding the squadron's service. The squadron probably disbanded near the end of the war, as most members apparently accepted paroles with their original unit of assignment. No separate muster rolls for this squadron are known to exist.

BIBLIOGRAPHY

Ambrose W. Hulett Letters. W. L. Skaggs Collection. Arkansas History
Commission, Little Rock, Arkansas.

Lawther's Squadron

Commander: Robert R. Lawther

Companies and Commanders

Company A: William H. McPike

Company B: Asbury Vandiver

Robert R. Lawther, formerly major of the 1st Missouri Cavalry Regiment, organized this unit about November 5, 1863, at Camden, Arkansas, under authority granted by Major General Sterling Price, commander of the District of Arkansas. Although Lawther referred to the unit as a battalion, it mustered but two companies and technically constituted only a squadron. The two companies, numbering 140 men in the aggregate, consisted primarily of Missourians exchanged following the surrender at Vicksburg, Mississippi, the previous July. The squadron existed only a short while, as the companies consolidated with the 11th Cavalry Battalion in late December near Camden, Arkansas, to form the 10th Cavalry Regiment. The unit had no known combat record during its brief existence. See the entry for the 10th Cavalry Regiment for the further service of the men of this squadron.

BIBLIOGRAPHY

Correspondence of General John S. Marmaduke. National Archives,
Washington, D.C.

*Trans-Mississippi Order and Letter Book, Brigadier-General John S.
Marmaduke.* Transcribed by Carolyn M. Bartels. Independence: Two
Trails, 2000.

D. Independent Companies

Champion's Company "Frost's Escort"

Commander: Captain John R. "Rock" Champion

John R. Champion recruited this company as the bodyguard for Brigadier General Daniel M. Frost, commanding officer of the 9th Division, Missouri State Guard, at Memphis, Tennessee, in late December 1861. Containing many St. Louis residents, the company likely mustered into state service on January 7, 1862, at Jacksonport, Arkansas, where Frost organized the few troops that had reported for duty from his military district. Champion's company departed Jacksonport with Frost's command in late January to join the main Missouri army under Major General Sterling Price at Springfield. Arriving at Springfield on February 11, the company retreated with the army into Arkansas the day following. The small unit, numbering only 25 troopers, participated in the battle at Pea Ridge, Arkansas, on March 7–8. It made a saber charge on the flank of the enemy during the engagement that stampeded a force intent on seizing Captain Henry Guibor's battery. The company wounded 8 Federals and possibly captured an enemy flag with the loss of 2 wounded. Following the Pea Ridge battle, Champion's company accompanied the Army of the West to Memphis, Tennessee, in mid-April. On April 26, the company, enlarged by recruits, mustered into Confederate service as Company H, 4th Cavalry Battalion (McCulloch's), subsequently the 2nd Cavalry Regiment. See the entry for the 2nd Cavalry Regiment for the further service of this company.

Bibliography

Confederate Organizations, Officers and Posts, 1861–1865, Missouri Units. Springfield: Ozarks Genealogical Society, 1988.

Wilson, Hunt P. "The Battle of Elkhorn." *Daily Missouri Republican,* St. Louis, Missouri, July 4 and July 11, 1885.

Clark's/Stallard's Company "Marmaduke's Escort"

Commander: Captain John C. Clark, killed July 4, 1863; David R.
Stallard

This company formed at Waverly, Lafayette County, Missouri on August
18, 1862, and joined the 5th Cavalry Regiment as Company D. It fought
with the regiment at Newtonia, Missouri, on September 30, 1862, without loss. In early December, during the Prairie Grove Campaign in northwestern Arkansas, it engaged the enemy at Cane Hill and Prairie Grove.
Stallard's company suffered casualties of 2 killed, 10 wounded, and 2 missing at Springfield and Hartville during Brigadier General John S.
Marmaduke's raid into southwest Missouri in January 1863. Marmaduke
detached the company from the 5th Regiment as his escort on May 15,
1863, following its participation in the general's raid into southeast
Missouri; it served in that capacity for the remainder of the war. The company fought at Helena, Arkansas, on July 4 and in defense of Little Rock
during August–September until the city fell to the Federals. A few members of the company accompanied Colonel Joseph O. Shelby when he
raided into western Missouri in October 1863.

During the spring of 1864, the company participated in the fighting
that opposed the advance of Major General Frederick Steele's Union army
into southern Arkansas. The company served throughout Major General
Sterling Price's expedition in Missouri in the fall of 1864, sometimes acting as the army's advance. Colonel Colton Greene, occasional commander
of Marmaduke's cavalry brigade during the operation, praised the company's steadfastness following the Confederate disaster at Mine Creek,
Kansas, on October 25. The prolonged Missouri campaign resulted in company losses of 6 dead, 14 wounded, and 17 missing. The Missouri expedition ended the company's combat career. Most survivors of the company
received paroles at Shreveport, Louisiana, on June 7, 1865.

BIBLIOGRAPHY

*Trans-Mississippi Order and Letter Book, Brigadier-General John S.
Marmaduke.* Transcribed by Carolyn M. Bartels. Independence:
Two Trails, 2000.

Corser's Company

Commander: Captain John W. Corser

Apparently organized in the spring of 1862, this company served as an unattached company in Major General Thomas C. Hindman's corps in northwest Arkansas in late 1862 and early 1863. Thereafter, it served as an independent company attached to Confederate headquarters at Little Rock, Arkansas. The company reported to Brigadier General John S. Marmaduke at Batesville for duty on March 30, 1863, under the provisions of Special Order No. 13. It appeared as an independent company in Marmaduke's Division through at least April 21, and then disappears from the records. It is possible that the company consolidated with Captain John C. Lee's company and became part of the 11th Cavalry Battalion as company G in July 1863.

Bibliography

Confederate Organizations, Officers and Posts, 1861–1865, Missouri Units. Springfield: Ozarks Genealogical Society, 1988.

Trans-Mississippi Order and Letter Book, Brigadier-General John S. Marmaduke. Transcribed by Carolyn M. Bartels. Independence: Two Trails, 2000.

Edmondson's Provost Guard

Commander: Captain Robert H. Edmondson

This unit appears to be a reorganization of the company Edmondson commanded as Provost Guard in the 2nd Division, Missouri State Guard. The company mustered into Confederate service at Van Buren, Arkansas on March 27, 1862, as the Provost Guard for the 2nd Missouri Brigade (Brigadier General Martin E. Green's) and accompanied the Army of the West to the Cis-Mississippi in mid-April. In mid-June 1862, the company merged into the 2nd Cavalry Regiment as Company H (2nd) and served the rest of the war with that regiment. See the entry for the 2nd Cavalry Regiment for the further service of the men of this company.

BIBLIOGRAPHY

Confederate Organizations, Officers and Posts, 1861–1865, Missouri Units.
Springfield: Ozarks Genealogical Society, 1988.

Peterson, Richard C., James E. McGhee, Kip A. Lindberg, and Keith I.
Daleen. *Sterling Price's Lieutenants: A Guide to the Officers and
Organization of the Missouri State Guard, 1861–1865.* Shawnee Mission:
Two Trails, 2007.

Jeffers's Company "Swamp Rangers"

Commander: Captain William L. Jeffers

This company, essentially a reorganization of Company A, 2nd Cavalry
Regiment, 1st Division, Missouri State Guard, formed in the spring of 1862
in Cape Girardeau County, Missouri. Sixteen of the recruits engaged a
superior force of the 12th Missouri State Militia Cavalry at Jackson on
April 9 and achieved a one-sided victory without casualties. Thereafter, the
recruits proceeded to New Madrid County, where they mustered into
Confederate service and elected officers on April 16. The company left
Missouri for Arkansas when pressed by operations of the 1st Wisconsin
Cavalry Regiment in Dunklin County in May. In Arkansas the unit
became Company B of Lieutenant Colonel Charles Matlock's Arkansas
Cavalry Battalion on June 16. On June 28, the company participated with
elements of the battalion in a successful attack on the enemy on White
River. When Matlock's battalion converted to infantry in early July,
Captain Jeffers resigned his commission and returned to Missouri, where
he recruited what became the 8th Missouri Cavalry Regiment. Some members of the company followed Jeffers, while others remained with Matlock
until July 18, when they transferred to Brigadier General James H.
McBride's command. The remnant of the "Swamp Rangers" served with
McBride until about August 15, at which time it consolidated with Captain
James Surridge's independent company near Batesville, Arkansas, to form
Company B, 3rd Cavalry Regiment. See the entry for the 3rd Cavalry
Regiment for the further service of this company.

BIBLIOGRAPHY

Nichols, Ray. "Eighth Missouri Cavalry." *Collage of Cape [Girardeau] County* 12 (September 1992): 1–7.

Ross, Kirby. *The Fight at Jackson Fairground: Confederate Victory against the Odds.* Topeka: Shunga Press, 2003.

Lee's Company "Hindman's Escort"

Commander: Captain John C. Lee

John C. Lee recruited this company in June 1862 for a regiment John C. Tracy attempted to organize. In all likelihood, the company participated in the battle at Lone Jack, Missouri, on August 16. Major General Thomas C. Hindman disbanded Tracy's command shortly after it returned to Arkansas following the Lone Jack engagement. Lee's company remained intact and subsequently served as Hindman's escort during the Prairie Grove Campaign in December. The company's escort duty ceased when Hindman left the department to return to the Cis-Mississippi in July 1863. Thereafter, the company merged into the 11th Cavalry Battalion (Young's) as Company G. See the entry for the 10th Cavalry Regiment for the further service of this company.

BIBLIOGRAPHY

Confederate Organizations, Officers and Posts, 1861–1865, Missouri Units. Springfield: Ozarks Genealogical Society, 1988.

Reeves's Company "Independent Missouri Scouts"

Commander: Captain Timothy Reeves

Timothy Reeves recruited this company primarily from veterans of the 3rd Infantry Regiment, 1st Division, Missouri State Guard, in early 1862. It crossed the Mississippi River after April 1, 1862, and joined the Army of the West at Memphis, Tennessee. The company performed duty for the office of the adjutant general on April 24; it then briefly joined a battalion commanded by Major Edward Ingraham. While at Corinth, Mississippi, on May 5, the company carried 72 men, present and absent, on its roll. Pursuant to the provisions of Special Order No. 102, Army of the West, dated June 1, the company moved to Ripley with other units to arrest stragglers and deserters. Reeves's men presumably continued to perform scout and like duties for the balance of the summer in Mississippi.

The company returned to the Trans-Mississippi about September 12, 1862, and scouted and served on outpost duty in southeast Missouri and northeast Arkansas. Reeves's company scouted into Missouri as far north as Iron County in search of intelligence regarding Union numbers and movements. During Brigadier General John S. Marmaduke's raid into southeast Missouri in late April 1863, Reeves's company composed the advance for Colonel George W. Carter's Texas cavalry brigade and fought at Patterson, Whitewater River, and Cape Girardeau. The company engaged a Union scouting party north of Doniphan on May 31, routing the enemy and capturing horses and equipment.

Reeves sought permission in June to enlarge his command. He began recruiting in southern Missouri and had 150 men enrolled at Cherokee Bay, Arkansas, by December 11. Reeves's command captured the Union garrison at Centerville, Missouri, on December 23 without loss. In turn, elements of the 3rd Missouri State Militia Cavalry Regiment surprised Reeves's camp on December 25 in Ripley County and routed the Confederates, killing, wounding, and capturing many of them. Reeves regrouped his command and fought several skirmishes along the Arkansas-Missouri line during the spring of 1864. At a date uncertain, but before June 7, Reeves commanded sufficient men to organize a battalion, subsequently the 15th Cavalry Regiment, and his "Missouri Scouts" became Company A of that organization. See the entry for the 15th Cavalry for the further service of this company.

BIBLIOGRAPHY

Collins, Andy. "To the Victor Belongs the Spoils." *Missouri Historical Review* 80 (January 1986): 176–95.

Roberts's Company "Frost's Escort"

Commander: Captain Leroy D. Roberts

This company mustered into Confederate service in the fall of 1862 as the result of a reorganization of Company A, Winston's Infantry Regiment, 5th Division, Missouri State Guard. In December it served as escort for Brigadier General Daniel M. Frost during the Prairie Grove Campaign. It ceased to act as Frost's escort at a date not of record, but likely around February 20, 1863, when Frost's brigade transferred from Little Rock to Fort Pleasant near Pine Bluff. Thereafter, the company operated as an independent command assigned to the Trans-Mississippi Department headquarters at Little Rock. Under the provisions of Special Order 13, District of Arkansas, dated March 30, 1863, the company reported to Brigadier General John S. Marmaduke for duty at Batesville, Arkansas. Soon thereafter, it merged into the 4th Missouri Cavalry Regiment as Company I (New) and served the balance of the war with that regiment. See the entry for the 4th Cavalry for the further service of this company.

BIBLIOGRAPHY

Confederate Organizations, Officers and Posts, 1861–1865, Missouri Units. Springfield: Ozarks Genealogical Society, 1988.

Trans-Mississippi Order and Letter Book, Brigadier -General John S. Marmaduke. Transcribed by Carolyn M. Bartels. Independence: Two Trails, 2000.

Savery's Company "Western Rangers"

Commander: Captain Phineas M. Savery

This company had a decidedly confusing record of service in the first year of the war. The company initially organized as the Provost Guard for headquarters, Missouri State Guard, per General Order No. 18 on August 14, 1861. The unit then became the "2nd Company of Independent Cavalry" per Special Order No. 153, December 3, 1861. Thereafter, under the provisions of Special Order 63, February 23, 1862, the company merged into the Missouri State Guard's "Body Guard Battalion." Special Order No. 66, dated March 1, directed the company to transfer to Colonel Thomas H. Rosser's provisional Confederate regiment, but for reasons unknown, the company never transferred. On March 3, the company, still in state service, became the Provost Guard for the Army of the West. On March 15, Savery received orders to organize a Provost Guard for Confederate service. He completed the organization about April 23, most likely at Memphis, Tennessee. The company again served as Provost Guard from May 10, until relieved on June 5, at which time it became part of Major General Dabney Maury's division. The company performed escort duties for Maury in the new assignment. On August 17, the company became Company I in the newly formed 2nd Missouri Cavalry Regiment. The company would subsequently be detached once again for escort duty and other service, but by September 10, 1863, returned to the regiment on a permanent basis. See the entry for the 2nd Cavalry Regiment for the further service of this company.

BIBLIOGRAPHY

Confederate Organizations, Officers and Posts, 1861–1865, Missouri Units. Springfield: Ozarks Genealogical Society, 1988.

Phineas M. Savery Papers. William R. Perkins Library, Duke University, Durham, North Carolina.

Smith's Company "Windsor Guards" or "Price's Escort"

Commander: Captain Epaminondas Smith

This company voluntarily served as Major General Sterling Price's escort after the battle of Boonville, Missouri, in June 1861 and received official assignment as such per Special Order No. 3, Missouri State Guard, dated July 12, 1861. It then became the "1st Company of Independent Cavalry" by Special Order No. 153, December 3, 1861, although it continued to serve as Price's escort company. The unit organized for Confederate service on January 26, 1862, at Springfield, Missouri. Per Special Order No. 63, February 28, 1862, the Body Guard and Provost Guard merged, which resulted in the creation of the "Body Guard Battalion" on March 2, which included this company. Smith's company continued to serve as Price's escort after the army transferred to the Cis-Mississippi in April 1862. On

August 17, the unit joined the newly formed 2nd Missouri Cavalry Regiment as Company I. The company continued as Price's escort, even after its assignment to the 2nd Cavalry. In fact, the company accompanied Price when he transferred to the Trans-Mississippi Department in March 1863 and served as his escort company until the end of the war.

BIBLIOGRAPHY

Confederate Organizations, Officers and Posts, 1861–1865, Missouri Units. Springfield: Ozarks Genealogical Society, 1988.

W. J. Thornton Letter. Entry 699A. Civil War Library/Museum, Philadelphia, Pennsylvania.

Surridge's Company

Commander: Captain James Surridge

This company consisted of men recruited from veterans of the 3rd Cavalry Regiment, 1st Division, Missouri State Guard. It included men from Madison and St. Francois counties. The date it initially mustered into Confederate service cannot be determined, but on August 15, 1862, it combined with a remnant of Captain William L. Jeffers's "Swamp Rangers" at Batesville, Arkansas, to form Company B, 3rd Cavalry Regiment. See the entry for the 3rd Cavalry Regiment for the further service of this company.

BIBLIOGRAPHY

Nichols, Ray. "Eighth Missouri Cavalry." *Collage of Cape [Girardeau] County* 12 (September 1992): 1–7.

Terry's Company

Commander: Captain William R. Terry

William R. Terry recruited this company in Callaway County in the fall of 1864. After several men enlisted, the company started for Glasgow in late October to join the Army of Missouri, at that time raiding through Missouri under command of Major General Sterling Price. En route to

Glasgow, the company mustered into Confederate service and elected Terry as captain. Unable to cross the Missouri River at Glasgow because of enemy activity in the area, the company marched back to Callaway County, hoping to unite with the recruit command of Caleb Dorsey. Scouts located Dorsey in Audrain County, just north of the Callaway County line, on November 3. That night, Terry's company camped close to Dorsey's recruits. The next morning, pickets spotted an enemy force of some 150 Union militiamen approaching the encampment. Being largely unarmed, Terry's men dispersed into small squads as the militia neared their position. A squad of eight of Terry's men sought safety in a barn located on a nearby farm. A contingent of the 67th Enrolled Missouri Militia surrounded the barn; the recruits surrendered without incident since they had little means of resistance. After the recruits surrendered, the commander of the militia, Major James C. Bay, ordered the prisoners executed, and seven of the eight were summarily shot to death. The company disintegrated after the events of November 4 and never joined the army as an intact unit.

BIBLIOGRAPHY

"The Brown Farm Massacre." *Fulton Gazette,* Fulton, Missouri, May 1, 1914.

133rd Anniversary of The Battle of Moore's Mill. N.p., 1995.

Woodson's Company
(Also known as Company A, 1st Cavalry Regiment)

Commander: Captain Charles H. Woodson

This company served in Virginia, the only Missouri Confederate unit to do so. Although often identified as Company A, 1st Missouri Cavalry Regiment, the unit had no connection whatsoever with that regiment. Confederate Secretary of War James Seddon granted former prisoners Charles H. Woodson and Edward H. Scott authority to raise a cavalry company from exchanged Missouri prisoners in late June 1863. They quickly recruited the company, which mustered into service about July 1 at Richmond, Virginia. The company consisted entirely of Missourians and represented various Missouri units of all branches of service. Since the men had no horses and could not easily procure them, the company spent its first several months of duty as infantry. On September 22, the Missourians temporarily became part of the 62nd Virginia Mounted Infantry Regiment and began service in Augusta County. As part of a larger force, the unit participated in a brief fight with Federals occupying Charles Town on October 18, until the garrison surrendered. Other small affairs against Federal cavalry raiders occupied the 62nd Mounted Infantry during the balance of 1863. In January 1864 Woodson's company moved to Harrisonburg for provost marshal duty, an assignment that lasted through the following April. Woodson's company faced its first major combat at New Market on May 15, once again serving with the 62nd Virginia Mounted Infantry. During the battle, the Missourians, only 62 in number, deployed in line fronting a battery of New York artillery. As the Confederates charged the Union position, they suffered heavy casualties. When the attack stalled, Woodson's men concentrated fire on the enemy artillerymen, wounded many of them, and temporarily silenced the battery. Another determined Confederate charge ensued, one that included the young cadets of the Virginia Military Institute, and the Federals retreated. While the casualties of Woodson's company at New Market are disputed, reliable sources indicate that at least 7 Missourians were killed or mortally wounded, and another 41 wounded, for a casualty rate of over 77 percent.

After seeing more infantry service, including a brief stint in the Richmond defensive perimeter by part of the company, the unit finally procured horses in June 1864. Once mounted, Woodson's company operated with Captain John Hanson McNeill's Rangers for a few weeks and then entered Maryland in early July as part of Major General Jubal Early's invading force. After returning from the Maryland operation, the Missourians spent the balance of the war engaged in hit-and-run raids on Union supply lines and scouting and skirmishing in the northern Shenandoah Valley. The company disbanded in April 1865 when the soldiers learned of the Confederate surrender at Appomattox. Thereafter, the troopers received paroles at various locations in northern Virginia. Approximately 85 men served in the company during its service to the Confederacy, and at least 8 died as a result of combat, while 1 succumbed to disease. In 1905, company survivors erected a small stone marker dedicated to "Woodson's Heroes" on the New Market battlefield. The marker still stands today, and on the monument is carved the following: *"This rustic pile / The simple tale will tell / It marks the spot / Where Woodson's Heroes fell."*

BIBLIOGRAPHY

Curran, Thomas F. "Memory, Myth, and Musty Records: Charles Woodson's Missouri Cavalry in the Army of Northern Virginia, Part I." *Missouri Historical Review* 94 (October 1999): 25–41.

———. "Memory, Myth, and Musty Records: Charles Woodson's Missouri Cavalry in the Army of Northern Virginia, Part II." *Missouri Historical Review* 94 (January 2000): 160–75.

Monachello, Anthony. "Strange Odyssey of the 1st Missouri." *America's Civil War* (March 1999): 26–33.

Price, William T. *Memorials of Edward Herndon Scott, M.D.* Wytheville: Jim Presgraves Books, 1974 .

E. Units That Failed to Complete Organization

Clark's Regiment "Clark's Recruits"

Commander: Henry E. Clark

Henry E. Clark, a recruiter with authority from the Confederate War Department, entered southeast Missouri in the late summer of 1862 to recruit a cavalry command. He subsequently reported that he successfully "equipped a regiment" (probably William L. Jeffers's battalion) and organized a total of 21 separate companies. The records suggest that other individuals recruited many of the units Clark claimed, although they may have been raised under his authority. Nothing confirms that Clark formally organized a regiment under his command, and in fact, Clark made no such claim in his subsequent correspondence. On October 26, 1862, Union cavalry unexpectedly attacked Clark's recruiting headquarters at Clarkton. The cavalrymen killed 12 of Clark's men, captured 39 others, including Clark, and dispersed most of the recruit companies. Some of the companies disbanded entirely, while others later joined existing or new organizations. After Clark's release from prison the following December, he returned to southeast Missouri and collected parts of eight companies he had recruited. On April 9, 1863, he organized them into a battalion commanded by Lieutenant Colonel Solomon G. Kitchen, which subsequently became the 7th Cavalry Regiment. This unit should not be confused with the infantry regiment organized by John B. Clark Jr. in the fall of 1862, also known as "Clark's Regiment."

Bibliography

Confederate Organizations, Officers and Posts, 1861–1865, Missouri Units. Springfield: Ozarks Genealogical Society, 1988.

Stanton, Donal J., Goodwin F. Berquist, and Paul C. Bowers, eds. *The Civil War Reminiscences of General M. Jeff Thompson.* Dayton: Morningside Press, 1988.

Coleman's Regiment

Commander: William O. Coleman

Companies and Commanders:

Company —: Stephen H. Darden, died as prisoner of war
August 13, 1862

Company —: Benjamin Holt

Company —: John W. Lennox

Company —: D. F. M. Sigler

Company —: Isaac D. Wilson

On June 20, 1862, William O. Coleman, a former regimental commander
in the 7th Division, Missouri State Guard, received appointment as colonel
in the Confederate service and authorization to organize a regiment of
Missouri cavalry. As Coleman was already in command of eight companies, five from Missouri and three from Arkansas, his orders provided that
he would retain the Missouri companies only and raise five additional companies of Missourians to complete his organization. The three Arkansas
companies subsequently left his command. Coleman never enlisted the
five additional companies required to complete his regiment. Major
General Thomas C. Hindman, department commander, soon ordered
Coleman to report to Brigadier General James H. McBride, commanding
in northeastern Arkansas, to serve under McBride's orders. Coleman
resisted serving under McBride, as he preferred independent command.
Although repeatedly ordered to report to McBride, Coleman obstinately
refused to comply. On July 31, Hindman dismissed Coleman from the
Confederate army and ordered his companies dismounted. The order took
time to take effect, but by late September, Coleman had no command.
His dismounted troops became part of Brigadier General Mosby M.
Parsons's Missouri infantry brigade, with many of them serving in the 10th
Missouri Infantry Regiment.

Bibliography

Confederate Organizations, Officers and Posts, 1861–1865, Missouri Units.
    Springfield: Ozarks Genealogical Society, 1988.

Schnetzer, Wayne H. *Men of the Tenth: A Roster of the Tenth Missouri Infantry,
    Confederate States of America.* Independence: Two Trails, n.d.

Dorsey's Regiment

Commander: Caleb W. Dorsey

Companies and Commanders:

Company —: (Lincoln, Pike) William Dorsey
Company —: (Lincoln, Pike) Benjamin Meade
Company —: (St. Charles) Miles Price
Balance of organization, if any, is unknown.

Sent forward to recruit by Brigadier General Joseph O. Shelby during Major General Sterling Price's 1864 Missouri Expedition, Caleb W. Dorsey proceeded to Pike County, his home territory. He eventually collected several hundred recruits in Pike and surrounding counties. In late October, while Price's army fought the enemy at Westport on the state's western border, Dorsey remained in distant Lincoln County, recruiting. Dorsey's presence drew the attention of Union commanders, locally and in St. Louis, who determined to destroy his force before it could cross the Missouri River and join Price. Several Union militia units in Audrain, Callaway, Lincoln, and St. Charles counties moved to track down and deal with Dorsey, but none could pinpoint the rebel command's position. Dorsey camped ten miles southeast of Fulton in Callaway County on November 5, preparatory to crossing the Missouri River. The next day, he captured a steamboat near dusk and began crossing his men at Cote Sans Dessein. A Union militia regiment finally tracked Dorsey's recruits to his camp but arrived too late to accomplish anything, for the last Confederate had already crossed the river; the Unionists found only smoldering camp-fires and abandoned equipment. The militia later captured and executed three of Dorsey's stragglers.

The precise movements of Dorsey's command after it crossed the Missouri are unknown, but he eventually led his recruits to Price's army in Texas, although the trek had greatly reduced the number of men on his rolls. After arrival in Texas, at a date unknown, Dorsey's recruits merged into Colonel Alonzo W. Slayback's battalion, Brigadier General Joseph O. Shelby's brigade, to increase that command to a regiment. Dorsey's companies consolidated with existing small companies to con-stitute companies A, C, and E of Slayback's Regiment. Many men of the regiment accepted paroles at Shreveport, Louisiana, in early June 1865.

BIBLIOGRAPHY

History of Callaway County, Missouri. St. Louis: National Historical Co., 1884.

Douglas's Regiment

Commander: William M. Douglas

Companies and Commanders:

Company F: (Howard) James Carson
Company: —— Blair
Company: —— Bliss
Company: —— Bly
Company: —— Caroder
Company: —— Corn
Company: —— Kennedy
Company: J. W. Owen

This recruit command formed during Major General Sterling Price's expedition into Missouri in the fall of 1864. Any formal regimental organization of the companies is very unlikely. The companies appear to have been enlisted primarily north of the Missouri River in late September and early October 1864. Once the companies crossed the Missouri at Rocheport, they joined Price's army in Saline County and became part of Colonel Charles Tyler's mostly unarmed brigade. The brigade guarded the army's wagon train until Price ordered the wagons destroyed following the Confederate defeat at Mine Creek, Kansas, on October 25. Douglas's command accompanied the army to Texas, losing perhaps half its number to disease and desertion during the difficult march. Reaching Texas at the end of November, Douglas's companies disbanded, and the men joined other cavalry and infantry units. An unofficial muster roll for only one company has been located for this unit; several soldiers of that company later served in Company F, 9th Missouri Sharpshooter Battalion. Prisoner of war rolls are the only other records located for the soldiers of this unit.

BIBLIOGRAPHY

Confederate Organizations, Officers and Posts, 1861–1865, Missouri Units. Springfield: Ozarks Genealogical Society, 1988.

"Tattler." "Away Back in War Days: An Old Confederate Soldier Tells of the Last Company to Leave Old Howard." *Pioneer Times* 6 (October 1982): 408–10.

Lawther's Partisan Ranger Regiment

Commander: Robert R. Lawther

Companies and Commanders:

Company A: (St. Louis) Charles T. Biser

Company —: (Callaway) Thomas J. Gibbs

Company —: (Cole, Maries) Thomas A. Lockett

Company —: (Cole) Henry A. Peabody

Company —: (Cole) James J. Reavis

Major Robert R. Lawther resigned his commission as major of the 1st Missouri Cavalry Regiment on June 15, 1862, after receiving authority from the Confederate War Department to raise a regiment of partisan rangers in the Trans-Mississippi. By late July 1862, Lawther had organized about 120 men into two companies along the Arkansas-Missouri border. Federal scouts reported Lawther moving north to join Colonel John A. Poindexter's recruit command north of the Missouri River, which is doubtful, but Lawther intended to recruit in Callaway, Cole, and Maries counties, among others. On the night of August 5, Lawther determined to strike an enemy camp south of Forsyth, Missouri. Union scouts learned of his intentions, and the camp prepared to receive the attack. Lawther's men struck the camp in the dark, only to discover it abandoned. Strong enemy fire from an adjacent ravine then shocked the Confederates, who hastily retreated with 3 killed and 10 wounded.

On August 28, Lawther's command, now increased to five companies and cooperating with recruits commanded by Colonel John Miscal Johnson, moved north from a camp south of Waynesville. The enemy attacked the Confederates near California House in Pulaski County and succeeded in dividing their column, with Johnson retreating south while Lawther continued north into Osage County. Pressed by a relentless Union pursuit, Lawther made a stand on or about September 1, and in a short fight suffered substantial losses, including 10 killed and several taken prisoner, Lawther among them. Further efforts to recruit the regiment ceased after Lawther's capture. Individual soldiers and some companies made their way to Arkansas, and many joined organized units. A remnant of Captain Reavis's company consolidated with soldiers of Foster's Light Battery to form Company A, 9th Missouri Sharpshooter Battalion, while a contingent of Captain Lockett's men filled out Company H, 10th Missouri Infantry Regiment.

BIBLIOGRAPHY

Confederate Organizations, Officers and Posts, 1861–1865, Missouri Units. Springfield: Ozarks Genealogical Society, 1988.

Nichols, Bruce. *Guerrilla Warfare in Civil War Missouri, 1862.* Jefferson: McFarland, 2004.

Schnetzer, Wayne H. *Men of the Tenth: A Roster of the Tenth Missouri Infantry, Confederate States of America.* Independence: Two Trails, n.d.

Phelan's Regiment
(Also unofficially known as the 6th Regiment)

Commander: William Gerald Phelan

Companies and Commanders:

Unknown

In the spring of 1862, William Gerald Phelan, formerly commander of the 2nd Infantry Regiment, 1st Division, Missouri State Guard, established a camp west of Bloomfield, Stoddard County, Missouri, for the purpose of organizing a cavalry regiment for Confederate service. He acted under authority granted by Brigadier General M. Jeff Thompson, commander of the 1st Division. Prisoner of war records and other sources reveal that Phelan had mustered at least four companies into Confederate service when the 1st Wisconsin Cavalry Regiment surprised his camp on May 11. The Federals killed 2 men in the attack and captured Phelan and some 30 others, while the remainder escaped. The regimental organization obviously had not been completed at the time of the Federal raid, and Phelan did not complete it at any time thereafter. Remnants of some of the companies appear to have been reorganized and subsequently incorporated into the 4th and 7th Missouri cavalry regiments.

BIBLIOGRAPHY

Cape Girardeau Eagle (Union Series). Cape Girardeau, Missouri, May 25, 1862.

Confederate Organizations, Officers and Posts, 1861–1865, Missouri Units. Springfield: Ozarks Genealogical Society, 1988.

Tracy's Regiment

Commander: John C. Tracy

Companies and Commanders

Company: ——— Allison

Company: G. C. Bowen

Company: Robert P. Bradley, killed August 16, 1862

Company: (Boone, Howard, Ray) William H. Frazier

Company: (Bates, Henry, St. Clair) Richard M. Hancock

Company: (Henry, Johnson, Pettis) John C. Lee

Company: James N. Thompson

Balance of organization, if any, is unknown.

John C. Tracy, a former lieutenant colonel in the 8th Division, Missouri State Guard, received authority to recruit for the Confederate army on June 4, 1862, from Major General Thomas C. Hindman. He began organizing a cavalry regiment from among Missourians in northern Arkansas; by June 24 he had enlisted about 200 men. Finding it difficult to enroll sufficient men to complete his regiment, Tracy set out on a recruiting expedition into Missouri in early August 1862. Ironically, for reasons unknown, Hindman withdrew Tracy's recruiting authority on August 6, about the time he left for Missouri. Tracy entered Missouri with John T. Coffee, who planned to recruit a regiment for the Missouri State Guard. Each man had between 250–300 men under arms for the expedition. Their movement into Missouri coincided with similar expeditions by other recruiting officers intent on bringing Missourians to the Confederate army that was organizing in northern Arkansas. Tracy and Coffee fought a successful skirmish with Union militia near Montevallo, in Vernon County, and then advanced north to a point near Lone Jack in Jackson County. On August 16, Tracy cooperated with other recruit commands in attacking an enemy force occupying Lone Jack. The Confederates initiated the battle with Tracy's troops on the left of the line, and after a fight of several hours' duration, they finally drove the Union command in retreat to Lexington. While Tracy's personal role in the battle is disputed, his men received praise for their part in the hard-won victory. In all likelihood, Tracy's men suffered considerable losses at Lone Jack, for he later wrote that the Southerners had been "shot all to pieces," but no casualty records for his unit have been found.

Unable to maintain a presence in Lone Jack owing to the approach of additional Union troops, the Confederate recruit commands, including Tracy's, retreated to Arkansas. While most commanders reported to a camp near Fayetteville to perfect their organizations, Tracy remained near the Missouri line. Hindman subsequently ordered Tracy to report to the camp, but he refused to do so, claiming that Hindman had no authority over his command. Shortly thereafter, Hindman relieved Tracy and placed his troops in other units. Captain John C. Lee's company remained intact and became Hindman's escort. Frazier's and Hancock's companies subsequently joined MacDonald's Cavalry Battalion. While one source indicates that three companies of Tracy's unit joined Colonel DeWitt C. Hunter's battalion to create the 11th Infantry Regiment, the rolls of that regiment do not support that conclusion. The available evidence demonstrates that Tracy neither enlisted sufficient men to constitute a regiment under Confederate law nor formally organized a regiment recognized by the Confederacy. Additionally, Tracy clearly never possessed a Confederate colonel's commission, and no record has been found of a regiment bearing his name after the Lone Jack battle.

Bibliography

Armstrong, John Wesley. "The Lone Jack Raid." *Rustic-Leader,* Lebanon, Missouri, May 12, 1881.

Confederate Organizations, Officers and Posts, 1861–1865, Missouri Units. Springfield: Ozarks Genealogical Society, 1988.

Luttrell, Henry C. "One More from Lone Jack." *Daily Missouri Republican,* St. Louis, Missouri, October 3, 1885.

Norton, Richard L., ed. *Behind Enemy Lines: The Memoirs and Writings of Brigadier General Sidney Drake Jackman.* Springfield: Oak Hills, 1997.

Major General Sterling Price. "Pap" to the Missouri Confederates who followed him. *Courtesy of John F. Bradbury Jr.*

Major General John S. Bowen. Died of disease after the fall of Vicksburg, Mississippi, 1863. *Courtesy of John F. Bradbury Jr.*

Brigadier General Mosby M. Parsons. Killed by guerrillas in Mexico following the surrender in 1865. *Courtesy of Civil War Museum at Wilson's Creek National Battlefield.*

Brigadier General M. Jeff Thompson, Missouri State Guard. Holding only a state commission, he nevertheless commanded Confederate troops. *Courtesy of John F. Bradbury Jr.*

Major James Harding, Quartermaster, 1st Missouri Brigade. Formerly quartermaster-general of the Missouri State Guard. *Author's collection.*

Sergeant Robert E. Young, 3rd Missouri Field Battery. He left the University of Missouri to join the army in 1861. *Courtesy of Edward Ziehmer.*

Colonel Solomon G. Kitchen, 7th Missouri Cavalry Regiment. Wounded in the face during the Missouri Expedition of 1864. *Author's collection.*

Colonel William L. Jeffers, 8th Missouri Cavalry Regiment. Captured at Mine Creek, Kansas, during the Missouri Expedition of 1864. *Author's collection.*

Colonel David Shanks, 12th Missouri Cavalry Regiment. Seriously wounded during the Missouri Expedition of 1864. *Credit:* Confederate Veteran *22 (1914): 123.*

Major James M. Parrott, 8th Missouri Cavalry Regiment. Died of disease in Little Rock, Arkansas, shortly after release from prison in 1865. *Author's collection.*

Lieutenant Washington L. Watkins, Assistant Adjutant, Jeffers's Missouri Cavalry Battalion. Captured in 1863. Released by order of General Ulysses S. Grant in 1865. *Courtesy of Margaret Harmon.*

Men of the 12th Missouri Cavalry Regiment. *Courtesy of Lone Jack Civil War Museum.*

Men of the 13th Missouri Cavalry Regiment, 1865. *Courtesy of Missouri Department of Natural Resources, DSP, Fort Davidson State Historic Site Collection.*

Colonel John B. Clark Jr., 9th Missouri Infantry Regiment. Subsequently a brigade commander of both infantry and cavalry. *Courtesy of Civil War Museum at Wilson's Creek National Battlefield.*

Lieutenant William H. Dunnica, 1st Missouri Infantry Regiment. Mortally wounded at Allatoona, Georgia, 1864. *Courtesy of Deborah Schreiber.*

Lieutenant John E. Wright, 2nd Missouri Infantry Regiment. Wounded during the 1864 Georgia Campaign. *Courtesy of Ronald K. Wright.*

Private Henry Clay Luckett, 2nd Missouri Infantry Regiment. Killed at Pea Ridge, Arkansas, 1862. *Courtesy of John E. Fayant.*

Lieutenant William H. Mansur, 3rd Missouri Infantry Regiment. Wounded and captured at Franklin, Tennessee, 1864. *Courtesy of Division of State Parks, Battle of Lexington Historic Site.*

Lieutenant Colonel Lebbeus A. Pindall, 9th Missouri Sharpshooter Battalion. His men led the way in four major battles. *Courtesy of Civil War Museum at Wilson's Creek National Battlefield.*

Captain Elbert Feaster, 11th Missouri Infantry Regiment. His devotion to duty was unwavering. *Courtesy of Kay White Miles.*

Captain David Thompson, 3rd Missouri Infantry Regiment. Captured in Missouri while on recruiting duty. *Courtesy of J. Dale West.*

Brigadier General Daniel M. Frost. Commanded the prewar militia in St. Louis and later led a division in the Confederate army. *Courtesy of J. Dale West.*

III

INFANTRY UNITS

A. REGIMENTS

1st Regiment (Bowen's/Rich's/Riley's)

Colonel: John Stevens Bowen, promoted brigadier general March 14, 1862; Lucius L. Rich, mortally wounded April 6, 1862, died August 9, 1862; Amos Camden Riley

Lieutenant Colonel: Lucius L. Rich, promoted colonel April 1, 1862; Amos Camden Riley, promoted colonel August 2, 1862

Major: Charles C. Campbell, resigned April 23, 1862; Hugh A. Garland

Companies and Commanders:

Company A: (New Orleans, St. Louis) J. Kemp Sprague, killed April 6, 1862; William C. P. Carrington

Company B: (St. Louis) Robert J. Duffy

Company C: (Memphis, St. Louis) David Hirsch, resigned October 27, 1861; John M. Muse, sent on recruiting service November 26, 1862 (Consolidated with Company F at date not on record.)

Company C (2nd): (St. Louis) Dudley F. Jackson, resigned July 17, 1862; Samuel A. Kennerly

Company D: (St. Louis) Martin Burke, promoted major March 6, 1862, and transferred; Lewis H. Kennerly, transferred to Company F July 7, 1862

Company E: (Mississippi, New Madrid, St. Louis) Olin F. Rice, resigned May 1, 1862

Company F: (St. Louis) Hugh A. Garland, promoted major May 16, 1862; Lewis H. Kennerly

Company G: (Pemiscot) John A. Gordon, resigned November 16, 1861; James H. McFarland

Company H: (New Madrid, Pemiscot) Tilford Hogan, resigned November 29, 1861; Bradford Keith

Company I: (New Madrid) Thomas J. Phillips, resigned October 13, 1861; Amos Camden Riley, promoted lieutenant colonel April 3, 1862; George W. Dawson, died of disease June 13, 1862

Company K: (Pemiscot) John E. Averill, resigned November 16, 1861; Charles L. Edmondson

This regiment bore the distinction of being the first Missouri unit of any type to enter Confederate service. John S. Bowen, a West Point graduate and Missouri Volunteer Militia officer captured at Camp Jackson on May 10, 1861, recruited the regiment at Memphis, Tennessee, in June 1861 under authority granted by President Jefferson Davis. Bowen enrolled large numbers of St. Louisans, including many exchanged prisoners taken at Camp Jackson; five companies primarily from the southeast Missouri "Bootheel" counties of New Madrid and Pemiscot, a mostly Irish company from New Orleans; and another contingent of Irishmen from Memphis. All the original field officers and many company commanders had been educated at West Point or private military institutions, while others had significant experience in the prewar Missouri militia, which resulted in the regiment possessing the most experienced leadership of any Missouri Confederate unit.

The 1st Missouri Infantry formally entered the Confederate army on June 22, 1861, at Camp Calhoun near Memphis. Although initially unarmed, the regiment nevertheless drilled near Memphis or at Fort Pillow until sent up the Mississippi River in mid-August to New Madrid, Missouri, to join Brigadier General Gideon J. Pillow's Army of Liberation. The regiment became exceptionally proficient in drill and employed the unique use of whistles to signal maneuvers rather than the bugles used by most units. In early September, the regiment transferred to Columbus, Kentucky, and finally received arms there on September 23. The regiment next spent several weeks at Camp Beauregard near Feliciana, Kentucky. On December 25, the regiment moved to Bowling Green, Kentucky, and later to Nashville, Tennessee. At the latter place, the 1st Infantry Regiment provided security in the aftermath of the Fort Donelson, Tennessee, surrender and performed the onerous task of destroying public property, including boats and bridges, when the Confederates abandoned the city to the enemy.

The regiment then joined the Army of Mississippi, commanded by General Albert Sidney Johnston, at Corinth, Mississippi. After performing routine duty around Corinth for several weeks, the 1st Missouri advanced with the army to Pittsburg Landing, Tennessee, where it experienced its first fighting at the battle of Shiloh on April 6–7, 1862. The regiment, led by Colonel Lucius Rich because of Bowen's promotion to brigade command, constituted part of Bowen's brigade in Major General John C. Breckinridge's Reserve Division; it was the only Missouri Confederate unit on the field. Closely engaged for two days, the 1st Infantry initially fought near and in the Peach Orchard and helped drive the Union defenders to Pittsburg Landing. The fighting in the Peach Orchard materially assisted in forcing the surrender of the Hornet's Nest, the strongpoint on the Federal left, along with 2,300 enemy soldiers. The 1st Missouri also fought hard on the second day of the battle, playing a major role in recapturing the abandoned guns of the 5th Company, Washington Artillery, a New Orleans battery. One of the last regiments on the field, and part of the army's rear guard as it retreated to Corinth, the 1st Infantry Regiment lost 48 killed, 130 wounded, and 29 missing of about 850 men engaged.

After Shiloh the regiment remained at Corinth until the Confederates abandoned the town, and then moved to Camp Price near Vicksburg. Although plans called for Bowen's brigade, including the 1st Missouri Infantry, to participate in General Breckinridge's attack on Major General Benjamin Butler's Federal command near Baton Rouge, Louisiana, the fighting ended before the brigade joined the division. The 1st Regiment next participated in the battle of Corinth on October 3–4 as part of Bowen's brigade in Major General Mansfield Lovell's division. The 1st Infantry fought on the Confederate right the first day of the battle as the Confederates drove the Federals from their outer defensive works, but it remained relatively inactive the next day. Known losses for the regiment, doubtless incomplete, included 4 killed and 3 wounded. The regiment served as part of the rear guard during the retreat from Corinth and engaged in skirmishing en route to the Hatchie River, where the army narrowly escaped Union pursuit.

Following the Corinth defeat, the 1st Infantry consolidated with the 4th Missouri Infantry on November 7, 1862, near Wyatt, Mississippi, owing to heavy losses in both regiments from battle, disease, and desertion; the regiments fought as a single unit for the remainder of the war. The consolidated regiment joined the 1st Missouri Brigade on that same date. Approximately 1,045 soldiers served in the 1st Infantry Regiment during the war, and regimental losses, including service in the consolidated regiment, totaled 141 killed in battle, 192 deaths by disease, 3 killed by accident, 1 drowned, and 1 murdered. About 200 members of the regiment deserted. See the entry for the 1st & 4th Infantry Regiment (Consolidated) for the subsequent service of the men of this command.

BIBLIOGRAPHY

Bock, H. Riley. "Confederate Col. A. C. Riley, His Reports and Letters, Part I." *Missouri Historical Review* 85 (January 1991): 158–81.

———. "Confederate Col. A. C. Riley, His Reports and Letters, Part II." *Missouri Historical Review* 85 (April 1991): 254–87.

———. "One Year at War: Letters of Capt. Geo. W. Dawson, C.S.A." *Missouri Historical Review* 73 (January 1979): 165–97.

Boyce, Joseph. "Battles of Corinth and Grand Gulf." *Daily Missouri Republican,* St. Louis, Missouri, September 6, 1884.

———. "First Day at Shiloh." *Daily Missouri Republican,* St. Louis, Missouri, January 7, 1884.

———. "The First Missouri." *Daily Missouri Republican,* St. Louis, Missouri, November 10, 1883.

———. "The First Missouri: Shiloh, The Second Day." *Daily Missouri Republican,* St. Louis, Missouri, May 3, 1884.

———. "The First Missouri Boys." *Daily Missouri Republican,* St. Louis, Missouri, August 29, 1885.

1st & 4th Regiment (Consolidated) (Riley's/Garland's)

Colonel: Amos Camden Riley; killed May 30, 1864; Hugh A. Garland, killed November 30, 1864

Lieutenant Colonel: Hugh A. Garland, promoted to colonel, May 30, 1864

Major: Hugh A. Garland, promoted lieutenant colonel May 1, 1863; Bradford Keith, killed August 26, 1864

Companies and Commanders:

Company A: William C. P. Carrington, killed May 16, 1863; Andrew J. Byrne, killed October 5, 1864 (Formerly Company A, 1st Infantry)

Company B: Francis McShane, disabled by wounds and then deserted July 8, 1863 (Formerly Companies A, F, and G, 4th Infantry)

Company C: Daniel Hays, sent to Trans-Mississippi on recruiting service, February 1, 1863 (Formerly Companies B and C, 4th Infantry)

Company D: Robert J. Duffy, promoted to major and assigned to recruiting service, dropped March 30, 1864; Joseph Boyce, wounded and captured November 30, 1864 (Formerly Companies B and D, 1st Infantry)

Company E: Norval Spangler, killed May 16, 1863; Aaron C. Patton, mortally wounded October 5, 1864, died December 24, 1864 (Formerly Companies E and H, 4th Infantry)

Company F: Lewis H. Kennerly (Formerly Companies E, F, and H, 1st Infantry)

Company G: James McFarland, disabled by wounds May 17, 1863; Bradford Keith, promoted major May 30, 1864; Goah W. Stewart, wounded and captured November 30, 1864 (Formerly Companies C [2nd] and G, 1st Infantry)

Company H: Jeptha D. Feagan, retired for wounds March 28, 1864 (Formerly Company K, 4th Infantry)

Company I: Matthew G. Norman, sent to Trans-Mississippi on recruiting service July 1863; Samuel A. Kennerly, killed September 5, 1864 (formerly Companies D and I, 4th Infantry)

Company K: Charles L. Edmondson (Formerly Companies I and K, 1st Infantry)

The 1st and 4th Missouri Infantry Regiments consolidated to form this unit on November 7, 1862, near Wyatt, Mississippi, as the result of heavy personnel losses in both organizations. The consolidated regiment joined the 1st Missouri Brigade the same day. Colonel Amos C. Riley assumed command, as Colonel Archibald MacFarlane, the senior colonel, had suffered a permanently disabling wound at Corinth, Mississippi, in October. After routine camp duty at Grenada and Jackson, Mississippi, for a few weeks, the regiment accompanied the brigade to Grand Gulf in early March 1863. There, the brigade constructed fortifications overlooking the Mississippi River. On April 4, the regiment accompanied the 2nd and 3rd Missouri Infantry Regiments and a section of Captain Henry Guibor's Missouri battery to Louisiana for the purpose of reconnoitering Federal movements south of Milliken's Bend. The Missourians skirmished with the enemy on occasion. Brigadier General John S. Bowen, commanding the division that included the 1st Missouri Brigade, ordered the Missourians back to Mississippi on April 15 because he feared Federal gunboats might cut them off from the army. During late April, the 1st & 4th Regiment occupied the Grand Gulf fortifications and sometimes exchanged fire with the enemy as the artillery dueled with Federal gunboats.

On April 30, the vanguard of Major General Ulysses S. Grant's army crossed the Mississippi River, landed at Bruinsburg, and moved toward Port Gibson, thereby initiating the final campaign for Vicksburg. Bowen rushed three brigades to Port Gibson to oppose the enemy advance and eventually called on the 1st Missouri Brigade for reinforcements. Colonel Francis M. Cockrell, the brigade commander, moved to Bowen's assistance with three regiments and some artillery, but the 1st & 4th Regiment performed guard duty at a bridge over Bayou Pierre and missed the battle. Overwhelmed by superior numbers, Bowen made a determined stand at Port Gibson on May 1 but withdrew as the day ended.

The 1st & 4th Regiment first encountered the enemy during the campaign at Champion Hill on May 16. There, the regiment participated in a bold attack by Bowen's division that shattered part of Grant's line. Colonel Riley led the veterans of the 1st & 4th in the desperate fighting, which cost the regiment heavy casualties. Unsupported in the fight by other units, Bowen's men encountered a Federal counterattack that drove the Confederates from the field. The 1st & 4th Infantry suffered losses of 46 killed or mortally wounded, 80 wounded, and 52 missing in the battle, the most of any 1st Missouri Brigade unit. Following the retreat from Champion Hill, the regiment manned entrenchments on the east bank of the Big Black River. On May 17, the Federals attacked the Confederate position, broke the center of the line, and forced the rebels into the Vicksburg defenses. Although initially held in reserve, the 1st Missouri Brigade, including the 1st & 4th Regiment, soon engaged the enemy. The Confederates repulsed Federal assaults on May 19 and 22 with considerable loss on both sides. In the attack on May 19, a regimental soldier captured the colors of the 8th Missouri Volunteer Infantry (Union). The regiment also rushed into the breach after a Federal mine tore a huge gap in the Confederate line on July 1.

The 1st & 4th Regiment's casualties tallied 34 killed and 59 wounded when the garrison surrendered on July 4, leaving merely 344 regimental members to be paroled. After being paroled at Vicksburg, the regiment moved to Demopolis, Alabama, to await exchange, which occurred September 12. A substantial number of men deserted the regiment after the fall of Vicksburg and never reported to Demopolis. In early October the brigade transferred to Meridian, Mississippi, where it joined Major General Samuel French's division. The brigade next moved to Mobile, Alabama. While at Mobile, the regiment won a drill competition between units of several states and received a stand of colors as a prize. The brigade returned to Mississippi, but only briefly, and then rounded up deserters in northern Alabama.

The 1st & 4th Regiment next participated in the Georgia Campaign of 1864, as General William T. Sherman's army targeted Atlanta. At the beginning of the campaign the 1st & 4th Infantry mustered merely 240 soldiers. The regiment fought at New Hope Church, Latimer House, Kennesaw Mountain, Smyrna, and along the Chattahoochee River, and was involved in the siege of Atlanta as well as numerous small skirmishes between mid-May and early September. Losses were 19 killed, 57 wounded, and 4 missing in the campaign. On May 30, Colonel Hugh A. Garland replaced Colonel Riley, who had been killed at New Hope Church. After the abandonment of Atlanta to the Federals, General John B. Hood, commander of the Army of Tennessee, moved his units northward. The 1st & 4th fought a heavy skirmish at Lovejoy Station on September 5, which cost the regiment 5 killed and an unknown number wounded. A month later, the regiment joined in General French's attack on the Federal garrison at Allatoona, Georgia. The 1st & 4th Regiment fought on the left center of the brigade as it rolled over the outer defenses of the Union position, but the main fortification could not be taken despite the Confederates' best efforts. Fearing possible Federal reinforcements, French withdrew his command and rejoined the main army. The 1st & 4th Infantry lost 5 killed, 37 wounded, and 2 missing in the fight.

Hood soon led his army north into Tennessee, while General Sherman started his famous march through Georgia. After missing an opportunity to perhaps destroy the enemy at Spring Hill, the Confederates found the Federals prepared for battle at Franklin on November 30. Hood sent his troops across an open field, with no artillery preparation, against the well-entrenched enemy. The 1st Missouri Brigade, with the 1st & 4th Regiment on the left center, charged valiantly and reached the federal line in the vicinity of Carter's cotton gin. Although repeated attacks occurred over the next five hours, all was in vain, and the Confederates fell in great numbers. The 1st & 4th Regiment, which had only about 100 men on the field, suffered near annihilation, with 35 killed or mortally wounded, 25 wounded, and 2 missing. The regiment also lost its flag when Colonel Hugh Garland fell mortally wounded with the colors.

The 1st & 4th Infantry followed the retreating Federal army to Nashville, but stayed there only briefly, for the 1st Missouri Brigade soon moved south to the Duck River to build fortifications. After the disastrous Tennessee Campaign, the brigade retreated to Mississippi and then moved to the defense of Mobile, Alabama. On April 9, 1865, a superior enemy force overwhelmed the garrison at Fort Blakely, including the 1st Missouri Brigade, and compelled its surrender after a short fight. The remnant of the 1st & 4th Regiment remained imprisoned at Ship Island, Mississippi, until the war ended shortly thereafter. The few men left in the regiment received paroles at Jackson, Mississippi, on May 13, 1865.

BIBLIOGRAPHY

Bock, H. Riley. "Confederate Col. A. C. Riley, His Reports and Letters, Part II." *Missouri Historical Review* 85 (April 1991): 254–87.

Boyce, Joseph. "Baker's Creek and Vicksburg Siege." *Daily Missouri Republican,* St. Louis, Missouri, December 5, 1884.

———. "The Capture of Fort Blakely." *Daily Missouri Republican,* St. Louis, February 12, 1887.

———. "The First Missouri: In Front of Sherman in Georgia." *Daily Missouri Republican,* St. Louis, May 11, 1885.

———. "The First Missouri Infantry, C.S.A.: Ship Island and Return to Missouri." *Daily Missouri Republican,* St. Louis, March 12, 1887.

———. "Missouri Confederates: Atlanta and Bloody Allatoona." *Daily Missouri Republican,* St. Louis, September 5, 1885.

———. "Missouri Confederates: The Tennessee Campaign." *Daily Missouri Republican,* St. Louis, January 30, 1886.

Merrifield, J. K. "Col. Hugh Garland—Captured Flags." *Confederate Veteran* 24 (1916): 551–52.

"Old Time War Letter." *Bates County Democrat,* Butler, Missouri, September 12, 1918.

2nd Regiment (Burbridge's/Cockrell's/Flournoy's)

Colonel: John Quincy Burbridge, resigned June 29, 1862; Francis Marion Cockrell, promoted to brigadier general, July 18, 1863; Peter Creed Flournoy

Lieutenant Colonel: Edward B. Hull, resigned May 8, 1862; Francis Marion Cockrell, promoted colonel, June 29, 1862; Robert D. A. Dwyer, died March 21, 1863; Pembroke S. Senteny, killed July 1, 1863; Thomas M. Carter

Major: Robert D. A. Dwyer, promoted lieutenant colonel June 29, 1862; Pembroke S. Senteny, promoted lieutenant colonel March 21, 1863; Thomas M. Carter, promoted lieutenant colonel July 20, 1863; William F. Carter

Companies and Commanders:

Company A: (Pike, Ralls) Pembroke S. Senteny, promoted major June 29, 1862; George D. Matthews

Company B: (Lincoln, Pike) Archer Bankhead, dropped May 8, 1862; John S. Wells

Company C: (Lincoln, St. Charles) Thomas M. Carter, promoted major March 22, 1863; Theodore L. Lanier

Company D: (Cole, Miller, Moniteau, Morgan) George Butler, dropped May 8, 1862; Samuel Livingston

Company E: (Atchison, Pettis) William A. Finney, resigned September 26, 1862; D. Franklin Koontz

Company F: (Jefferson, Laclede, Pike, St. Charles) William F. Carter, promoted major July 20, 1863; Claudius M. B. Thurmond

Company G: (Monroe, Ralls, Shelby) Thomas B. Wilson, dropped November 24, 1863; Thompson Alford

Company H: (Johnson) Francis Marion Cockrell, promoted lieutenant colonel May 12, 1862; James W. Selby, mortally wounded October 4, 1862, died October 18; James C. Douglass, retired for wounds, ca. 1863

Company I: (Boone, Callaway) Richard H. Carter, dropped May 8, 1862; William H. Hall, mortally wounded October 4, 1862, died October 22; James A. Glanville

Company K: (Chariton, Linn, Sullivan) Peter Creed Flournoy, promoted colonel July 20, 1863; George W. Sandusky, retired for wounds, February 1865.

This regiment completed its organization at Springfield, Missouri, on January 16, 1862, and became part of the 1st Missouri Brigade, commanded by Colonel Henry Little. Veterans of the Missouri State Guard filled its ranks. Originally designated the 1st Infantry, the regiment thereafter became the 2nd Infantry since Colonel John S. Bowen's regiment, formed earlier, had precedence. In less than a month after organization, the Missourians yielded possession of Springfield to an advancing Union army and retreated into northwest Arkansas. The 2nd Infantry deployed several times to assist the rear guard in checking the enemy pursuit until the army reached Cove Creek, Arkansas. In early March, the regiment advanced with Major General Earl Van Dorn's Army of the West to attack the Union army near Pea Ridge, and after an exhausting march met the enemy near Elkhorn Tavern on March 7. The 1st Missouri Brigade, including the 2nd Infantry, pushed the Federals back considerably on March 7, capturing their camp and two pieces of artillery. The second day of the battle belonged to the Federals, for they launched a heavy counteroffensive and, after hard fighting, drove the Confederates from the field. Recorded regimental losses included 46 killed or mortally wounded, 49 wounded, and 15 missing over two days of combat, but the adjutant reported aggregate casualties of 150, and actual losses may have been greater.

After the defeat at Pea Ridge, the Confederates retreated to Frog Bayou, near Van Buren, to rest and recuperate. Eventually ordered to the Cis-Mississippi, the Confederates marched across Arkansas to Des Arc and boarded steamers for shipment to Memphis, Tennessee. The 2nd

Infantry departed Des Arc on April 10 aboard the *H. D. Mears.* After arrival in Memphis, the regiment accompanied the brigade by rail to Corinth, Mississippi, on April 28. In early May, because of sickness and desertion, the 2nd Infantry mustered only 590 soldiers present of 923 listed on the rolls. The regiment participated in a light skirmish with the enemy on May 9 near Farmington. The Confederate army evacuated Corinth at the end of May, when a large Federal force threatened the town, and retreated to Baldwyn.

Over the next few months the regiment performed routine duty in camps in northern Mississippi. It arrived on the field too late to participate in the battle at Iuka on September 19. The 2nd Infantry fought hard in the attack on Corinth on October 3–4. On October 3, the Missourians drove the Federals into their inner works but at a high cost in casualties. The next day the 1st Missouri Brigade launched a daring attack on Battery Powell, finally capturing it and several artillery pieces, but the brigade could not withstand enemy enfilading artillery fire and a subsequent counterattack, which resulted in the abandonment of both the captured position and cannons. The 2nd Infantry suffered losses of 47 killed or mortally wounded, 107 wounded, and 91 missing in the battle.

The regiment spent the next few months in winter camps with no fighting. In March, the regiment accompanied the brigade to Grand Gulf, a strongpoint on the Mississippi River, and constructed artillery emplacements and defensive positions. In early April, the 2nd Infantry crossed the Mississippi River to Louisiana with two other regiments and a battery to observe enemy movements west of the river. That assignment lasted over a week and involved some light skirmishing before the troops returned to Grand Gulf. The 2nd Regiment remained at Grand Gulf on May 1, when part of the 1st Missouri Brigade marched to Port Gibson to counter Major General Ulysses S. Grant's movement from the Mississippi River at the beginning of the Vicksburg Campaign. The regiment engaged the enemy at Champion Hill on May 16, when the 1st Missouri Brigade attacked Grant's line and drove it back in disorder in the pivotal battle of the campaign. Lacking reinforcements on its right, the brigade, including the 2nd Infantry, fell back in turn to a Federal counterattack. The 2nd Infantry, which fought on the left center of the brigade line, suffered losses of 10 killed, 35 wounded, and 38 missing in the battle. The Federals routed the Confederates at the Big Black River on May 17 and drove them into the Vicksburg fortifications. Once inside the defensive perimeter, the 1st Missouri Brigade constituted the reserve, but only for a short while, for the regiments soon moved to threatened positions on the line. The 2nd Missouri deployed at the 27th Louisiana Lunette on May 19 to help repel a large-scale attack by Major General William T. Sherman's corps. Half the regiment fought at the same position on May 22, while the other companies remained in reserve.

On July 1, a mine exploded beneath the 2nd Infantry's position and caused several casualties. The Confederates received paroles after the Vicksburg garrison surrendered on July 4, including 356 members of the 2nd Infantry. The siege had been costly for the regiment, as its casualties amounted to 35 killed or mortally wounded and 75 wounded. The regiment accompanied the brigade to Demopolis, Alabama, after the surrender to await exchange, which occurred September 12. Several regimental members deserted to the Trans-Mississippi Department following the surrender; many of them subsequently performed service in Missouri units in that theater. Owing to heavy losses in the units of the 1st Missouri Brigade, the regiments consolidated at Demopolis on October 1, 1863, per Special Order No. 17, Headquarters, Paroled Prisoners. The ten companies of the 2nd Infantry consolidated into six and joined a remnant of the 6th Infantry to form the 2nd & 6th Missouri Infantry Regiment (Consolidated), an organization that endured to the end of hostilities. Some 1,120 men served in the 2nd Infantry during the war, including its period of service in the consolidated regiment. Regimental losses included 199 battle deaths, 133 deaths from disease, 3 killed by accident, 1 shot escaping capture, and 1 suicide. About 141 men deserted the regiment. See the entry for the 2nd & 6th Infantry Regiment (Consolidated) for the further service of the men of this regiment.

BIBLIOGRAPHY

Anderson, Ephraim McDowell. *Memoirs: Historical and Personal; Including the Campaigns of the First Missouri Confederate Brigade.* Edited by Edwin Bearss. Dayton: Morningside Press, 1972.

Depp, Thomas. "Personal Experiences at Pea Ridge." *Confederate Veteran* 20 (1912): 17–20.

Dudley, W. B. "An Old Missouri Johnnie." *Confederate Veteran* 39 (1931): 197–98.

"Gen. Francis M. Cockrell Obituary." *Confederate Veteran* 24 (1916): 101.

Northway, Martin. "Band of Brothers." *Missouri Life* (June 2004): 40–46.

"Story of the Civil War as Told by Charles E. Smith, Confederate Veteran." *Star,* St. Louis, Missouri, May 14, 1924.

"Was in the Siege of Vicksburg." *Centralia Fireside Guard,* Centralia, Missouri, March 16, 1917.

2nd & 6th Regiment (Consolidated) (Flournoy's)

Colonel: Peter Creed Flournoy

Lieutenant Colonel: Thomas M. Carter, disabled by wound November 30, 1864; Stephen Cooper

Major: William F. Carter, killed October 5, 1864

Companies and Commanders:

Company A: John S. Wells, captured November 30, 1864 (Formerly Companies B and H, 2nd Infantry)

Company B: John M. Hickey, wounded and captured November 30, 1864 (Formerly Companies H and F, 6th Infantry)

Company C: John D. Parsons, captured November 30, 1864 (Formerly Companies G, I, and K, 6th Infantry)

Company D: Albert A. Woodard, killed November 30, 1864 (Formerly Companies C and D, 6th Infantry)

Company E: James A. Glanville, disabled by wound June 17, 1864 (Formerly Company I, 2nd Infantry)

Company F: Theodore L. Lanier, wounded and captured November 30, 1864 (Formerly Companies C and F, 2nd Infantry)

Company G: Thompson Alford, wounded and captured October 5, 1864 (Formerly Companies D and G, 2nd Infantry)

Company H: William H. Moss, wounded and captured November 30, 1864 (Formerly Companies A, B, and E, 6th Infantry)

Company I: Claudius M. B. Thurmond, wounded and captured November 30, 1864 (Formerly Company A, and parts of F and I, 2nd Infantry)

Company K: D. Franklin Koontz, captured November 30, 1864 (Formerly Companies E and K, 2nd Infantry)

After the surrender at Vicksburg on July 4, 1863, the Missouri troops moved to a parole camp at Demopolis, Alabama, to await exchange, which occurred on September 12. On October 6, the 2nd Infantry and 6th Infantry regiments consolidated to form the 2nd & 6th Missouri Infantry Regiment (Consolidated) under the provisions of Special Order No. 17, Headquarters, Paroled Prisoners. Heavy losses in both regiments to battle, disease, and desertion mandated the consolidation, which continued for the remainder of the war. Colonel Peter C. Flournoy, commander of the 2nd Infantry, assumed leadership of the consolidated regiment. The regiment recuperated from the Vicksburg ordeal at Demopolis for several weeks; it soon received new uniforms and Enfield rifles and prepared for more combat.

On October 19, the regiment joined the 1st Missouri Brigade's move to Meridian, Mississippi, where the Missourians remained until shipped back to Alabama in early January 1864. Another movement to Meridian occurred on February 5 for the purpose of opposing the advance of Major General William T. Sherman, but no significant fighting developed for the Missourians. The regiment returned to Alabama with the brigade to round up deserters and guerrillas in the northern part of the state. The next combat for the regiment occurred in the prolonged Atlanta Campaign, as the Confederates sought to stop the advance of Sherman's army toward that vital city. The brigade fought with Major General Samuel French's division during the campaign. At the beginning of operations, the 2nd & 6th Regiment mustered 560 soldiers, the most of any regiment in the 1st Missouri Brigade. Although it was subjected to artillery fire and engaged in light skirmishing as the campaign got underway, the regiment's first significant fight occurred at Latimer House north of Kennesaw Mountain on June 18. The brigade then retreated to Kennesaw Mountain and established a defensive line. On June 27, the Federals assaulted the Confederate position, but hard fighting by the rebels drove them back with heavy losses. When the Confederate commander, General Joseph E. Johnston, elected to abandon the Kennesaw line, the Missourians retreated toward Atlanta, fighting at Smyrna, along the Chattahoochee River, and at Peachtree Creek before occupying defensive positions northwest of the city.

For the next several weeks, the regiment endured nearly constant artillery barrages and fought several heavy skirmishes before the

Confederates evacuated Atlanta. The regiment then moved with the army to a new position near Lovejoy Station. The Atlanta Campaign took a heavy toll on the regiment, as reported casualties tallied 12 killed, 126 wounded, and 58 missing. In early October, General John B. Hood, the Army of Tennessee commander, ordered French's division to attack a strong Federal position at Allatoona, Georgia. The division assaulted the position on October 5 and successfully drove the enemy from their outer defenses into a strong center fortification. The 2nd & 6th Infantry occupied the left of the brigade line as the Confederates pressed forward, but despite a strong effort, the rebels could not carry the main fort. French, fearing enemy reinforcements, withdrew his division and moved back to the main army. The failed assault on Allatoona cost the 2nd & 6th Regiment 16 killed, 62 wounded, and 13 missing. Once back with the army, the regiment marched north into Tennessee, when Hood determined to reclaim the state for the Confederacy. After a botched attempt to trap the enemy at Spring Hill, the Confederates pursued the enemy to Franklin.

When the Confederates arrived at Franklin on November 30, they found the Federals ensconced in strong breastworks on the south edge of town. Throwing caution to the wind, Hood ordered an assault against the enemy late that afternoon. His divisions deployed in the face of the enemy, and with no artillery preparation stepped off the line and marched toward the Federal position. The 1st Missouri Brigade, with the 2nd & 6th Infantry on the left of the line, moved forward with flags flying as the brigade band struck up "Dixie." The charge that followed decimated the regiment. Hitting the Federal line near the Carter cotton gin, the Missourians faced a devastating firestorm of shot and shell that tore into their lines with terrible effect. Although some few made it into the breastworks, most fell before they closed with the enemy. After five hours of desperate fighting, the bloodletting finally ended when the Federals withdrew to Nashville, leaving the Confederates in possession of the field. The 2nd & 6th Infantry counted losses of 46 killed or mortally wounded, 57 wounded, and 61 missing and presumed captured, for a casualty rate of over 60 percent of those that entered the fight. Many of the prisoners doubtless suffered wounds as well. The Federals captured the regiment's flag, which is now in the collections of the Missouri State Museum. Despite the heavy toll of the battle, the regiment moved on to Nashville with the army on December 2. The regiment stayed there only briefly, for on December 10, the small

Missouri brigade moved south to construct fortifications along the Duck River. The brigade rejoined the army, which had suffered a humiliating defeat at Nashville, in Mississippi in early January 1865.

After a quiet winter in Mississippi, the brigade moved to the defense of Mobile, Alabama, in late March 1865. At Mobile the brigade manned a thin defensive line at Fort Blakely on the eastern shore of the bay. On April 9, the day that General Robert E. Lee surrendered the Army of Northern Virginia, Fort Blakely fell to a superior enemy force after a brief fight. The Federals transported the captured Missourians to Ship Island, Mississippi, where they languished as prisoners until sent to Jackson, Mississippi, for final parole in May.

BIBLIOGRAPHY

Franklin, Ann York. *The Civil War Journal of Lt. George R. Elliott, 2nd & 6th Missouri Infantry, Company F, 1862–1864.* Louisville: Privately printed, 1997.

Hickey, John M. "The Battle of Franklin." *Confederate Veteran* 17 (1909): 14.

Weidemeyer, John M. "Recollections of the Surrender and Home-Coming." In *Reminiscences of Women of Missouri during the Sixties,* 288–89. Dayton: Morningside Press, 1988.

3rd Regiment (Rives's/Pritchard's/Gause's)

Colonel: Benjamin Allen Rives, mortally wounded March 7 and died March 11, 1862; James Alfred Pritchard, mortally wounded October 4, and died October 20, 1862; William Randall Gause, sent to Trans-Mississippi Department on detached service September 1863

Lieutenant Colonel: James Alfred Pritchard, promoted colonel March 7, 1862; William Randall Gause, promoted colonel November 6, 1862; Finley L. Hubbell, mortally wounded May 16 and died June 3, 1863

Major: Finley L. Hubbell, promoted lieutenant colonel November 6, 1862; James K. McDowell, promoted lieutenant colonel May 28, 1863; Robert J. Williams

Companies and Commanders:

Company A: (Ray) Robert J. Williams, promoted major May 28, 1863; Obediah Taylor

Company B: (Gentry, Ray) William Randall Gause, promoted lieutenant colonel May 8, 1862; Thomas J. Patton, dropped January 27, 1864

Company C: (Carroll and Ray) James K. McDowell, promoted major November 6, 1862; Gwinn McCuiston

Company D (1st): (Clay) David Thompson (Disbanded August 12, 1862)

Company D (2nd): (Clay, Lafayette) Jesse L. Price (Formerly Company G [1st], Erwin's Battalion. Added to regiment around August 9, 1862)

Company E: (Daviess, DeKalb) Anderson C. Smith, dropped January 20, 1864; George W. Covell

Company F: (Daviess, Randolph, Ray) Thomas G. Lowry

Company G: (Buchanan, Jackson) John W. Kemper, mortally wounded October 4 and died October 31, 1862; William B. Adams

Company H: (Carroll, Grundy, Livingston) William G. Mirick, dropped May 8, 1862; John W. Bagby

Company I: (Clay, Chariton, Ray) William P. McIlwaine, killed May 16, 1863; William M. Chamberlain

Company K: (Macon, Randolph) Aurelius E. Samuel, killed September 15, 1863 while recruiting in Missouri; James Rutter

This regiment mustered into Confederate service at Springfield, Missouri, on January 17, 1862. It contained many veterans of the 3rd, 4th, and 5th divisions of the Missouri State Guard. Initially numbered the 2nd Infantry, the designation changed to the 3rd Infantry after the discovery that two other regiments had precedence. The regiment joined the 1st Missouri Brigade following organization. On February 12, the regiment retreated with the Missouri army to Cove Creek, Arkansas, when Springfield became untenable because of the advance of a numerically superior Federal army. During the hurried retreat the regiment deployed with the rear guard on occasion and skirmished with the pursuing enemy.

Major General Earl Van Dorn, Confederate commander in the Trans-Mississippi, ordered an advance on March 3, and the 3rd Regiment marched northward from Cove Creek with the 1st Missouri Brigade toward the enemy near Pea Ridge, Arkansas. The Confederates and Missouri State Guard troops in Major General Sterling Price's division approached

Elkhorn Tavern early on March 7, with the 3rd Infantry deployed in the center of the brigade line. By 9:00 a.m. they encountered the enemy near the tavern and found themselves fully engaged within an hour. The Confederates enjoyed success that day, pushing the Federal line back and then repelling an enemy counterattack in the afternoon. During the day, the 3rd Infantry assisted in capturing two enemy cannons. At nightfall, the rebels established a line in the former camps of the Federals and lay on their arms with victory seemingly at hand. Matters took a decided turn for the worse on March 8, for the Federals had defeated another wing of the army at nearby Leetown the previous day, which enabled a concentration against Price's division. After fighting briefly that morning, the enemy's superior artillery, and an attack by their rejuvenated infantry, drove the Confederates into retreat. The 3rd Infantry reported losses of 39 killed or mortally wounded, 45 wounded, and 33 missing, but the actual casualties may have been greater. Colonel Benjamin A. Rives fell mortally wounded in the battle; James A. Pritchard succeeded him in command. The army retreated to near Van Buren, Arkansas, and regrouped after the defeat.

In late March, the troops marched across Arkansas to Des Arc for transport up the Mississippi River to Memphis, Tennessee. The 3rd Regiment arrived in Memphis on April 7 and remained eight days until it moved to Corinth, Mississippi. In a strength report dated May 5, the 3rd Infantry mustered but 450 present of 754 soldiers on the rolls. While in the Corinth area, the regiment deployed for the fight at Farmington on May 9 but never closely engaged the enemy. The 3rd Infantry accompanied the army south when the Confederates evacuated Corinth in late May. For the next three months the regiment performed duty in camps in northern Mississippi. Although placed in line of battle at Iuka, Mississippi, on September 19 and exposed to artillery fire, the regiment saw no fighting. The 3rd Infantry engaged the enemy at Corinth on October 3–4 during the Confederate effort to capture that place. On October 3, the regiment attacked the Federals and pushed their line back with light casualties. The day following, the 3rd Infantry joined in a desperate attack on Battery Powell and suffered heavy losses as the strong Federal position fell to the Missourians, along with several pieces of artillery. The Missourians did not hold the redoubt long, though, for the enemy shelled the position with enfilading artillery fire and launched a strong counterattack. The regiment hurriedly withdrew from the field with 11 killed, 65 wounded, and 16 missing, and counted 14 mortally wounded in the latter categories. Colonel James A. Pritchard fell mortally wounded in the battle; William R. Gause succeeded Pritchard as regimental commander. The regiment escaped further disaster at Davis Bridge on the Hatchie River by avoiding a Federal movement that threatened their line of retreat.

In early 1863, the 3rd Regiment moved to the Vicksburg area, where it guarded the bridge over the Big Black River. The brigade moved to Grand Gulf on the Mississippi River in early March to construct fortifications. On April 5, the 3rd Infantry joined other Missouri troops already in Louisiana to reconnoiter the advance of Federal troops in that vicinity. Several small clashes between the opposing forces occurred before the Missourians returned to the east side of the river in mid-April. During encounters with the Federal gunboats at Grand Gulf later that month, the regiment lost 1 killed and 3 wounded. On May 1, the 3rd Infantry and two other Missouri regiments marched from Grand Gulf to assist in opposing a Federal attack near Port Gibson, Mississippi. The advancing Federals, the vanguard of Major General Ulysses S. Grant's army, had landed at Bruinsburg to initiate the final campaign for Vicksburg. The Confederates, outnumbered three to one, fought well at Port Gibson, but they could not stop Grant's advance. The rebels retreated late in the day, having delayed the enemy as long as possible. The 3rd Infantry counted losses of 3 killed, 12 wounded, and 9 missing in the battle.

The regiment next engaged the enemy at Champion Hill, the pivotal battle of the Vicksburg Campaign. On May 16, the 3rd Regiment, aligned in the center of the brigade, joined a charge that broke the enemy line and threatened defeat for Grant's army. Without reinforcements, the Confederate attack slowed, and then an enemy counterattack forced the rebels to withdraw from the fight. The 3rd Infantry suffered casualties of 36 killed or mortally wounded, 63 wounded, and 44 missing in the close contest. The next day the Federals routed the Confederates from a defensive position on the east bank of the Big Black River and pushed them into Vicksburg.

For the next forty-seven days, the 3rd Regiment endured almost constant bombardment and fighting as the Vicksburg siege unfolded. Although often in a reserve role, the regiment assisted in repulsing a Federal attack on the Stockade Redan on May 22 and resisted other assaults in June and July. With no hope of relief, the Vicksburg garrison surrendered on

July 4. The siege operation cost the regiment 35 killed or mortally wounded, and 20 additional wounded. Only 258 men of the regiment received paroles at Vicksburg, while perhaps a hundred left for the Trans-Mississippi after the surrender. Some had tired of fighting, while others merely wanted to visit home; most of these soldiers never returned to the regiment.

After being paroled, the regiment moved with the brigade to Demopolis, Alabama, to await exchange, which occurred on September 12. The Missouri troops reorganized at Demopolis because of heavy battle losses in previous fighting, deaths by disease, and desertions. Under the provisions of Special Order No. 17, Headquarters, Paroled Prisoners, dated October 6, 1863, the 3rd Infantry reorganized into four companies and consolidated with four like companies of the 5th Infantry to form the 3rd & 5th Missouri Infantry Regiment (Consolidated). The men served in the consolidated regiment for the balance of hostilities. About 1,020 soldiers served in the 3rd Infantry during the war, including the period of consolidation with the 5th Infantry. Regimental losses included 213 battle deaths, 117 lost to disease, 1 dead by accident, 2 murdered, and 1 executed by courts-martial. Some 150 soldiers deserted the regiment, mostly after the surrender of the Vicksburg garrison, and many of them saw subsequent service in units in the Trans-Mississippi Department. See the entry for the 3rd & 5th Infantry Regiment (Consolidated) for the further service of the men of this regiment.

BIBLIOGRAPHY

"'A Few Letters Home from the Battlefield': Letters of Confederate Sergeant Phillip Henry Gill." *Kearney Courier,* Kearney, Missouri, December 17, 1988.

Bradley, James. *The Confederate Mail Carrier.* Mexico: Privately printed, 1894.

Cleveland, Charles Boarman. "With the Third Missouri Regiment." *Confederate Veteran* 31 (1923): 18–20.

Erwin, W. J. " The Genius and Heroism of Lieut. K. H. Faulkner." *Confederate Veteran* 14 (1906): 497–98.

Hubbell, Finley L. "Diary of Lieut. Col. Hubbell of 3rd Regiment Missouri Infantry, C.S.A." *The Land We Love* 6 (1867): 97–105.

Payne, A. M. "The Battle of Pea Ridge." *Carthage Press,* Carthage, Missouri, April 26, 1917; May 3, 1917.

Renfro, Henry. "Civil War Letters, 1862–1865." *Richmond Missourian,* Richmond, Missouri, June 26, 1930; July 3 and 10, 1930.

Trigg, S. C. "Fighting around Vicksburg." *Confederate Veteran* 12 (1904): 120.

3rd & 5th Regiment (Consolidated) (McCown's)

Colonel: James C. McCown

Lieutenant Colonel: James K. McDowell, killed August 30, 1864

Major: Owen A. Waddell, mortally wounded October 5 and died October 6, 1864; Robert J. Williams, disabled by wound October 5, 1864

Companies and Commanders:

Company A: Patrick Canniff, killed November 30, 1864 (Formerly Companies E and F, 5th Infantry)

Company B: Jesse L. Price, sent on detached service September 1864 (Formerly Companies D, I, and K, 3rd Infantry)

Company C: Ben Eli Guthrie (Formerly Companies I and K, 5th Infantry)

Company D: John W. Bagby (Formerly Companies A and H, 3rd Infantry)

Company E: Gwinn McCuistion, disabled by wound October 5, 1864 (Formerly Companies C and F, 3rd Infantry)

Company F: Samuel G. Hale, killed November 30, 1864 (Formerly Companies B, C, and K, 5th Infantry)

Company G: Barnett J. Atkisson, killed November 30, 1864 (Formerly Companies A, D, G, and H [2nd], 5th Infantry)

Company H. George W. Covell, wounded and captured November 30, 1864 (Formerly Companies B, E, and G, 3rd Infantry)

Following the surrender at Vicksburg on July 4, 1863, the Missouri troops moved to a parole camp at Demopolis, Alabama. After being exchanged on September 12, the regiments, decimated by death and desertion, consolidated under the provisions of Special Order No. 17, Headquarters, Paroled Prisoners, dated October 6, 1863. The 3rd and 5th infantry regiments joined to form the 3rd & 5th Missouri Infantry Regiment (Consolidated), and the soldiers fought in this organization for the balance of the war. The troops received new Enfield rifles and accoutrements while at Demopolis in anticipation of returning to combat.

On October 16, the 1st Missouri Brigade, including the consolidated 3rd & 5th Infantry, traveled by rail to Meridian, Mississippi, for duty with Major General Samuel French's division. In early January, the brigade rushed to Mobile, Alabama, to deal with a rumored mutiny of Confederate troops at that locale. The brigade returned to Mississippi in February to contend with the advance of Major General William T. Sherman on Meridian, but it did not engage the enemy before moving to Demopolis again. The 3rd & 5th Regiment joined in corralling deserters in northern Alabama before marching to Georgia in May as the Atlanta Campaign got underway. At the start of the prolonged campaign in Georgia, the regiment mustered only 340 men. On May 19, the 3rd & 5th Infantry skirmished with the enemy near Cassville and then on May 25 engaged in a hard fight at New Hope Church. The regiment fought at Latimer House and next occupied rifle-pits in the Kennesaw Mountain line. The 3rd & 5th Infantry helped repel a strong Federal attack on their position at Kennesaw on June 19 and suffered significant casualties in doing so. By mid-July the 1st Missouri Brigade held defensive works just northwest of Atlanta. Over the next two months the regiment endured nearly constant bombardment by enemy artillery and frequently engaged in skirmishing. When the Confederates abandoned Atlanta in early September, the brigade moved to Lovejoy Station, and a skirmish there on September 6 ended the campaign. The casualties of the 3rd & 5th Infantry during the Atlanta Campaign totaled 25 killed, 98 wounded, and 6 missing.

On October 5, General French marched his division to Allatoona, Georgia, to assault a strongly fortified Union position. The 1st Missouri Brigade, with the 3rd & 5th Infantry on the right center of the line, charged forward and quickly captured the Federals' outer works, but, despite a gallant effort, could not penetrate the main fortification. General French, fearing Federal reinforcements, withdrew his men and marched to rejoin the main army. The failed attack cost the 3rd & 5th Infantry 18 killed, 53 wounded, and 5 missing. In late October, the army entered Tennessee, as General John B. Hood had determined to redeem the state for the Confederacy. After a long march through dreary winter weather, the 1st Missouri Brigade arrived at Franklin on November 30 to discover a well-entrenched enemy prepared for battle. Hood decided to fight despite the Federals' admirable defensive position and ordered an attack. The 1st Missouri Brigade deployed for battle with the 3rd &

5th Infantry on the right center of the line. Probably no more than 150 men stood in the regimental ranks that day. When the signal to move forward came, the Missourians charged through a storm of artillery and small-arms fire. Few of them ever made it to the Federal line. After five hours of bloody fighting, the Federal army withdrew from the field, leaving the wrecked Confederate army behind. The 3rd & 5th Infantry suffered near annihilation at Franklin, for it counted 36 dead, 34 wounded, 27 wounded prisoners, and 16 missing, for total casualties of 113. The regiment followed the army to Nashville but remained there only a short time before the 1st Missouri Brigade marched to the Duck River to build fortifications.

The brigade rejoined the army, which had suffered a disastrous defeat at Nashville, in Mississippi in early January 1865. After a stay of a few weeks near Tupelo, the 3rd & 5th Regiment moved with the brigade to the defense of Mobile, Alabama, in early February. It eventually joined the brigade in the revetments of Fort Blakely on the eastern shore of Mobile Bay. On April 9 a large Federal force captured the Blakely garrison after a brief fight. Transported to a makeshift prison on Ship Island, Mississippi, the Missourians remained prisoners until released in early May. They then proceeded to Jackson, Mississippi, where they received paroles to finally end their military service to the Confederacy.

Bibliography

Bradley, James. *The Confederate Mail Carrier.* Mexico: Privately printed, 1894.

Cleveland, Charles Boarman. "With the Third Missouri Regiment." *Confederate Veteran* 31 (1923): 18–21.

Erwin, W. J. " The Genius and Heroism of Lieut. K. H. Faulkner." *Confederate Veteran* 14 (1906): 497–98.

———. "Perilous Undertaking of Two Brothers." *Confederate Veteran* 15 (1907): 308–9.

Guthrie, Ben Eli. "Notes on Co. I, 5th Missouri Infantry Regiment." In *History of Randolph and Macon Counties, Missouri,* 861–65. St. Louis: National Historical Co., 1884.

Renfro, Henry. "Civil War Letters, 1862–1865." *Richmond Missourian,* Richmond, Missouri, June 26, 1930; July 3 and 10, 1930.

Roberts, Frank Stovall. "With the Third Missouri." *Confederate Veteran* 31 (1923): 84.

Trigg, S. C. "Why the Band Played at Franklin." *Confederate Veteran* 12 (1904): 120.

4th Regiment (MacFarlane's)

Colonel: Archibald A. MacFarlane, permanently disabled by wounds October 3, 1862

Lieutenant Colonel: Waldo P. Johnson, sent to Missouri on recruiting service, August 1862, resigned December 7, 1863

Major: Stephen W. Wood, resigned August 1862

Companies and Commanders:

Company A: (Taney) James Walker, dropped May 15, 1862; Francis McShane

Company B: (Howell) William Howard, dropped June 12, 1862; Daniel W. Nicks

Company C: (Fulton County, Arkansas; Ozark County, Missouri) Daniel Hays

Company D: (Oregon) J. Posey Woodside, disabled by wounds October 4, 1862

Company E: (Henry, Laclede) Norval Spangler, killed May 16, 1863; James H. Wickersham

Company F: (Christian) Henderson P. Greene, sent to Trans-Mississippi on recruiting service November 1, 1862

Company G: (Dallas) Richard C. Newport, sent to the Trans-Mississippi on recruiting service October 25, 1862

Company H: (Cass) John H. Britts, dropped April 4, 1862; Phillip W. Fulkerson, dropped May 15, 1862; Aaron C. Patton

Company I: (Oregon, Reynolds) William A. Farris, dropped June 15, 1862; Matthew G. Norman

Company K: (Marion, Monroe) Jeptha D. Feagan

This regiment mustered into Confederate service on April 28, 1862, at Memphis, Tennessee. The regimental organization resulted from the consolidation of the battalions of Majors Archibald MacFarlane and Waldo P. Johnson and a Missouri State Guard company commanded by Captain Jeptha D. Feagan. Regimental members came from south-central and southwest Missouri, although Feagan's company originated in the extreme northeast part of the state. A considerable number of the troops had previous service in the Missouri State Guard in the 7th and 8th divisions, while Feagan's company, a 2nd division unit, converted directly to Confederate service. After forming, the regiment moved by rail to Corinth, Mississippi, with the Army of the West. It mustered 547 soldiers, rank and file, present at that locale on May 5. The regiment deployed on May 9 at the fight at Farmington but did not engage the enemy. The Confederate army evacuated Corinth in late May as the large Federal army of Major General Henry W. Halleck threatened to overwhelm the Confederate position. The 4th Infantry spent the balance of the summer months drilling and preparing for combat in camps in northern Mississippi as part of Brigadier General Martin E. Green's 2nd Missouri Brigade. Several members of the regiment died from disease during the sultry summer months.

At the battle of Iuka, Mississippi, on September 19, the 2nd Missouri Brigade remained in reserve and suffered no reported losses. In early October, the 4th Infantry moved with the army to engage the enemy at Corinth. Colonel MacFarlane led his troops in the attack against the Federal lines on October 3, and after a hard fight, the men drove the enemy into their inner works on the outskirts of Corinth. The day following, the regiment participated in a determined charge directed at Battery Powell. Although initially successful, in less than an hour the troops gave way to heavy enemy artillery fire and a strong counterattack and withdrew from the field with substantial losses. The 4th Infantry reported casualties of 15 killed, 87 wounded, and 27 missing in the battle. Colonel MacFarlane suffered a disabling wound in the fighting and never again actively commanded the regiment. During the retreat from Corinth, the regiment barely evaded the pursuing enemy at the fight for Davis Bridge on the Hatchie River. Badly battered by the fighting at Corinth and greatly reduced in numbers by battle losses, disease, and desertion, the 4th Infantry consolidated with the 1st Infantry on November 7, 1862, near Wyatt, Mississippi, and served as the 1st & 4th Infantry Regiment (Consolidated), 1st Missouri Brigade, for the balance of the war. Some 880 men served in the 4th Infantry from the initial organization until the final surrender. During the regiment's service, including the period of consolidation with the 1st Infantry, it suffered 118 battle deaths, 126 deaths from disease, 3 killed in accidents, and 2 murdered. Approximately 180 soldiers deserted the regiment, primarily after the surrender of Vicksburg, and many of them saw service thereafter in Trans-Mississippi units. A Van Dorn pattern flag that belonged to this unit is held by the Museum of the Confederacy, Richmond, Virginia. See the entry for the 1st & 4th Infantry Regiment (Consolidated) for the further service of the men of this unit.

BIBLIOGRAPHY

Bacon, Charles E. "War Times at Iuka, Mississippi." *Confederate Veteran* 11 (1903): 120.

Lenox, David F. *Personal Memoirs of a Missouri Confederate Soldier and His Commentaries on the Race and Liquor Questions.* Texarkana: Privately printed, ca. 1906.

"Major John H. Britts." *Confederate Veteran* 18 (January 1910): 36.

Joseph R. Mothershead Diary. Tennessee State Library and Archives, Nashville, Tennessee.

"Old Time War Letter." *Bates County Democrat,* Butler, Missouri, September 12, 1918.

5th Regiment (McCown's)

Colonel: James C. McCown

Lieutenant Colonel: Robert S. Bevier, assigned to recruiting duty in Richmond, Virginia, October 1, 1863

Major: Owen A. Waddell

Companies and Commanders:

Company A: (Johnson) Owen A. Waddell, promoted major September 1, 1862; Royal D. Stokely, died of wounds July 2, 1863; Barnett J. Atkisson

Company B: (Macon, Marion) Carter M. Smith, deserted February 9, 1862; Mark Trumper, resigned December 10, 1862; Samuel G. Hale

Company C: (Polk) Asbury C. Bradford, died of disease ca. December 22, 1863

Company D: (Polk) Alexander C. Lemmon

Company E: (Franklin, Gasconade) James W. Fair, mortally wounded October 3 and died December 4, 1862; Matthew Townsend

Company F: (Linn, St. Louis) Patrick Caniff

Company G: (Henry) Stephen D. Coale, died as a prisoner ca. 1863

Company H (1st): (Johnson) Charles H. Thomas, resigned January 6, 1863; Noah Grant, detached for duty as post commandant May 10, 1863

Company H (2nd): (Exchanged prisoners, very mixed) Harvey G. McKinney, killed May 16, 1863

Company I: (Johnson, Macon) Ben Eli Guthrie

Company K: (Dunklin, Stoddard) David Y. Pankey, dropped April 13, 1863; Ferrell B. Spicer

This regiment formed at Saltillo, Mississippi, on September 1, 1862, by adding Captain David Y. Pankey's company, formerly of Major Isaac N. Hedgpeth's battalion, to an existing battalion commanded by Lieutenant Colonel James McCown. At the regiment's initial muster it counted 618 soldiers on its rolls, a majority of whom had earlier service in the Missouri State Guard. Although organized after the 6th Missouri Infantry Regiment, it nevertheless received the designation of the 5th Infantry Regiment. The regiment joined the 1st Missouri Brigade for duty after organization.

When the Federals attacked Iuka, Mississippi, on September 19, the regiment deployed in line of battle but never closely engaged the enemy. Nonetheless, artillery fire and light skirmishing resulted in regimental casualties of 1 killed and 4 wounded before the Confederates withdrew. The 5th Infantry participated in the fighting at Corinth, Mississippi, on October 3–4. On the first day, the regiment moved forward with the brigade with light losses as the enemy fell back into their defensive positions on the outskirts of Corinth. The next day, the 5th Regiment joined in a charge against Battery Powell, a strong redoubt bristling with artillery. The Confederates carried the position, driving the enemy into Corinth and capturing several pieces of artillery, but at a heavy price in casualties. Moreover, the success lasted only forty minutes, for the Federals rallied and directed heavy artillery fire onto the position, launching a strong counterattack that sent the rebel Missourians in full retreat. The 5th Infantry paid a high cost for the abbreviated success, with 25 men killed or mortally wounded and 62 others wounded or missing. The regiment retreated with the army southward and avoided further losses when the army barely escaped a second Federal column at the battle for Davis Bridge on the Hatchie River.

Following the carnage at Corinth, the regiment enjoyed relatively quiet times in winter quarters in northern Mississippi. In early March 1863, the 5th Infantry moved with the brigade to Grand Gulf, south of Vicksburg, and constructed artillery positions on the Mississippi River. About a month later, the regiment joined two other Missouri regiments and a battery on the west bank of the river for the purpose of tracking Federal movements south of Milliken's Bend. The Missourians engaged in some skirmishing with the enemy before returning to Grand Gulf in mid-April. On May 1, Major General Ulysses S. Grant advanced toward Port Gibson after crossing the Mississippi with a considerable force in the first move of the final campaign for Vicksburg. Brigadier General John S. Bowen defended Port Gibson with three brigades, but he soon called for reinforcements. The 5th Infantry and two Missouri regiments marched to Bowen's assistance. The 5th Missouri fought exceptionally well at Port Gibson, winning laurels for its role in a charge that stymied a Federal flank movement that could have been disastrous for Bowen's outnumbered army. The regiment paid a price for its fighting prowess, however, as its casualties tallied 17 killed, 19 wounded, and 31 missing before the Confederates left the field in defeat. The 5th Infantry moved with Bowen's division to a position east of Vicksburg after the battle of Port Gibson.

On May 7, a company of 100 exchanged prisoners, all Missourians, joined the regiment as a second Company H. The 5th Regiment next experienced combat on May 16, when the 1st Missouri Brigade made a remarkable charge that broke Grant's line at Champion Hill and almost resulted in an important Confederate victory. But Bowen's men received no support after driving back the Federals and soon gave way to a counterattack and left the field defeated. The 5th Infantry lost 4 killed, 49 wounded, and 37 missing in the close contest. The next day the Federals routed the Confederates from their defensive position east of the Big Black River and drove the demoralized rebels into the Vicksburg fortifications. The 1st Missouri Brigade assumed the role of the strategic reserve once inside the Vicksburg lines. The Missourians soon joined the fighting, as they reinforced threatened points along the defensive perimeter.

The 5th Infantry helped repel major Federal assaults on May 19 and 22. On June 25, the regiment rushed into a large gap in the line created by the explosion of a mine beneath the 3rd Louisiana Redan. The rebels beat back the Federals with hard fighting as they attempted to exploit the breach in the line. Another mine blew a huge hole in the line on July 1, but no enemy assault followed on this occasion. The Vicksburg garrison, destitute of provisions and with no relief in sight, surrendered on July 4, after forty-seven days of siege. The extended campaign cost the 5th Regiment 20 killed and 52 wounded. Also, some men left the regiment after the capitulation, never to return. Some 276 regimental soldiers received paroles following the surrender and then accompanied the brigade to a camp in Demopolis, Alabama, to await exchange.

On October 6, nearly a month after being exchanged, the 5th Infantry reorganized into a mere four companies and consolidated with four companies of the 3rd Infantry to form the 3rd & 5th Missouri Infantry Regiment (Consolidated), per the provisions of Special Order No. 17, Headquarters, Paroled Prisoners. The men of the 5th Regiment served in the consolidated regiment until hostilities ceased. About 774 men fought in the 5th Infantry during the war, including the period of consolidation with the 3rd Infantry. Regimental losses included 156 battle fatalities, 123 deaths from disease, 2 killed accidentally, and 1 killed in a personal dispute. Some 182 men deserted the regiment, many of whom subsequently served in units in the Trans-Mississippi Department. See the entry for the 3rd & 5th Regiment (Consolidated) for the further service of the men of this regiment.

Bibliography

Bevier, Robert S. *History of the First and Second Missouri Confederate Brigades, 1861–1865, 861–65.* St. Louis: Bryan, Brand & Co., 1879.

Guthrie, Ben Eli. "Notes on Co. I, 5th Missouri Infantry Regiment." In *History of Randolph and Macon Counties, Missouri.* St. Louis: National Historical Co., 1884.

William A. Ruyle Letter. Western Historical Manuscript Collection, University of Missouri–Rolla, Rolla, Missouri.

Avington Wayne Simpson Diary. Western Historical Manuscript Collection, University of Missouri, Columbia, Missouri.

Tucker, Phillip Thomas. *Westerners in Gray: The Men and Missions of the Elite Fifth Missouri Infantry Regiment.* Jefferson: McFarland, 1995.

6th Regiment (Erwin's/Hedgpeth's)

Colonel: Andrew Eugene Erwin, killed June 25, 1863; Isaac Newton Hedgpeth, permanently disabled by wound October 3, 1862, and never assumed field command

Lieutenant Colonel: Isaac Newton Hedgpeth, promoted colonel July 7, 1863; Stephen Cooper

Major: Joseph P. Vaughn, killed October 3, 1862; Stephen Cooper, promoted lieutenant colonel June 25, 1863; Jeptha Duncan, made prisoner May 16, 1863

Companies and Commanders:

Company A: (Cass, Jackson) Francis M. McKinney, killed October 3, 1862; William H. Oldham, disabled by wound May 16, 1863

Company B: (Jackson, Lafayette) Samuel F. Taylor, killed October 3, 1862; Edwin T. Starke, relieved October 4, 1863

Company C: (Boone, Howard) Stephen Cooper, promoted major November 26, 1862; John H. Cooper, sent on detached service after July 4, 1863

Company D: (Cape Girardeau, Stoddard) Albert A. Woodard

Company E: (Jackson, Johnson) Jeptha Duncan, promoted major June 25, 1863; William H. Moss

Company F: (Cass, St. Clair) John M. Wiedemeyer

Company G: (Clay, Platte) John B. Clark, resigned April 16, 1863; James Synnamon

Company H: (Howard) John M. Hickey

Company I: (Cape Girardeau, Scott) John D. Parsons

Company K: (Cape Girardeau, Ripley, Wayne; State of Arkansas) Alvah G. Kelsey, killed October 3, 1862; Ebenezer G. Liles

This regiment mustered into service at Guntown, Mississippi, on or about August 26, 1862, after the consolidation of seven companies of Lieutenant Colonel Eugene Erwin's battalion (A–C and E–H) with three others drawn largely from Major Isaac N. Hedgpeth's battalion. Two of the three latter companies (I and K) transferred directly from Hedgpeth's unit, while Captain Samuel S. Harris's artillery company, also part of Hedgpeth's battalion, merged with Captain Robert McDonald's artillery company to form Company D. Neither of the artillery companies ever had cannons and had served as infantry for several months. At the organization, the ten companies mustered about 690 men, rank and file. The regiment soon joined Brigadier General Martin E. Green's brigade in Brigadier General Henry Little's division.

On September 19, the regiment deployed with the brigade at Iuka, Mississippi, and endured considerable artillery fire but did not actively engage in the fighting. The 6th Infantry experienced its first combat in the battle at Corinth, Mississippi, on October 3–4. On the first day of the battle, the regiment lost many soldiers killed and wounded as the brigade charged Federal positions and drove the enemy into their inner works. The day following, the 6th Infantry assaulted Battery Powell with the brigade, and after hard fighting, carried the position, along with several pieces of artillery. The Confederates held the hard-won redoubt for about forty minutes before enfilading artillery fire and a strong enemy counterattack drove them from the field with heavy casualties. In the two days of carnage at Corinth, the 6th Regiment sustained losses of 40 killed, 130 wounded, and 53 missing; the latter categories included 11 additional soldiers with mortal wounds. The regimental leadership suffered terribly, as 29 officers and 22 noncommissioned officers fell killed, wounded, or missing in the fierce fighting. On the retreat from Corinth, the regiment barely eluded the pursuing Federals during an engagement at Davis Bridge on the Hatchie River. On October 22 the 6th Infantry became part of the 1st Missouri Brigade, Brigadier General John S. Bowen's division. The winter months passed quietly as the regiment occupied camps in northern Mississippi and performed routine duty.

With the coming of spring, the 6th Infantry marched with the brigade to Grand Gulf on the Mississippi River below Vicksburg. At Grand Gulf the regiment constructed fortifications and on occasion fired into Federal gunboats and transports. On May 1, the regiment moved to Port Gibson to oppose the advance of Major General Ulysses S. Grant's Federal army as the final campaign to capture Vicksburg began. Badly outnumbered but not outfought, the Confederates could only hope to delay Grant's move inland from the Mississippi River. The 6th Infantry engaged the enemy all day at Port Gibson and won accolades from Brigadier General

Martin E. Green for a strong performance, but the rebels finally retreated as darkness fell. The regiment next fought at Champion Hill, the pivotal battle of the Vicksburg Campaign, on May 16. The 6th Infantry participated in one of the grand charges of the war that day, as Bowen's division drove the Federals in disorder for nearly a mile, seriously threatening defeat for Grant's entire army. However, all was for naught, for the division received no support in its assault, and enemy reinforcements first stymied Bowen's advance and then sent the Confederates reeling in defeat with a strong counterattack. The next day, May 17, the Confederates suffered another setback when their defensive line along the east bank of the Big Black River gave way, causing them to retreat into the Vicksburg fortifications.

For the next forty-seven days the regiment served in the trenches of Vicksburg, enduring almost constant bombardment by enemy artillery, short rations, and little rest. On May 22 and June 25, the regiment assisted in repulsing major Federal attacks and suffered considerable loss in the fighting, including Colonel Erwin, the regimental commander, who was shot to death. The Federals undermined the 6th Regiment's position and detonated a large mine on July 1. Eleven regimental members suffocated after being covered with dirt as a result of the explosion. The Vicksburg garrison surrendered on July 4, and the survivors of the regiment received paroles. The campaign cost the 6th Infantry dearly, for from May 1 through July 4 the regiment suffered losses of 46 killed, 189 wounded, and 132 missing, more than 60 percent of the unit's strength when the campaign began. The 6th Infantry survivors, numbering only 216 men, moved with the brigade to Demopolis, Alabama, to await exchange. On October 6, after being exchanged, the 6th Infantry reorganized into only four companies, and under the provisions of Special Order No. 17, Headquarters, Paroled Prisoners, consolidated with the 2nd Infantry to form the 2nd & 6th Missouri Infantry Regiment (Consolidated), an arrangement that lasted for the balance of the war. Approximately 708 men served in the ranks of the 6th Infantry from late August 1862 until hostilities ceased, which included the period of consolidation with the 2nd Regiment. Of that number, 192 died in battle and 67 are known to have perished from disease. Other losses included 81 soldiers that transferred to other units and 138 deserters; many of the latter enlisted in units in the Trans-Mississippi Department. A Van Dorn pattern battle flag carried by the regiment at Corinth and through the Vicksburg Campaign, and secreted out of Vicksburg by Colonel Erwin's widow, went on display at the Corinth National Battlefield Park in 2006. See the entry for the 2nd & 6th Infantry Regiment (Consolidated) for the further service of the men of this unit.

Bibliography

Baldwin, Ugenus. "Historical Sketch of Organization, Marches, Engagements of Co. C, 6th Regiment Missouri Infantry." Manuscript. Missouri State Archives, Jefferson City, Missouri.

"Colonel Eugene Erwin." *Confederate Veteran* 4 (1896): 264.

Curran, Thomas F. "'On the Road to Dixie': A Missouri Confederate's Review of the Civil War at Its Midpoint." *Missouri Historical Review* 91 (January 2002): 69–92.

Franklin, Ann York. *The Civil War Journal of Lt. George R. Elliott, 2nd & 6th Missouri Infantry, Company F, 1862–1864.* Louisville: Privately printed, 1997.

John M. Leach Diary. Typescript. Western Historical Manuscript Collection, University of Missouri–Rolla, Rolla, Missouri.

Payne, James E. "Missouri Troops in the Vicksburg Campaign." *Confederate Veteran* 36 (1928): 302–3, 340–41, 377–79.

———. "Recreation in Army Life." *Confederate Veteran.* 38 (1930): 388–90.

———. "The Sixth Missouri at Corinth." *Confederate Veteran* 36 (1928): 462–65.

———. "Skylarking along the Lines." *Confederate Veteran* 38 (1930): 96.

Synnamon, James. "A Veteran with Many Wounds." *Confederate Veteran* 21 (1913): 582.

Weidemeyer, John M. "Memoirs of a Confederate Soldier." In *Reminiscences of Women of Missouri during the Sixties,* 61–68. Dayton: Morningside Press, 1988.

7th Regiment (Franklin's)

See Units That Failed to Complete Organization

7th Regiment (Jackman's/Caldwell's/Lewis's)

Redesignated the 16th Regiment. See the entry for that regiment.

8th Regiment (Hunter's/Burns's)

Redesignated the 11th Regiment. See the entry for that regiment.

8th Regiment (Mitchell's)

Colonel: Charles Samuel Mitchell

Lieutenant Colonel: John S. Smizer

Major: W. H. L. Frazier, resigned February 18, 1863; John W. Smizer, promoted lieutenant colonel January 23, 1863; John W. Hill

Companies and Commanders:

Company A: (Dallas, St. Louis) John W. Smizer, promoted major August 8, 1862; Joseph J. Leddy, cashiered June 7, 1863; John W. Hill, promoted major November 6, 1863; James T. Otey

Company B: (St. Louis, Texas) Charles L. Johnson, absent without leave January 21, 1863, reported dead.

Company C: (Texas) Joseph H. Mooney, dropped April 14, 1863; William Dings

Company D: (Crawford, Gasconade, Phelps) Eathan A. Pinnell

Company E: (Dent, Phelps) William Skiles, absent without leave July 23, 1863; James McClure

Company F: (Newton, Pulaski, Saline) James P. Daugherty

Company G: (Barry, Lawrence, McDonald, Newton) Amry M. Curry

Company H: (McDonald, Newton) John Carroll, absent without leave on August 13, 1863; 2nd Lieutenant Jesse H. Rogers

Company I: (Barry) James Montgomery

Company K: (Barry, Lawrence, McDonald, Newton) Elias O. Bowen, resigned December 30, 1863; Josiah Rodgers, resigned August 29, 1864

This regiment initially organized August 7, 1862, in Oregon County, Missouri, as a mounted unit. It contained many soldiers recruited in central and south-central Missouri; a substantial number had served in the

6th and 7th Divisions, Missouri State Guard. The regiment mustered into Confederate service on September 2, near Evening Shade, Arkansas. By order of Major General Theophilus Holmes, Trans-Mississippi Department commander, the regiment dismounted and converted to infantry on September 12. In September, some ladies of Batesville, Arkansas, furnished the regiment a banner, which was a variant of the first Confederate national flag. Due to a decrease in numbers caused by soldiers leaving to join other units, the companies consolidated, and the regiment reorganized as a battalion of six companies on October 19, which became the 7th Infantry Battalion. Ordered to join the army organizing near Fort Smith, Arkansas, the regiment marched west on October 27. The battalion arrived at Camp Massard, the headquarters of Brigadier General Mosby M. Parsons's brigade, on November 28. The following day the battalion consolidated with the three companies of Major W. H. L. Frazier's southwest Missouri battalion. Mitchell's enlarged battalion moved north with Parsons's command toward Prairie Grove, Arkansas, on December 3, where it would experience its first combat. Parsons's brigade occupied a position on the Cane Hill road at the beginning of the battle on December 7. As the fight developed, the Missourians moved to the battlefield to confront Union reinforcements. Deployed on the left of the line when Parsons's brigade charged Federals attacking its front, Mitchell's battalion initially remained in reserve. When later ordered forward, it joined the fight without hesitation. The Federals soon gave way in retreat; the Missourians pressed on until heavy enemy artillery fire stalled the attack. Parsons's men then fell back to their original line and assumed a defensive posture. Since the Confederate commander, Major General Thomas C. Hindman, decided not to renew the fight the next day, the army retreated toward Van Buren around midnight. Mitchell's battalion, which entered the battle with 450 men, counted its battle losses as 1 killed and 19 wounded. Parsons later complimented the battalion for the "gallant and conspicuous" part it played in the engagement.

On December 23, men taken from companies of Frazier's original battalion formed a new company and increased Mitchell's battalion to regimental size. Special Order No. 27, Headquarters, Trans-Mississippi Department, dated January 23, 1863, formalized the regimental organization. At the beginning of 1863, the regiment marched with the army toward Little Rock. Mitchell's regiment transferred from Parsons's brigade to another commanded by Colonel John B. Clark Jr. while en route. Upon arrival at Little Rock, the brigade established winter quarters. On February 7, Mitchell's men boarded the steamer *Arkansas* and sailed to White's Bluff, some sixty-five miles down river. Later that month the brigade moved fifteen miles further downriver to Fort Pleasant, near Pine Bluff, where it guarded the Arkansas River approach to Little Rock. Clark's brigade, less Mitchell's regiment, marched to the Mississippi River on June 12 to operate against Federal shipping. Mitchell's men remained on duty at Fort Pleasant until the brigade returned a month later. On July 23, word arrived that the Confederate War Department had designated the regiment the 8th Infantry.

The regiment next moved with the brigade to Little Rock to defend the capital against Major General Frederick Steele's approaching army. The Confederates constructed entrenchments north of the Arkansas River, which the infantry occupied. Steele wisely avoided the fortifications and attacked the city from the southeast. Outflanked and in danger of being cut off, the infantry abandoned the trenches and marched southward as the Confederates yielded the city to the Federals on September 10. Initially encamped at Arkadelphia following the loss of Little Rock, the 8th Infantry moved with the brigade in October to Camp Bragg near Camden and established winter quarters. On December 15, Special Order 177, Headquarters, Price's Division, confirmed the war department's designation of the regiment as the 8th Infantry. Over the winter months the regiment performed routine military duties in camp. In the spring of 1864, Federal Major General Nathaniel Banks initiated the Red River Campaign with the intention of capturing Shreveport, Louisiana, and then moving on into Texas. The 8th Infantry marched toward Shreveport with the army preparatory to meeting Banks's invading force.

By late March, Clark's brigade occupied a camp south of Shreveport. On March 25, under the provisions of Special Order No. 73, Headquarters, Trans-Mississippi Department, General Parsons formed a Missouri infantry division consisting of his brigade and Clark's. The 8th Infantry remained in Clark's 1st Brigade in the division. The new division marched south on April 3 to augment the army commanded by Major General Richard Taylor as he sought to halt the Union offensive. The army engaged the enemy at Pleasant Hill, Louisiana, on April 9. Clark's brigade, including the 8th Infantry, deployed on the right of the Confederate line and initiated the fight. As the brigade charged forward, it overwhelmed the Federal skirmishers and then shattered an enemy brigade, taking many prisoners and capturing two artillery batteries. As the Missourians pressed their advantage, they were suddenly exposed to heavy flank fire as part of a Union corps attacked their right. Outflanked and exposed to a terrific fire, Clark's brigade, and then the units to its left, sought safety in retreat. Before the Confederates could be rallied, the Federals had retreated southward. The 8th Infantry suffered casualties of 16 killed or mortally wounded and 60 wounded in the engagement.

After resting for five days, the army turned north to deal with Major General Frederick Steele's force at Camden, Arkansas. Twenty-four hours before the rebels arrived, Steele abandoned the town and retreated toward Little Rock. For two rain-soaked days, three Confederate infantry divisions pursued the fleeing Federals until Steele made a stand at Jenkins's Ferry on the Saline River. When Parsons's division reached Jenkins's Ferry on the morning of April 30, the Missourians discovered an Arkansas brigade already engaging Steele's army in the flooded bottomlands. The division moved forward, with Clark's brigade on the left, and reinforced the Arkansans. After fighting on the left of the line for nearly an hour, the Missourians moved to the right, but the Federals retreated across the Saline before they could be engaged again. Battle losses for the 8th Infantry amounted to 7 killed and 22 wounded. The 8th Infantry experienced no further significant combat during the war. The Missourians camped in southern Arkansas and northwestern Louisiana for the balance of hostilities, while faraway events determined their fate. The men of the 8th Infantry received paroles at Alexandria, Louisiana, on June 7, 1865, and then boarded the steamer *Judge Fletcher* for the long trip to Missouri. The losses for the regiment totaled 25 battle fatalities and 141 dead from disease.

Bibliography

Banasik, Michael, ed. *Serving with Honor: The Diary of Captain Eathan Allen Pinnell of the Eighth Missouri Infantry Regiment (Confederate)*. Iowa City: Camp Pope Bookshop, 1999.

"Capt. James McClure." *Confederate Veteran* 33 (1925): 107.

"Col. Charles S. Mitchell." In *Memorial and Biographical History of Dallas County, Texas*, 973–75. Chicago: Lewis Publishing Co., 1878.

Coleman, R. B. "Where the Eighth Missouri Surrendered." *Confederate Veteran* 33 (1925): 155, 158.

Curry, Ray Cornelius, and Charles Ray Richardson, eds. *Civil War Memories of A. M. Curry*. Abilene: Hardin-Simmons University Press, 1988.

"From a Correspondent." *Confederate Veteran* 10 (1902): 266.

McNamara, J. H. "From Arkadelphia to Pleasant Hill: Parsons' Missouri Brigade in the Red River Campaign." *Daily Missouri Republican,* St. Louis, Missouri, November 6, 1886.

———. "Incidents in the Campaign against Steele in Arkansas." *Daily Missouri Republican,* St. Louis, Missouri, July 16, 1887.

———. "Missouri Confederates." *Daily Missouri Republican,* St. Louis, Missouri, December 5, 1885.

"Where the Eighth Missouri Surrendered." *Confederate Veteran* 33 (1925): 204.

9th Regiment (Clark's)

Colonel: John Bullock Clark Jr.

Lieutenant Colonel: Michael W. Buster

Major: James Quinn Morton

Companies and Commanders

Company A: (Boone, Carroll, Howard, Platte, Randolph) Harry H. Hughes

Company B: (Adair, Clark, Knox, Lewis, Monroe, Schuyler) William T. Bond

Company C: (Boone, Cooper, Montgomery, Randolph) John B. Bowles

Company D: (State of Arkansas) John F. Ross (Formerly Company B, and parts of F and H, Clarkson's Battalion)

Company E: (State of Arkansas) Leftwich H. Stone, resigned December 1, 1862; W. B. Cox (Formerly Company A and part of G, Clarkson's Battalion)

Company F: No record of such a company in regiment

Company G: (State of Arkansas) Joseph B. Forrester (Formerly Companies D and E and parts of F and G, Clarkson's Battalion)

Company H: (Boone, Callaway) David W. Craig

Company I: (State of Arkansas) John F. Winfrey (Formerly Company C, Clarkson's Battalion)

Company K: No record of such a company in regiment

The organization of this regiment resulted from Special Order No. 38, District of Arkansas, November 10, 1862, which directed John B. Clark Jr., former commander of the 3rd Division, Missouri State Guard, to take charge of four companies of Missouri recruits (A–C, H) and march to Fort Smith. Many of the recruits had belonged to cavalry units formed by John A. Poindexter, Joseph C. Porter, and Henry Snider north of the Missouri River the previous summer. The order further provided that Clark unite those companies with four companies (actually eight companies consolidated into four), formerly of Colonel James J. Clarkson's Independent Ranger Battalion, then commanded by Lieutenant Colonel Michael W. Buster. Most members of these companies were Arkansans. The newly formed unit mustered into service at Fort Smith on November 16. Although denominated a regiment, Clark's command consisted of only eight companies, which violated Confederate law and the specific orders of the corps commander, Major General Thomas C. Hindman. Technically, the unit constituted only a battalion. Evidence suggests the existence of two other companies near the time of organization, but they cannot definitely be established as part of the regiment. The regiment eventually became part of an independent brigade commanded by Brigadier General John S. Roane, primarily a Texas organization. On December 1, the regiment's strength amounted to 594 officers and men.

Clark's Regiment first engaged the enemy at Prairie Grove on December 7. Although initially deployed in reserve against a possible attack from the direction of Cane Hill, Roane's brigade moved forward to the left of the Confederate line late in the day. When Brigadier General James G. Blunt's Union troops attacked the rebel left, Brigadier General Mosby M. Parsons's Missouri brigade boldly charged the enemy. Clark's Regiment soon joined the action when sent forward to reinforce Parsons's men. The Missourians successfully repulsed Blunt's attack, but their charge eventually faltered; faced with heavy enemy artillery fire, the Confederates withdrew to their original position. Nearly out of ammunition and food, the Confederates abandoned the field that night and retreated to near Van Buren, Arkansas. The fight cost Clark's Regiment 3 killed, 20 wounded, and 3 missing. On December 28, the army marched toward Little Rock.

The regiment joined a new brigade under command of Colonel Clark on January 4, 1863, while en route to the capital city, which they reached twelve days later. The regiment's stay at Little Rock ended on February 7, when the regiment boarded a steamer and traveled down the Arkansas

River to White's Bluff. Less than two weeks later, the regiment sailed to Day's Bluff on the *Granite State* and moved into a camp known as Fort Pleasant. At Fort Pleasant the brigade guarded the river approach to Little Rock with other units. On June 12, part of Clark's brigade, including the 9th Infantry, marched to the Mississippi River to operate against Federal shipping. The mixed force attacked a Federal flotilla on June 22, inflicting severe damage on transports and a gunboat while killing several boat guards and crewmen. On June 27, Clark's command took a position at Gaines Landing, Arkansas, and again attacked the Federals' boats with some success. Learning of an approaching Union ground force, the Confederates retreated to Fort Pleasant, arriving there on July 13. The regiment received word of its designation as the 9th Infantry by the Confederate War Department on July 23. The regiment moved with the brigade in late July to Little Rock, threatened at the time by Major General Frederick Steele's Federal army. At Little Rock the regiment helped build fortifications north of the Arkansas River in anticipation of a Federal attack. But the Missourians never engaged the enemy, for on September 10 the Confederates abandoned the city to the Federals and retreated to a camp near Arkadelphia. On September 30, at Arkadelphia, the regiment reorganized per Special Order No. 171, District of Arkansas. Under the provisions of the order, the six companies of the 8th Battalion (Musser's) replaced the four companies formerly belonging to Clarkson's Battalion, which formed into a new Arkansas battalion. The reorganized regiment remained under the command of Colonel Clark. See the 9th Regiment (Reorganized) for the further service of the men of this organization.

BIBLIOGRAPHY

Edwin E. Harris Correspondence. Gilder Lehrman Institute of American History, New York Historical Society, New York, New York.

Haimerl, David L. *Clarkson's Battalion, C.S.A.: A Brief History and Roster.* Independence: Two Trails, 2005.

Moore, John C. "John B. Clark, Jr." In *Missouri*, by Moore, 206–8, vol. 12 of *Confederate Military History,* ed. Clement A. Evans. Wilmington: Broadfoot, 1988.

9th Regiment (Reorganized) (Clark's/Musser's)

Colonel: John Bullock Clark Jr., promoted brigadier general
March 4, 1864; Richard H. Musser

Lieutenant Colonel: Richard H. Musser, promoted colonel April 12,
1864; Richard Gaines

Major: Richard Gaines, promoted lieutenant colonel April 12, 1864;
Harry H. Hughes

Companies and Commanders:

Company A: (Adair, Buchanan, Linn) Joseph N. Miller, disposition
unknown; William F. Carter

Company B: (Boone, Carroll, Howard, Platte, Randolph, St.
Charles) Harry H. Hughes, promoted major April 12, 1864;
George H. Willis

Company C: (Adair, Boone, Clark, Knox, Monroe, Schuyler)
William T. Bond, disposition unknown, W. R. Banes

Company D: (Boone, Montgomery, Randolph) John D. Bowles,
resigned August 15, 1864; Walter W. Stone

Company E: (Boone, Callaway) David W. Craig, resigned
January 13, 1864; George R. Brooks

Company F: (Platte) Alexander D. Ellis, resigned January 29, 1864,
Fielding Y. Doke

Company G: (Lafayette, Saline, St. Louis) Franklin S. Robertson,
transferred to cavalry at date not of record; Robert H. Edmondson,
dropped July 11, 1864

Company H: (Cass, Saline, St. Clair) David Herndon Lindsay

Company I: (Chariton, Jasper, Montgomery, Pike, Vernon)
James C. Wallace

Company K: (Chariton, Miller) John Hanna

Special Order No. 171, District of Arkansas, September 30, 1863, created
this regiment by consolidating the four Missouri companies of Clark's
Regiment (B–E), previously designated the 9th Infantry by the Con-
federate War Department, with the 8th Battalion (Musser's) at a camp near
Arkadelphia, Arkansas. The regiment became part of Brigadier General
Thomas F. Drayton's brigade on October 12 and moved with it to Camp

Bragg, Ouachita County, Arkansas, on October 20, to establish winter quarters. On December 15, Special Order 177, Headquarters, Price's Division, confirmed the war department's designation of the unit as the 9th Infantry. The regiment spent the winter months inactive, occupied primarily in performing routine camp duties. On January 12, Colonel Clark took temporary command of the brigade, with Lieutenant Colonel Richard H. Musser assuming regimental command. The brigade broke camp on January 29 and moved to one in Hempstead County, Arkansas, dubbed Camp Sumter. In mid-March, the regiment marched toward Shreveport, Louisiana, as the army prepared to defend the city from a Federal army approaching from the south under Major General Nathaniel Banks. By March 25, the regiment had crossed the Red River and encamped just south of Shreveport. On that same date, Brigadier General Mosby M. Parsons organized the two Missouri brigades, his own and Clark's, into a small division under the provisions of Special Order No. 73, Headquarters, Trans-Mississippi Department. The 9th Infantry remained in Clark's brigade, while Richard H. Musser retained regimental command.

On April 3, the division left Shreveport to reinforce the army of Major General Richard Taylor, then contending with Banks's army near Mansfield. After a hard march, the Missourians reached Pleasant Hill, Louisiana, on April 9 and deployed for battle late that afternoon. Parsons's division composed the right of the Confederate line, with Clark's brigade, including the 9th Infantry, located on the extreme right. The brigade charged forward and captured most of the enemy skirmishers occupying a ditch along their front. The Missourians continued on, and although receiving enemy fire on their right flank, shattered a Union brigade, captured two artillery batteries, and rushed toward the hamlet of Pleasant Hill. The flank fire increased considerably; then, part of Major General Andrew J. Smith's Federal corps emerged from a concealed position and attacked the Confederate right in force. The 9th Infantry took the brunt of Smith's assault, veered to the left seeking safety, and then retreated in considerable disorder. The Confederates eventually rallied behind their original position, but by then, darkness covered the field, and the Federals withdrew to end the battle. The regiment's reported casualties totaled 5 killed and at least 108 wounded at the engagement, although Musser later estimated his losses at about 175.

After a short respite, the Missouri division moved north with the army toward Camden, Arkansas, intending to attack the Union force there; however, the Federals evacuated the position and retreated toward Little Rock as the Confederates reached Camden. After some delay in crossing the Ouachita River, the Confederates pursued Major General Frederick Steele's army northward. Parsons's division arrived at Jenkins's Ferry on the Saline River on April 30 to find an Arkansas division fighting Steele's force in a bottomland flooded by recent rains. The division deployed, with Clark's brigade on the left, and moved forward about 300 yards where it engaged the enemy for a half hour. Ordered to the right of the line, the Missourians could not renew the fight before the Federals withdrew across the Saline. The battle cost the 9th Infantry 7 killed and 45 wounded. Jenkins's Ferry essentially ended the combat career of the 9th Regiment; it spent the remainder of the war in camps in southern Arkansas and northern Louisiana. The men of the regiment received paroles at Alexandria, Louisiana, on June 7 and then boarded the steamer *B. L. Hodge* for shipment to Missouri. Regimental losses during the war included 27 soldiers killed or mortally wounded, while another 131 succumbed to disease.

Bibliography

McNamara, J. H. "From Arkadelphia to Pleasant Hill: Parsons' Missouri Brigade in the Red River Campaign." *Daily Missouri Republican,* St. Louis, Missouri, November 6, 1886.

———. "Incidents in the Campaign against Steele in Arkansas." *Daily Missouri Republican,* St. Louis, Missouri, July 16, 1887.

———. "Missouri Confederates." *Daily Missouri Republican,* St. Louis, Missouri, December 5, 1885.

Moore, John C. "John B. Clark, Jr." In *Missouri,* by Moore, 206–8, vol. 12 of *Confederate Military History,* ed. Clement A. Evans. Wilmington: Broadfoot, 1988.

Musser, Richard H. "The Battle of Pleasant Hill, La." *Daily Missouri Republican,* St. Louis, Missouri, December 26, 1885.

"Richard H. Musser." In *History of Howard and Chariton Counties,* 761–64. Missouri St. Louis: National Historical Co., 1883.

9th Regiment (White's/Ponder's)

Redesignated the 12th Regiment. See the entry for that regiment.

10th Regiment (Subsequently known as the 10th Consolidated Regiment) (Steen's/Pickett's/Moore's)

Colonel: Alexander Early Steen, killed December 7, 1862; Alexander Corbin Pickett, defeated in special election December 2, 1863; William M. Moore

Lieutenant Colonel: William C. Chappell, killed December 7, 1862; William M. Moore, promoted colonel December 2, 1863; Simon Harris, killed April 30, 1864; Elijah H. Magoffin

Major: Alexander Corbin Pickett, promoted colonel December 7, 1862; Simon Harris, promoted lieutenant colonel December 2, 1863; Elijah H. Magoffin, promoted lieutenant colonel ca. July 21, 1864; Benjamin Holt

Companies and Commanders:

Company A: (Macon, Marion, Monroe, Platte, Randolph) William M. Moore, promoted lieutenant colonel December 7, 1862; George W. McChristy

Company B: (Clark, Clay, Franklin, Knox, Pettis, Platte, Scotland, St. Louis) Elijah H. Magoffin, promoted major December 2, 1863; John B. Musgrove

Company C: (Douglas, Texas, Wright) Benjamin Holt, promoted major July 21, 1864

Company D: (Dent, Phelps) John W. Lenox, accidentally killed September 23, 1863; Elias D. Wright

Company E: (Maries, Phelps) John M. Johnson, on detached service as recruiter, resigned September 2, 1863, for disability; Campbell Greenup, deserted November 14, 1862; Alexander Trammel

Company F: (Fulton County, State of Arkansas; Lawrence) Isaac D. Wilson, died December 2, 1862; John C. McKinney, transferred at date not of record (Company transferred and became Company M, 38th Arkansas Infantry Regiment)

Company F (2nd): (Iron, Madison, Ripley, Washington) Richard B. Overton, disposition unknown; A. C. Hancock (Formerly companies B, C, F, G, and K, 12th Infantry Regiment)

Company G: (Hickory, Phelps, Pulaski) Moses J. Bradford, died as prisoner of war February 13, 1865 (Consolidated with Company K at date not of record)

Company G (2nd): (Butler, Carter, Reynolds, Ripley, St. Francois, Wayne) James B. McGhee (Formerly companies A, D, E, H, and I, 12th Infantry Regiment)

Company H: (Gasconade, Maries, Osage) Simon Harris, promoted major December 7, 1862; Jacob A. Love

Company I: (St. Louis, Jefferson) D. F. M. Sigler, resigned March 12, 1863; John McDaniel

Company K: (Maries, Miller) John Still, resigned March 23, 1863; Henry Y. Brockman

This regiment organized at Camp Mulberry, situated east of Fort Smith, Arkansas, on November 10, 1862. The genesis of the regiment appears to have been a battalion, commanded by Alexander E. Steen, formed from William O. Coleman's disbanded cavalry outfit; John M. Johnson's mounted recruits; and a few men recruited by others. The unit attained full regimental strength when two companies, made up of remnants of John W. Priest's and John H. Winston's Missouri State Guard regiments, consolidated with Steen's battalion. In late July, the soldiers of the latter companies had returned from duty in the Cis-Mississippi with Brigadier General Mosby M. Parsons. After final organization, the regiment contained some 650 indifferently armed soldiers, many with prior service in the 2nd, 5th, and 6th divisions of the Guard. Alexander E. Steen, a former regular army officer and general in the Guard, assumed command. The regiment immediately became part of Parsons's brigade in Brigadier General Daniel M. Frost's division.

In early December, the regiment marched northward with the brigade in the initial movement of the Prairie Grove Campaign. While part of the brigade engaged an enemy cavalry force on Reed's Mountain late on December 6, Steen's regiment did not take part in the fighting. On December 7, Parsons's brigade deployed to prevent an attack from Cane Hill, as the balance of the army engaged the enemy at Prairie Grove. Later that day, the brigade moved forward to the main Confederate line of battle. Late in the afternoon, units of Major General James G. Blunt's Army of the Frontier attacked Parsons in force. Parsons in turn charged the advancing Federals with his entire brigade, led by Steen's and Colonel James D. White's regiments. The Confederates drove the enemy back some three hundred yards before heavy enemy artillery fire stalled the charge.

Parsons's units withdrew to their original position and established a defensive perimeter for the night. The Confederate attack proved very costly for Steen's regiment, for it lost 31 killed or mortally wounded, including Steen and Lieutenant Colonel Chappell, 62 wounded, and 3 missing. The Confederate commander, Major General Thomas C. Hindman, withdrew the army from the field at midnight, declining to continue the battle the next morning. Alexander C. Pickett replaced Steen as regimental commander. The army retreated to Van Buren, Arkansas, where it remained until early January 1863, when it moved to Little Rock. Pickett's regiment occupied winter quarters at Little Rock until the following spring.

On May 3, 1863, Major General Sterling Price, division commander, designated Pickett's regiment as the 10th Infantry Regiment in Special Order No. 30. Later that month, the regiment moved north with Price's infantry division toward Jacksonport, Arkansas. In late June the division moved to assault the Federal garrison at Helena on the Mississippi River. After a difficult twelve-day march across the flooded delta region of eastern Arkansas, the Confederates arrived near Helena and prepared to assault the enemy positions at daybreak on July 4. Parsons's attack on the earthworks atop Graveyard Hill ("Battery C") was delayed because of a mix-up in orders, but once the Missourians charged forward, they made quick work of the defending Federals. The brigade then moved into Helena. Unnoticed by Parsons's men, the other columns had made little headway against the enemy. Consequently, the Missourians, without adequate support, experienced a tremendous crossfire of small arms and artillery to their front and flanks. Unable to endure the punishing fire, Parsons's regiments had little choice but to retire. Many of the Missourians could not withdraw, and the Federals made them prisoners. After five hours of intense combat, the Confederates retreated from the field in defeat. The 10th Infantry suffered near annihilation in the fighting, losing 11 killed, 41 wounded, and 237 captured. Two days after the battle, the strength of the regiment totaled only 236 present for duty.

The 10th Infantry next participated in the defense of Little Rock. The infantry constructed entrenchments north of the Arkansas River as a Union army under Major General Frederick Steele approached the city in August. But the regiment did no fighting, as Steele bypassed the defenses and attacked the city from the southeast. Parsons's brigade retreated from the city on September 10 and moved to southern Arkansas near Arkadelphia. On November 22, Special Order No. 215, District of Arkansas, directed that the remnant of the 12th Regiment, numbering less than 200 men, consolidate into two companies and be attached temporarily to the 10th regiment. The two companies replaced companies F and G: the former transferred to the 38th Arkansas Infantry Regiment, while the latter consolidated with company K. On December 15, Special Order 177, Headquarters, Price's Division, confirmed the earlier designation of the unit as the 10th Infantry.

The regiment spent the winter months quartered in southern Arkansas at various camps. In late March 1864, General Parsons organized a Missouri division composed of his brigade and one commanded by Colonel John B. Clark Jr. The 10th Infantry joined the 2nd brigade under Colonel Simon P. Burns. In early April, the brigade moved to reinforce Major General Richard Taylor as he strove to halt the advance of Major General Nathaniel Banks's Federal army toward Shreveport, Louisiana, during the Red River Campaign. After a hard march, the brigade joined the army at Pleasant Hill, Louisiana, on April 9. That afternoon, the brigade deployed for battle, with Burns's brigade on the left of Clark's. The Missourians, occupying the Confederate right, successfully charged the enemy, essentially destroying a Union brigade in its front. But an unforeseen Federal attack on the division's right quickly overwhelmed Parsons's men, who retreated in considerable disorder. By the time the Confederates rallied, the Union army had abandoned the field. The 10th Regiment's battle losses tallied 10 killed and 25 wounded.

Parsons's division next turned north and marched toward Camden, then occupied by another Federal army under General Frederick Steele. Before the Confederates could invest Camden, Steele abandoned the position and marched for Little Rock. In pursuit of Steele's fleeing army, the Confederates finally overtook the Federals at Jenkins's Ferry on the Saline River. Early on April 30, in a driving rainstorm, Parsons's weary troops moved into line to reinforce an Arkansas division. Burns's brigade, which included the 10th Infantry, deployed on the left of Clark's brigade and moved forward into battle. Burns's brigade aligned on the right of the Arkansans and within an hour pushed the enemy back some distance in heavy fighting. The brigade, often maneuvering in knee-deep water, then received orders to fall back to permit a Texas division to move forward. After having accomplished that maneuver, the brigade then moved to support the Texans' right. Before the Missourians could renew the fight, the enemy crossed the Saline on pontoons, ending the battle. The engagement cost the 10th Infantry 3 killed, including Lieutenant Colonel Simon Harris, and 8 wounded.

The battle at Jenkins's Ferry effectively ended the regiment's combat. The consolidation of the two companies of the 12th Infantry into the 10th Regiment became permanent on September 29. The consolidated regiment spent the remainder of the war in camps in southern Arkansas and near Shreveport, Louisiana. The men of the 10th Infantry received paroles at Shreveport on June 8, 1865, and then boarded the steamer *E. H. Fairchild* for shipment to Missouri. In a final act of defiance, a few soldiers tore the regimental flag into pieces and distributed them to regimental members as souvenirs. During the course of the war the regiment's losses included 61 battle deaths, 198 dead from disease, and 2 killed accidentally.

BIBLIOGRAPHY

Allardice, Bruce S. "Alexander Early Steen." In *More Generals in Gray*, 215–17. Baton Rouge: Louisiana State University Press, 1995.

Bennett, John A. "Diary of a Confederate Soldier." *Missouri Cash-Book,* Jackson, Missouri, July 29, 1897.

Bright, J. L. "The Red River Again." *Daily Missouri Republican,* St. Louis, Missouri, June 5, 1886.

———. "Two Forced Marches." *Daily Missouri Republican,* St. Louis, Missouri, November 21, 1885.

"Col. W. M. Moore." *Confederate Veteran* 36 (1928): 64.

Robert J. Christie Jr. Memoir. Unpublished typescript in the possession of James Denny, Jefferson City, Missouri.

Grubbs, James L. "The Last Company that Surrendered." *Daily Missouri Republican,* St. Louis, Missouri, January 9, 1886.

McNamara, J. H. "From Arkadelphia to Pleasant Hill: Parsons' Missouri Brigade in the Red River Campaign." *Daily Missouri Republican,* St. Louis, Missouri, November 6, 1886.

———. "Incidents in the Campaign against Steele in Arkansas." *Daily Missouri Republican,* St. Louis, Missouri, St. Louis, Missouri, July 16, 1887.

———. "Missouri Confederates." *Daily Missouri Republican,* St. Louis, Missouri, December 5, 1885.

Schnetzer, Wayne H. *Men of the Tenth: A Roster of the Tenth Missouri Infantry, Confederate States of America.* Independence: Two Trails, n.d.

Wood, W. H. "The Battle of Helena." *Daily Missouri Republican,* St. Louis, Missouri, January 16, 1886.

11th Regiment (Hunter's/Burns's)
(Formerly the 8th Regiment)

Colonel: DeWitt Clinton Hunter, resigned February 4, 1863; Simon Pierce Burns, appointed commander of 2nd Brigade, Brigadier General Mosby M. Parsons's Division, March 24, 1864.

Lieutenant Colonel: Simon Pierce Burns, promoted colonel March 24, 1863; Thomas H. Murray

Major: Thomas H. Murray, promoted lieutenant colonel March 24, 1863; James Phillips

Companies and Commanders:

Company A: (Jasper, Lawrence) James Phillips, promoted major March 24, 1863; John F. Gibson

Company B: (Barry) Joseph G. Peevey, resigned September 2, 1863; William McBride

Company C: (Barry) John S. Herriford, resigned November 17, 1863; William Trower, resigned at date not of record in 1865

Company D: (Benton, Hickory) Elbert S. Feaster

Company E: (Cedar, Vernon) William M. Lowe, resigned January 7, 1863; James McKill

Company F: (Lawrence) David C. Howard

Company G: (Cedar, Polk) Morris W. Mitchell

Company H: (Buchanan, Platte, Ray) Jackson Cooper, mortally wounded December 7, 1862, died January 3, 1863; John P. Quesenberry, resigned at date not of record in 1865; Benjamin F. Davis (Formerly Company F, 35th Arkansas Infantry Regiment)

Company I: (Cass) Amos S. Bradley

Company K: (Cass, Greene, Jasper, Newton) Benjamin G. Johnson

In the summer of 1862, DeWitt C. Hunter initiated recruitment of this regiment from the mounted unit he had commanded in the 8th Division, Missouri State Guard. By the end of July, he had perhaps 300 men in camp at Frog Bayou near Van Buren, Arkansas. Unable to complete his organization, Hunter joined other recruiters in an expedition into Missouri to gather more men. After several days of recruiting, the recruit commands camped near Lone Jack in Jackson County. On August 16, the joint forces attacked a Union column at Lone Jack; Hunter's men fought on the right of the Confederate line. After a prolonged fight, the enemy retreated to Lexington. Hunter's command suffered known losses of 5 killed and 8 wounded in the engagement. A growing Union buildup in the area forced the Confederates to ride for safety in Arkansas. Still lacking sufficient men to form a regiment after returning from Missouri, Hunter organized a battalion of 700 men on August 31. The battalion organized as infantry, since Major General Thomas C. Hindman, commander in northwest Arkansas, dismounted many units recruited for cavalry service. Within two weeks, Hunter received additional men from other recruit commands, and on September 15, he reorganized his battalion as a regiment at Camp Massard. The regiment became part of Brigadier General Mosby M. Parsons's Missouri infantry brigade.

The regiment initially engaged in combat at Prairie Grove on December 7. While Parsons's brigade first deployed to protect the army from an attack from Cane Hill, it moved forward to the main battle line in the afternoon. Subsequently, the brigade countercharged an advancing Union battle line and drove it considerably until the attack faltered because of stiff resistance, including heavy artillery fire. The Confederates then returned to their original position and prepared a defensive line. Hunter's regiment suffered casualties of 19 killed or mortally wounded and 32 wounded in the fight. General Hindman, the Confederate commander, decided to withdraw from the field at midnight because of shortages in ammunition and other supplies. The army retreated to near Van Buren; after a short stay, it moved to Little Rock. Parsons's brigade established winter quarters at Little Rock and remained there until the following spring. Colonel Hunter resigned his commission in early February; Simon P. Burns subsequently replaced Hunter as regimental commander. On May 3, 1863, by Special Order No. 30, Major General Sterling Price, division commander, designated Burns's regiment as the 8th Infantry.

The regiment moved with the army to Helena in late June, as the Confederates planned to capture the garrison and relieve Federal pressure on Vicksburg. In the attack on Helena early on July 4, Parsons's brigade assaulted a fortification atop Graveyard Hill. The charging Missourians, along with an Arkansas brigade, captured the Federal position after hard fighting and then proceeded into Helena proper. Since the brigades on their flanks made no forward progress, Parsons's men found themselves subjected to heavy fire to their front and on both flanks. The Missourians could not long withstand the punishing fire and withdrew to Graveyard Hill. The retreat continued as the Confederate commander, Lieutenant General Theophilus Holmes, called off the fight. Burns's regiment lost 15 killed, 78 wounded, and 66 missing in the battle. The army retreated to Des Arc on the White River and subsequently to Little Rock, where the brigade built defensive works north of the Arkansas River.

In August, a Union army commanded by Major General Frederick Steele threatened the capital city. Although the infantry brigades manned the fortifications in anticipation of battle, Steele sidestepped their position. Parsons's brigade evacuated Little Rock without a fight on September 10 and retreated south to Arkadelphia. In October, the brigade established winter quarters near Camden and later relocated to Spring Hill in January 1864. Special Order No. 177, Headquarters, Price's Division, renumbered Burns's unit as the 11th Regiment on December 15. General Parsons organized a small division consisting of his brigade and another commanded by Colonel John B. Clark Jr. on March 24, 1864. The 11th Regiment became part of the 2nd brigade, under Colonel Burns, while Lieutenant Colonel Thomas H. Murray assumed command of the regiment.

By early April, Major General Richard Taylor contended with a large Union army determined to take Shreveport, Louisiana, and then move into Texas as part of the Red River Campaign. Parsons's division marched to reinforce Taylor's army. After a forced march, the Missouri division reached Taylor near Pleasant Hill, Louisiana, on April 9. In the battle that followed, Parsons's division fought on the right of the Confederate line, with Burns's brigade deployed to the left of Clark's. The Missourians' attack shattered a Union brigade, resulting in the capture of artillery and many prisoners. Just when it seemed the day was won, part of a Federal infantry corps smashed into Parsons's right flank and drove the Missourians from the field in disorder. Before the division could be reformed, the Federals had escaped to the south. The 11th Regiment counted losses of 10 killed or mortally wounded and 39 other wounded at Pleasant Hill.

After a respite of five days, the regiment marched with Parsons's division to Camden, Arkansas, then occupied by General Frederick Steele's Federal army. Outnumbered and bereft of provisions, Steele evacuated

Camden on April 27, retreating north toward Little Rock. Twenty-four hours later, the rebels pursued and finally overtook the Federals astraddle the Saline River at Jenkins's Ferry on April 30. The Missourians moved into the flooded river bottom to reinforce an Arkansas division, with Burns's brigade, including the 11th Infantry, eventually deployed on the left of Clark's brigade. Aligned on the right of the Arkansans, Burns's men pushed forward, sometimes up to their knees in water, for a quarter of a mile in heavy fighting. The brigade then fell back to allow Major General John G. Walker's Texas division to engage the enemy. Burns's brigade supported the Texans' right. Before the Missourians could renew the fight, the Federals crossed the Saline and escaped to Little Rock. The engagement resulted in casualties for the 11th Infantry of 2 killed and 15 wounded.

The regiment experienced no further serious combat after the battle at Jenkins's Ferry and camped in southern Arkansas and near Shreveport, Louisiana, for the balance of the war. The 11th Infantry was paroled at Shreveport on June 8, 1865, and then boarded a steamer for shipment to Missouri. During the war the regiment lost 69 men killed in battle and 164 to disease.

Bibliography

McNamara, J. H. "From Arkadelphia to Pleasant Hill: Parsons' Missouri Brigade in the Red River Campaign." *Daily Missouri Republican,* St. Louis, Missouri, November 6, 1886.

———. "Incidents in the Campaign against Steele in Arkansas." *Daily Missouri Republican,* St. Louis, Missouri, July 16, 1887.

———. "Missouri Confederates." *Daily Missouri Republican,* St. Louis, Missouri, December 5, 1885.

"[Moses] Roberts Diary." *Blue and Grey Chronicle* 6 (June 2002): 11–15; 7 (October 2003): 14–16; 7 (April 2004): 12–16; 7 (June 2004): 10–12; 9 (July 2006): 1–11.

Schnetzer, Wayne. *Men of the Eleventh: A Roster of the Eleventh Missouri Infantry, Confederate States of America.* Independence: Two Trails, 1999.

Simpson, T. W. "Three Years in the C.S.A." *Bolivar Herald,* Bolivar, Missouri, August 30, 1917.

12th Regiment (White's/Ponder's)
(Formerly the 9th Regiment)

Colonel: James Daniel White, reassigned to provost marshal duty August 28, 1863; Willis Miles Ponder, made prisoner April 18, 1864

Lieutenant Colonel: Willis Miles Ponder, promoted colonel August 28, 1863; Benjamin Holmes

Major: Thomas B. Sandford, killed July 4, 1863; Benjamin Holmes, promoted lieutenant colonel August 28, 1863; Richard C. Berryman

Companies and Commanders:

Company A: (Randolph County, Arkansas; Ripley) Willis Miles Ponder, promoted lieutenant colonel October 23, 1862; Richard B. Overton

Company B: (Iron, Madison, Washington) Henry Smith, deserted April 10, 1863; Benjamin Cross

Company C: (Iron, Madison, St. Francois, Washington) Richard C. Berryman, promoted major August 28, 1863; James A. Carson

Company D: (Reynolds, St. Francois, Washington) William H. Talbot, died March 12, 1863; Joseph C. Esselman

Company E: (Wayne) Benjamin Holmes, promoted major July 4, 1863; James B. McGhee

Company F: (Iron, Madison) Thomas D. Lashley, died January 20, 1863; Daniel T. Launius, killed July 4, 1863; John M. Peace

Company G: (Randolph County, Arkansas; Ripley) H. A. Canada, resigned before October 28, 1862; Dennis W. Reynolds

Company H: (Carter, Ripley, Wayne) Harrison Bennett, resigned June 8, 1863; Daniel P. Patterson

Company I: (Butler, Ripley, Wayne) S. M. Stephenson, resigned May 26, 1863; Carroll Epps

Company K: (Ripley) David Gardner, resigned before March 2, 1863; John E. Clark

The 12th Regiment is doubtless the most problematic of all Missouri Confederate infantry units to understand in terms of organizational chronology. The regiment initially organized near Couch's Spring, south of Alton, Oregon County, Missouri, in late August 1862. Recruited primarily in the eastern Ozarks of Missouri, many of the men had served in the 1st Division, Missouri State Guard. James D. White, a former battalion commander in that division, recruited the regiment by authority of Major General Thomas C. Hindman, district commander. After organizing the unit, White moved the command to Pocahontas, Arkansas. In mid-September, part of the regiment engaged in a skirmish north of Pocahontas, losing 2 killed and an unknown number wounded. The regiment marched toward Yellville, Arkansas, on October 10 and formally mustered into Confederate service at that locale on October 22. Shortly thereafter, the able-bodied of the regiment moved with other troops under Brigadier General Mosby M. Parsons to Camp Massard near Van Buren. In early November, the regiment joined Colonel Alexander E. Steen's brigade in General Parsons's division; thereafter, Parsons assumed command of the brigade, while Brigadier General Daniel M. Frost took over the division.

On November 30, the brigade moved northward with the army toward Prairie Grove. Lieutenant Colonel Willis M. Ponder commanded the regiment in lieu of Colonel White, who remained ill in camp. The regiment deployed on Reed's Mountain with the brigade on December 6 but did not take part in the skirmish that occurred there that evening. Parsons's brigade occupied a position on the Cane Hill road early on December 7 to protect the army from an attack from that direction, while the balance of the army met the enemy near Prairie Grove Presbyterian Church. The brigade moved forward to the battle line in mid-afternoon. As daylight faded, Major General James G. Blunt's Federal division moved on Parsons's position, only to be met by a countercharge led by Ponder's and Colonel Alexander E. Steen's regiments, and then by the entire brigade. The Missourians pushed the enemy back a considerable distance, but their attack stalled when confronted with Blunt's artillery. Parsons withdrew the brigade under heavy fire and established a defensive perimeter near his original line. General Hindman, commander of the Confederate forces, elected to abandon the field that night, as his men possessed insufficient ammunition to continue the fight. Ponder reported regimental losses of 15 killed or mortally wounded and another 57 wounded in the fight.

The Confederates retreated to Van Buren after Prairie Grove, but in early January 1863 they marched to Little Rock and established winter quarters. On May 3, Special Order No. 30, Headquarters, Price's Division, designated the unit as the 9th Infantry Regiment. Colonel White returned from sick leave and resumed command of the regiment on June 11. By early July, the army had moved to Helena, preparatory to attacking that garrison. The Confederates hoped the capture of Helena would draw enemy troops from the Vicksburg siege. When the assault began at daybreak on July 4, Parsons's brigade charged "Battery C," a fortification on Graveyard Hill. The Missourians quickly captured the position, and the raising of the flag of the 9th Infantry atop the hill first signaled the success. Driving on into Helena without flank support, Parsons's men received heavy artillery and rifle fire directed at their front and both flanks. Many retreated to Graveyard Hill; others surrendered to the Federals. The Confederates abandoned the attack after five hours of fighting and made their way back to Little Rock. White's regiment suffered 12 battle deaths, 50 wounded, and an unknown number missing at Helena. Following the battle, the regiment reported only 168 men present for duty. In August, the brigade constructed and occupied entrenchments north of the Arkansas River in anticipation of a Federal movement against the capital. Late that month, Colonel White left the regiment for a new assignment; Lieutenant Colonel Ponder succeeded to command. After the Federals bypassed the Confederate defensive positions in early September, the rebel infantry retreated to southern Arkansas without a fight, as Little Rock fell to the enemy.

On November 22, Special Order No. 215, Headquarters, District of Arkansas, consolidated the remnant of the 12th Regiment into two companies and temporarily attached them to a similarly depleted 10th Infantry Regiment. Whether this consolidation continued until the following September, when it became permanent, is impossible to determine from existing sources. What is certain is that the regiment continued to be reported as a separate unit whether or not it remained attached to the 10th Infantry. Special Order No. 177, Headquarters, Price's Division, renumbered the regiment as the 12th Infantry on December 15. When General Parsons joined his old brigade with that of Colonel John B. Clark Jr. to form a small division in late March 1864, Colonel Simon P. Burns's 2nd Brigade included the 12th Regiment as a separate entity.

In early April, the Missouri division marched to reinforce General Richard Taylor's army, then confronting a large enemy force south of Shreveport, Louisiana. The Missourians joined Taylor near Pleasant Hill on April 9. When Taylor deployed his army for battle later that day,

Parsons's division occupied the Confederate right. Parsons's men charged the enemy to initiate the battle; the Missourians swept the enemy from their front and moved into Pleasant Hill. At the moment victory seemed certain, a heavy fire enfiladed Parsons's right flank, causing the Missouri division to soon recoil in disorderly retreat. The Federal army abandoned the field and retreated southward before the Confederate troops could be rallied. Reported casualties for the 12th Regiment during the battle included 4 killed and 10 wounded.

After a few days' rest, the army moved north toward Camden, Arkansas, then held by Major General Frederick Steele's Federal army. Arriving at Camden shortly after Steele had evacuated the town, the Confederates marched in pursuit. On April 30, the rebels encountered Steele deployed in a strong position on the south bank of the flooded Saline River at Jenkins's Ferry. Parsons's two brigades soon entered the battle to assist an Arkansas division already engaged with the enemy. Burns's brigade, including the 12th Infantry, aligned on the right of the Arkansans and moved forward, slowly advancing across the submerged battlefield under withering fire. But the Confederates could not break the Union line, and soon Burns's brigade received orders to withdraw to permit a Texas division to take the front. Burns's men did so. Later, the Missourians moved to support the Texas brigades, but the Federals escaped over the Saline before the fighting could be renewed. The casualties of the 12th Regiment at Jenkins's Ferry totaled 1 killed and 2 wounded, both mortally.

After the battle at Jenkins's Ferry, the Missouri division moved to southern Arkansas and saw no further serious fighting. On September 29, the two companies of the 12th Infantry permanently consolidated with the 10th Infantry as companies F and G, and the 12th Infantry officially ceased to exist as a separate organization. The division eventually moved to camps near Shreveport, Louisiana. The consolidated 10th Infantry was paroled at Shreveport on June 8, 1865. The men traveled to Missouri aboard the steamer *E. H. Fairchild*. Incomplete records indicate that during its service the 12th Regiment suffered 36 battle deaths and 101 deaths due to disease, while Federals authorities executed 3 others.

BIBLIOGRAPHY

Banasik, Michael, ed. *Serving with Honor: The Diary of Captain Eathan Allen Pinnell of the Eighth Missouri Infantry Regiment (Confederate)*. Iowa City: Camp Pope Bookshop, 1999.

Confederate Organizations, Officers and Posts, 1861–1865, Missouri Units.
Springfield: Ozarks Genealogical Society, 1988.

Lackey, W. S. C. "Sergeant Ancil Matthews in the Civil War." Unpublished
typescript. Missouri State Archives, Jefferson City, Missouri.

"Last Roll Call—Another Civil War Veteran Gone." *Prospect-News,*
Doniphan, Missouri, August 30, 1900.

McNamara, J. H. "From Arkadelphia to Pleasant Hill: Parsons' Missouri
Brigade in the Red River Campaign." *Daily Missouri Republican,* St.
Louis, Missouri, November 6, 1886.

————. "Missouri Confederates." *Daily Missouri Republican,* St. Louis,
Missouri, December 5, 1885.

16th Regiment (Jackman's/Caldwell's/Lewis's/Cumming's) (Formerly the 7th Regiment)

Colonel: Sidney Drake Jackman, resignation accepted October 25,
1862; Josiah Hatcher Caldwell, resigned March 24, 1863; Levin
Major Lewis, assigned to duty as brigadier general by General
Edmund Kirby Smith May 16, 1865; Pleasant W. H. Cumming

Lieutenant Colonel: Levin Major Lewis, promoted colonel
March 24, 1863; Pleasant W. H. Cumming, promoted to colonel
ca. May 16, 1865

Major: Pleasant W. H. Cumming, promoted lieutenant colonel
March 24, 1863; Jesse P. Herrell, resigned before February 17, 1865;
John G. Stemmons

Companies and Commanders:

Company A: (Clay, Jackson, Johnson, Monroe) Henry Y. C.
Brooking

Company B: (Benton, St. Clair) Benjamin N. Cocke

Company C: (Bates, Boone, Callaway, Johnson) Jesse P. Herrell,
promoted to major on March 24, 1863; George W. Perry, killed
July 4, 1863; Samuel Smith

Company D: (Johnson) David M. Raker

Company E: (Newton) James W. Bullard, resigned November 17,
1862; Stephen W. Warner

Company F: (Henry, Johnson) James H. Gillett, resigned May 28, 1863; John E. Strong

Company G: (Dade) John G. Stemmons, promoted major February 17, 1865

Company H: (McDonald) D. T. Lauderdale, died March 7, 1863; Pleasant McGhee

Company I: (Bates, Henry) Ephraim Allison, resigned April 17, 1863; James C. Martin

Company K: (Henry) Frederick P. Bronaugh

In the summer of 1862, Jeremiah V. Cockrell and Sidney D. Jackman began recruiting a cavalry regiment from among Missouri exiles in northwest Arkansas. Unable to enlist sufficient men to complete the regiment, they received permission to undertake a recruiting expedition into western Missouri. Other recruiters joined the expedition and marched for Missouri on August 1. Over the next several days, large numbers of volunteers joined the Missourians' ranks. The recruit commanders established a camp in Jackson County near Lone Jack on August 15. Learning that a Union cavalry command had occupied the village, the Confederates concluded to attack the next day. Jackman led the men recruited for Cockrell's regiment, as the latter visited his home. The Confederates formed a battle line west of Lone Jack, with Jackman's men holding the center, and attacked Lone Jack early in the morning. After a severe fight that lasted several hours, the outnumbered enemy retreated to Lexington. Jackman's command incurred known losses of 22 killed, 21 wounded, and 3 missing. Faced with a growing concentration of Union forces in the area, the Confederates retreated to Arkansas, barely ahead of the enemy.

Major General Thomas C. Hindman, district commander, dismounted most of the units after their arrival in Arkansas. This regiment mustered into Confederate service on August 31, near Fayetteville, under the command of Jackman, for Cockrell returned to Missouri to recruit cavalry. Subsequently, Hindman likewise accepted Jackman's resignation on October 25 to allow him to recruit in Missouri; Josiah H. Caldwell succeeded to regimental command. After a period of preparation for combat, the regiment marched to attack the enemy in early December as part of Brigadier General Mosby M. Parsons's Missouri infantry brigade. On the evening of December 6, Parsons's brigade skirmished with enemy scouts on Reed's Mountain, but Caldwell's men did not participate in the action. General Hindman's I Corps engaged the Federals at Prairie Grove the following day. Although Parsons's brigade initially served in reserve to prevent a flank or rear attack, it moved to the front later in the day. After a late arrival on the field, Major General James G. Blunt's Federal division attacked the left of the Confederate line. Parsons countercharged the advancing Federals with his entire brigade, with Caldwell's regiment in the left center of the Missouri formation. Parsons's men shoved the enemy back about three hundred yards, but the Missourians' charge faltered when they encountered heavy enemy artillery fire. Parsons withdrew his men back to his original position and established a defensive line. The attack cost Caldwell's regiment 11 killed or mortally wounded and 37 wounded. Hindman, his army low on ammunition and other supplies, withdrew from the field at midnight. The army retreated to Van Buren, where it remained until early January 1863; it then marched to Little Rock and established winter quarters.

Caldwell's regiment suffered severely from disease over the next few months, with over 100 men dying in camp and hospitals. Colonel Caldwell resigned his commission March 23; Levin M. Lewis replaced him in command of the regiment. Major General Sterling Price, division commander, designated the regiment as the 7th Infantry on May 3, in Special Order No. 30. In late June, the army moved toward Helena with the intention of capturing the river town and relieving Federal pressure on Vicksburg. After a march slowed by high water, the Confederates attacked the Helena garrison early on July 4. Parsons's brigade quickly took their objective atop Graveyard Hill and proceeded into the town proper. But without adequate support, the Missourians soon experienced heavy enemy fire on their front and flanks. Unable to withstand the Federal firepower, Parsons's men attempted to withdraw, but many could not and became prisoners. Those that escaped joined the army in retreat after five hours of intense combat. The casualties for Lewis's regiment at Helena tallied 34 killed or mortally wounded, 106 wounded, and 54 missing, leaving only 325 effective men present for duty after the battle. The prisoners included a wounded Colonel Lewis; Lieutenant Colonel Pleasant W. H. Cumming assumed temporary regimental command.

Returning to Little Rock, the regiment assisted in building defensive positions north of the state capital as Major General Frederick Steele's

Federal army threatened the city in August. Although the infantry expected to fight Steele's army, he sidestepped their position and attacked Little Rock from the southeast. Parsons's brigade left their entrenchments on September 10 and retreated into southern Arkansas near Arkadelphia. On December 15, Special Order 177, Headquarters, Price's Division, redesignated the regiment as the 16th Infantry. The regiment quartered in southern Arkansas at various camps during the winter months.

In late March 1864, General Parsons organized a Missouri division composed of his brigade, under Colonel Simon P. Burns, and another commanded by Colonel John B. Clark Jr. The 16th Infantry joined the 2nd brigade under Colonel Burns. The division moved to reinforce Major General Richard Taylor in early April as he attempted to stop the advance of Major General Nathaniel Banks's Federal army toward Shreveport during the Red River Campaign. The division joined Taylor's army near Pleasant Hill on April 9, after a forced march. In the afternoon the division deployed for battle, with Burns's brigade on the left of Clark's. Parsons ordered his brigades forward, and the Missourians' advance overran a Union brigade and continued on into the village of Pleasant Hill. Suddenly, a Federal flank attack on the division's right overpowered the Missourians, who soon retreated in disorder. Before Parsons and his officers could rally the men, the Union army had abandoned the field. The 16th Regiment's battle losses amounted to 1 killed and 24 wounded.

After a brief rest, Parsons's division marched north toward Camden, Arkansas, then occupied by Federal army of General Frederick Steele. Steele abandoned Camden just before the Confederates reached the town and rapidly retreated toward Little Rock. The Confederates doggedly pursued Steele's army through driving rainstorms and finally overtook the Federals at Jenkins's Ferry on the Saline River. On April 30, Parsons's division moved to reinforce an Arkansas division already engaged with the enemy. Burns's brigade, which included the 16th Infantry, deployed on the left of Clark's brigade and moved forward. Burns aligned his brigade on the right of the Arkansans, and the Confederates sloshed forward a quarter mile across the flooded battlefield in heavy fighting. Burns then withdrew his brigade to make way for a Texas division to move forward. The brigade then moved back up to support the Texans' right, but before the brigade could reengage, Steele's army crossed the Saline on a pontoon bridge, ending the battle. The engagement cost the 16th Infantry 10 killed and 20 wounded.

The 16th Infantry experienced no other serious combat after the battle at Jenkins's Ferry. The regiment camped in southern Arkansas and near Shreveport, Louisiana, for the balance of the war. Colonel Lewis returned to the regiment from captivity in the spring of 1865. On May 16, General E. Kirby Smith, Trans-Mississippi Department commander, assigned Lewis to duty as a brigadier general. Lieutenant Colonel Cumming received promotion to colonel and commanded the 16th Infantry until the war ended. Paroled at Shreveport on June 8, 1865, the men of the regiment then boarded a steamer for the trip home to Missouri. The 16th Infantry suffered more fatalities during the war than any other Missouri Confederate unit. The losses included 83 men killed or mortally wounded in battle, 253 lost to disease, 2 executed for desertion, and 3 executed by Union authorities.

BIBLIOGRAPHY

Carlock, L. L. H. "A Bit of Civil War History." *Greenfield Vedette,* Greenfield, Missouri, March 28, 1918.

Cassell, T. W. "Gen. Levin M. Lewis." *Confederate Veteran* 15 (1907): 346–47.

The Civil War Diaries of Irvin Parker and C. B. Lotspeich. Compiled by Robert E. Kennedy and Robert Lotspeich. Pleasant Hill: Pleasant Hill Historical Society, 2001.

McNamara, J. H. "From Arkadelphia to Pleasant Hill: Parsons's Missouri Brigade in the Red River Campaign." *Daily Missouri Republican,* St. Louis, Missouri, November 6, 1886.

———. "Incidents in the Campaign against Steele in Arkansas." *Daily Missouri Republican,* St. Louis, Missouri, July 16, 1887.

———. "Missouri Confederates." *Daily Missouri Republican,* St. Louis, Missouri, December 5, 1885.

Norton, Richard L., ed. *Behind Enemy Lines: The Memoirs and Writings of Brigadier General Sidney Drake Jackman.* Springfield: Oak Hills, 1997.

B. Battalions

Bevier's Battalion (Possibly known as the 3rd Battalion)

Major: Robert S. Bevier

Companies and Commanders

Company A: (Marion) Carter M. Smith, deserted February 9, 1862; Mark Trumper

Company B: (Franklin) James W. Fair

Company C: (Linn, St. Louis) Patrick Caniff

Company D: (Johnson) Charles H. Thomas

Robert S. Bevier, a former regimental commander in the Missouri State Guard, organized this battalion at Springfield, Missouri, on January 28, 1862. Recruited primarily from veterans of the Guard, soldiers from the 2nd, 8th, and 9th Divisions quickly filled the company rosters. After the battalion formed, it joined the 2nd Missouri Brigade under the command of Brigadier General William Y. Slack. The battalion retreated from Springfield to northwest Arkansas with General Sterling Price's troops in mid-February, when the Missourians abandoned the town in the wake of a threatening Federal advance. When Major General Earl Van Dorn led the Army of the West to Pea Ridge, Arkansas, to attack a Federal army in early March, Bevier's battalion marched northward with the 2nd Missouri Brigade. On March 7, the battalion deployed with the 2nd brigade on the right of the Confederate line near Elkhorn Tavern, where it quickly came under intense enemy fire. The battalion assisted in silencing the enemy and subsequently helped repel Federal cavalry that threatened the brigade's right flank. Later in the day, the battalion joined in a general Confederate advance that drove the Federals back a considerable distance before the attack broke off. Although exposed to heavy artillery fire, the battalion was not engaged on the day following, as the Confederates withdrew from the field before Bevier's unit could close with the enemy. The battalion retreated with the army to a camp at Frog Bayou near Van Buren. Losses for the battalion in the fight amounted to 1 killed, 9 wounded, and 5 missing.

On March 23, while still encamped at Frog Bayou, the battalion consolidated with five companies formerly of Rosser's Battalion to create a new battalion commanded by Lieutenant Colonel James McCown. The reason for the companies leaving Rosser's outfit is not known. See the entry for McCown's Battalion for the further service of the soldiers of this battalion.

BIBLIOGRAPHY

Bevier, Robert S. *History of the First and Second Missouri Confederate Brigades, 1861–1865*. St. Louis: Bryan, Brand & Co., 1879.

William A. Ruyle Letter. Western Historical Manuscript Collection, University of Missouri–Rolla, Rolla, Missouri.

Clark's Battalion

Major: John Bullock Clark Jr.

Company A: (Boone, Howard) Stephen Cooper

Company B: (Howard) John M. Hickey

This battalion may have never completed its organization. The commander, John B. Clark Jr., led the 3rd Division of the Missouri State Guard at the battle of Pea Ridge in March 1862 and then crossed the Mississippi River with the Army of the West in April. It appears that Clark soon began recruiting a unit for Confederate service from among the state troops in his division. Apparently only two companies, containing some 120 men, had mustered into the battalion by May 15, 1862. The Missouri Confederate units reorganized about that time under the Conscription Act at Corinth, Mississippi. Clark's two companies soon merged into Lieutenant Colonel Eugene Erwin's battalion, which organized on or about May 16, thus ending the very brief existence of this unit. Clark subsequently returned to the Trans-Mississippi Department, where he eventually recruited a regiment for service in that theater. See the entry for Erwin's Battalion for the further service of the men of this battalion.

BIBLIOGRAPHY

Confederate Organizations, Officers and Posts, 1861–1865, Missouri Units. Springfield: Ozarks Genealogical Society, 1998.

Erwin's Battalion (Also known as the 3rd or 5th Battalion)

Lieutenant Colonel: Andrew Eugene Erwin

Major: Joseph P. Vaughn

Companies and Commanders

Company A: (Cass, Jackson) Jeremiah V. Cockrell, dropped May 17, 1862; Jeptha Duncan

Company B: (Jackson, Johnson, Platte) Francis M. McKinney

Company C: (Jackson, Lafayette) Samuel F. Taylor

Company D: (Cass, St. Clair) David P. Fleming, dropped May 17, 1862; John M. Weidemeyer

Company E: (Boone, Howard) Stephen Cooper

Company F: (Howard) John M. Hickey

Company G (1st): (Clay, Lafayette) Jesse L. Price (Added to the battalion in June, this company transferred to the 3rd Infantry Regiment ca. August 9, 1862)

Company G (2nd): (Clay, Johnson, Platte) John B. Clark (Added to the battalion to replace Price's company as G, ca. August 9, 1862)

This battalion initially organized at Corinth, Mississippi, on or about May 16, 1862, by the addition of two companies (E, F) formerly commanded by Major John B. Clark Jr. to the four remaining companies in Lieutenant Colonel Thomas H. Rosser's battalion, and the election of new field officers. Most men of Cooper and Hickey's companies served in the 3rd Division, Missouri State Guard, and had fought at the battle of Pea Ridge, Arkansas, the previous March. On May 5, the companies of Rosser's old battalion, which had arrived in Mississippi on April 28, mustered 281 men present, but it is likely that the additional two companies increased the enrollment to some 400. The newly formed battalion remained at Corinth in garrison until the Confederates abandoned that post to the enemy in late May. The battalion performed routine military tasks, including drill and guard duty, at different camps in northern Mississippi for the next three months. While it was encamped at Guntown during the summer months, the local ladies presented the battalion with a Van Dorn pattern battle flag that subsequently became the regimental banner of the 6th

Missouri Infantry Regiment. Captain Jesse L. Price's company joined the battalion sometime in June, and when it subsequently transferred to the 3rd Infantry Regiment around August 9, Captain John B. Clark's company replaced it. At Guntown, on August 26, three additional companies joined the battalion to form a regiment commanded by Colonel Erwin, designated the 6th Infantry. See the entry for the 6th Infantry Regiment for the further service of the men of this battalion.

BIBLIOGRAPHY

Curran, Thomas F. "'On the Road to Dixie': A Missouri Confederate's Review of the Civil War at Its Midpoint." *Missouri Historical Review* 91(January 2002): 69–92.

Franklin, Ann York. *The Civil War Journal of Lt. George R. Elliott, 2nd & 6th Missouri Infantry, Company F, 1862–1864.* Louisville: Privately printed, 1997.

John M. Leach Diary. Typescript. Western Historical Manuscript Collection, University of Missouri–Rolla, Rolla, Missouri.

Frazier's Battalion (Also known as 1st Battalion)

Major: W. L. H. Frazier

Companies and Commanders:

Company A: (Barry, Lawrence, McDonald, Newton) Amry M. Curry

Company B: (McDonald, Newton) John Carroll

Company C: (Barry) James Montgomery

This short-lived unit apparently organized, without proper legal authority, when three independent companies of mostly unarmed recruits united to form the battalion about October 6, 1862, at Elm Springs, Arkansas. The companies, containing 240 men in the aggregate, had been recruited in southwest Missouri and then moved into Arkansas to join the Confederates organizing there. After drilling for a few weeks at Elm Springs, the battalion marched on or about October 15 to a camp near Clarksville where it received arms and accoutrements; it later moved on to Camp Massard, ten miles south of Van Buren, to join other newly formed Missouri units. At Camp Massard, Brigadier General Mosby M. Parsons labored to fully organize and prepare the units that constituted his Missouri infantry brigade for combat. After reaching Parsons's camp, Frazier's battalion combined with the six companies of the 7th Infantry Battalion (Mitchell's) on November 29, 1862, to create Mitchell's Regiment, subsequently the 8th Infantry Regiment. Frazier's companies became companies G, H, and I of the consolidated unit under the original officers. Notably, the consolidation of Frazier's and Mitchell's battalions had not been officially authorized, and the resultant organization did not possess the ten companies required by Confederate law to be a regiment. Frazier's battalion had no known combat record before it consolidated with the 7th Battalion. See the entry for the 8th Infantry Regiment for the further service of the men of this battalion.

BIBLIOGRAPHY

Banasik, Michael, ed. *Serving with Honor: The Diary of Captain Eathan Allen Pinnell of the Eighth Missouri Infantry Regiment (Confederate)*. Iowa City: Camp Pope Bookshop, 1999.

Curry, Ray Cornelius, and Charles Ray Richardson, eds. *Civil War Memories of A. M. Curry*. Abilene: Hardin-Simmons University Press, 1988.

Hedgpeth's Battalion (Also known as 1st Battalion)

Major: Isaac Newton Hedgpeth

Companies and Commanders:

Company A: (Bollinger, Stoddard) Jason H. Hunter

Company B: (Dunklin, Stoddard) William L. Watkins, disposition unknown; David Y. Pankey

Company C: (Cape Girardeau, Ripley, Wayne; State of Arkansas) Isaac Newton Hedgpeth, promoted major July 10, 1862; Alvah G. Kelsey

Company D: (Cape Girardeau, Stoddard) Samuel S. Harris

Company E: (Cape Girardeau, Scott) John D. Parsons

The companies of this battalion underwent several organizational changes in the summer of 1862. In April, five infantry and three artillery companies, all recruited from the 1st Division, Missouri State Guard, accompanied Brigadier General M. Jeff Thompson to Memphis, Tennessee. The companies performed duty at Forts Pickering and Pillow, Tennessee, beginning in late April, and served as "marines" aboard the Confederate River Defense Fleet at the engagement at Plum Point Bend on May 10, 1862, losing 2 killed and 8 wounded in the fight. Because of a decrease in numbers, the five infantry companies consolidated into three (A–C) on May 30. General Thompson intended that all of the companies would again sail with the Confederate River Defense Fleet at Memphis on June 6, 1862, but an unexpected attack by the Federal fleet prompted the boats to depart the wharf before the troops could board. The units moved to Mississippi before Memphis fell to the Federals and performed routine guard and outpost duty. On July 2, the batteries of Samuel S. Harris and John D. Parsons, neither of which possessed artillery pieces, joined the three infantry companies to form this battalion. After organization, the five companies carried about 300 men present on the rolls. Thereafter, on July 10, the battalion consolidated with the 1st Confederate Infantry Battalion to create a regiment commanded by Colonel George H. Forney and known as the 1st Confederate Infantry Regiment. Although the regiment made marches in anticipation of battle, the opportunity for combat always proved elusive.

The assignment of the Missourians to the 1st Confederate Infantry Regiment soon ended, for Special Order No. 17, dated August 25, 1862, Headquarters, District of Tennessee, detached the five companies from the regiment, assigned them to Brigadier General Martin E. Green's infantry brigade, and ordered them to report to Brigadier General Henry Little at Guntown, Mississippi, for further orders. At Guntown the companies received still another assignment, with Companies A and B consolidating to form Company K, 5th Missouri Infantry Regiment, while Companies D (after merger with Robert McDonald's artillery company), E, and C became companies D, I, and K, respectively, of the 6th Missouri Infantry Regiment. The companies served with these regiments as infantry for the balance of the war. See the separate entries for the 5th and 6th Infantry Regiments for the further service of the soldiers of this battalion.

BIBLIOGRAPHY

Confederate Organizations, Officers and Posts, 1861–1865, Missouri Units.
Springfield: Ozarks Genealogical Society, 1998.

McGhee, James E., ed. *General M. Jeff Thompson's Letter Book, July 1861–June 1862*. Independence: Two Trails, 2004.

Stanton, Donal J., Goodwin F. Berquist, and Paul C. Bower, eds. *The Civil War Reminiscences of General M. Jeff Thompson*. Dayton: Morningside Press, 1988.

Hughes's Battalion (Also known as 2nd Battalion)

Major: John Taylor Hughes

Companies and Commanders:

Company A: (Clay, Lafayette) Jesse L. Price

Company B: (Clay, Johnson, Platte) Joseph P. Carr, resigned March 20, 1862; John B. Clark

Company C: Unknown

This battalion consisted of remnants of the command organized by John T. Hughes, a former regimental commander in the Missouri State Guard, at Springfield, Missouri, in January 1862. The company rosters included many soldiers recruited from the 5th and 8th Divisions of the Missouri State Guard. Hughes's command constituted a part of Brigadier General William Y. Slack's 2nd Missouri Brigade and fought at Pea Ridge, Arkansas, on March 7–8, 1862. Hughes led both Confederate and Missouri State Guard companies on March 7, which deployed on the right of the 2nd brigade, occupying the extreme right of the Confederate line. Shortly after taking position, the command received heavy fire but quickly silenced it. Hughes's men likewise helped scatter Union cavalry seeking to outflank their position. Later in the day, the unit participated in a general advance by the rebel forces that drove the Federals back a considerable distance. In the advance, Hughes's troops captured an enemy flag. Less active on March 8, Hughes's men retreated with the army when the Federals won the day with a determined artillery and infantry attack. Hughes reported casualties of 1 killed, 3 wounded, and 4 missing for the two days of combat, but the losses were likely greater.

The command retreated after the battle to Frog Bayou near Van Buren, Arkansas. While encamped at Frog Bayou, Hughes's command decreased considerably in numbers, likely due to the organization of new Confederate units. Hughes's troops proceeded with the Army of the West to Memphis, Tennessee, in April and later that month moved to Corinth, Mississippi. By May 15, Hughes commanded a battalion of only three companies, mustering about 150 soldiers present for duty. Hughes advised Major General Sterling Price on that date that his men desired to maintain their separate organization rather than consolidate with another unit. But consolidation could not be avoided, and the battalion organization soon ended. From the few records available, it appears that the battalion disbanded sometime in June 1862. The companies commanded by Price and Clark eventually merged into Lieutenant Colonel Eugene Erwin's battalion, while the disposition of the third company is unknown. See the entry for Erwin's battalion for the further service of the men of this unit.

BIBLIOGRAPHY

Confederate Organizations, Officers and Posts, 1861–1865, Missouri Units. Springfield: Ozarks Genealogical Society, 1988.

Duncan, Charles V., Jr. *John T. Hughes—From His Pen.* Modesto: Privately printed, 1991.

Johnson's Battalion (Also known as 1st Battalion)

Major: Waldo Porter Johnson

Companies and Commanders:

Company A: (Cass) John H. Britts, dropped April 4, 1862; Philip W. Fulkerson

Company B (1st): (Clay, Platte) Joseph P. Carr (Reassigned to Hughes's Battalion before March 7, 1862)

Company B (2nd): (Henry, Laclede) Norval Spangler (Added to the battalion ca. March 25, 1862, after consolidating with Captain Stephen W. Wood's company)

Company C: (Christian) Henderson P. Greene

Company D: (Dallas) Richard C. Newport

This battalion mustered into Confederate service with four companies (A, B [1st], C, D) around March 3, 1862, at the Missouri Confederate encampment at Cove Creek, Arkansas. Most recruits had previously served in the 8th Division, Missouri State Guard. It became part of the 3rd Missouri Brigade, commanded by Colonel Colton Greene. On March 7, the first day of the battle of Pea Ridge, the brigade deployed between the 1st Missouri Brigade and Colonel Thomas Rosser's battalion of the 2nd Missouri Brigade in support of the 3rd Missouri Light Artillery near Elkhorn Tavern. An artillery exchange opened the battle for the 3rd brigade, and the initial fire wounded several men, including Major Johnson. The brigade eventually charged forward as part of a general movement and pressed the Union line back, capturing the enemy's camp. A fight then developed in an open field, and the 3rd brigade suffered numerous casualties. With the coming of darkness, the brigade, including Johnson's battalion, bivouacked in the captured enemy encampment. The following morning, the Federals launched a massive artillery barrage and moved a large body of infantry toward the Confederate line. The 3rd brigade fought furiously for a while, but the enemy infantry and artillery fire broke the Confederate line. Soon thereafter, the brigade abandoned its position and retreated. One of the last units to leave the field, the brigade marched with the army in retreat to Frog Bayou near Van Buren, Arkansas. The known losses of the battalion in the battle amounted to 7 killed or mortally wounded, 15 wounded, and 9 missing.

The battalion transferred to the artillery brigade of the Army of the West on March 20. About March 25, Captain Norval Spangler's company, which had fought at Pea Ridge with troops under Brigadier Daniel M. Frost, joined the battalion. Johnson's Battalion transferred to the Cis-Mississippi with the army in April. On April 28, the battalion consolidated with Major Archibald MacFarlane's battalion and Captain Jeptha Feagan's Missouri State Guard company to form the 4th Infantry Regiment at Memphis, Tennessee. See the entry for the 4th Infantry Regiment for the further service of the men of this battalion.

BIBLIOGRAPHY

Jines, Billie, ed. "Civil War Diary of Henderson P. Greene." *Flashback* 17 (1967): 15–18.

"Major John H. Britts." *Confederate Veteran* 18 (January 1910): 36.

"Waldo Porter Johnson." In *Biographical Directory of the American Congress, 1774–1949*, 1380–81. Washington: Government Printing Office, 1950.

MacFarlane's Battalion

Major: Archibald A. MacFarlane

Companies and Commanders

Company A: (Howell) William Howard

Company B: (Fulton County, State of Arkansas; Ozark)
Daniel Hays

Company C: (Oregon) James Posey Woodside

Company D: (Oregon, Reynolds) William A. Farris

This battalion, recruited in counties along the southern Missouri border beginning in early February 1862, included many veterans of the 1st and 2nd Infantry Regiments, 7th Division, Missouri State Guard, in its ranks. The battalion likely organized at the end of that month at Mammoth Spring, Fulton County, Arkansas, as MacFarlane had three companies mustered into service there by February 28. In March, MacFarlane remained at Mammoth Spring, cooperating with William O. Coleman in further recruitment along the Arkansas-Missouri line. By the middle of the month, MacFarlane and Coleman established a rendezvous for recruits on the Spring River near Mammoth Spring. About 600 soldiers had gathered near the Spring River Mill on March 13, when Federal cavalry attacked their encampment. A prolonged fight, known as the battle of South Fork, occurred after the Confederates established a defensive perimeter in a nearby swamp. Unwilling to penetrate too far into the marshes, the Federals, after maneuvering and fighting awhile, finally withdrew with 3 killed and 12 wounded. The Federal commander, who made the only report of the engagement, estimated rebel losses at about 100 in killed, wounded, and prisoners, clearly an exaggeration. The known casualties of MacFarlane's three companies tallied 5 killed, 8 wounded, and 4 taken prisoner.

Pursuant to orders issued on April 8, MacFarlane moved his battalion to Des Arc, Arkansas, where the troops boarded boats and sailed to Memphis, Tennessee, to join other Missouri units in Major General Earl Van Dorn's Army of the West. Several men deserted before reaching Des Arc, and some stragglers remained in Arkansas. Captain William Farris's company joined the battalion about April 26 at Memphis. On April 28, the day many troops moved to Corinth, Mississippi, the battalion consolidated with Major Waldo P. Johnson's battalion and Captain Jeptha D. Feagan's Missouri State Guard company to form the 4th Missouri Infantry Regiment. See the entry for the 4th Infantry Regiment for the further service of the men of this battalion.

BIBLIOGRAPHY

McGhee, James E., ed. *General M. Jeff Thompson's Letter Book, July 1861–June 1862.* Independence: Two Trails, 2004.

Monks, William. *A History of Southern Missouri and Northern Arkansas, Being an Account of the Early Settlements, the Civil War, the Ku-Klux, and Times of Peace,* edited by John F. Bradbury Jr. and Lou Wehmer. Fayetteville: University of Arkansas Press, 2003.

McCown's Battalion (Also known as 2nd or 4th Battalion)

Lieutenant Colonel: James C. McCown
Major: Robert S. Bevier

Companies and Commanders:

Company A: (Johnson) Owen A. Waddell

Company B: (Macon, Marion) Mark Trumper

Company C: (Polk) Asbury C. Bradford

Company D: (Polk) Alexander C. Lemmon

Company E: (Franklin, Gasconade) James W. Fair

Company F: (Linn, St. Louis) Patrick Caniff

Company G: (Henry) Stephen D. Coale

Company H: (Johnson) Charles H. Thomas

Company I: (Johnson, Macon) Ben Eli Guthrie

This battalion organized in a camp at Frog Bayou near Van Buren, Arkansas, on March 23, 1862, by consolidating the four companies of Major Robert S. Bevier's battalion with five companies that had previously served in Lieutenant Colonel Thomas H. Rosser's battalion. The reason the companies withdrew from Rosser's battalion is not recorded. All of the companies had fought at the battle of Pea Ridge, Arkansas, on March 7–8. After a relatively brief period of rest, the new battalion departed Frog Bayou on March 24 and marched for Des Arc, Arkansas, with the Army of the West, which had been ordered to Memphis, Tennessee. After arrival at Des Arc on April 7, the battalion sailed on the steamer *Hartford City* the next day and reached Memphis four days later. Almost immediately, the battalion boarded a train for shipment to Corinth, Mississippi.

McCown's unit, mustering 476 present on the rolls on May 5, remained in the Corinth vicinity for a few weeks while the Confederate army gathered. On May 9, the battalion moved to Farmington with the 1st Missouri Brigade and engaged in skirmishing with the Federal advance, suffering only light casualties. The Confederates evacuated Corinth in late May as a large Federal army approached the rebel position and threatened to overwhelm the smaller Confederate force. For the balance of the summer the battalion occupied different camps in northern Mississippi, performing routine military duties and preparing for combat.

On September 1, at Saltillo, a company of southeast Missourians commanded by Captain David Y. Pankey, formerly part of Major Isaac N. Hedgpeth's battalion, joined McCown's battalion as a tenth company. With the addition of that company, McCown's battalion reorganized into the 5th Infantry Regiment, 1st Missouri Brigade. See the entry for the 5th Infantry Regiment for the further service of the men of this battalion.

Bibliography

William A. Ruyle Letter. Western Historical Manuscript Collection, University of Missouri–Rolla, Rolla, Missouri.

Tucker, Phillip Thomas. *Westerners in Gray: The Men and Missions of the Elite Fifth Missouri Infantry Regiment.* Jefferson: McFarland, 1995.

Mitchell's Battalion (Also known as 7th Battalion)

See the entry for the 8th Infantry Regiment (Mitchell's).

Musser's Battalion (Also known as 8th Battalion)

Lieutenant Colonel: Richard H. Musser
Major: Richard Gaines

Companies and Commanders:

Company A: (Adair, Buchanan, Linn) Joseph N. Miller
Company B: (Platte, St. Louis) Alexander D. Ellis
Company C: (Carroll, Lafayette, Saline) Franklin S. Robertson
Company D: (Cass, Saline, St. Clair) D. Herndon Lindsay
Company E: (Chariton, Montgomery, Pike) James C. Wallace
Company F: (Chariton, Miller) John Hanna
Company G: James Kelley

Lieutenant Colonel Waldo P. Johnson, 4th Missouri Infantry Regiment, assumed oversight of the recruitment of Missourians in the Trans-Mississippi in August 1862. He eventually established a camp on Horsehead Creek in Johnson County, Arkansas, where he organized Missourians into companies. On November 17, Johnson reported that he had organized three companies of 80 men each; he recommended Richard H. Musser be given command of the companies for the purpose of forming a battalion or regiment. Musser, formerly judge advocate of the 3rd Division, Missouri State Guard, fought with the Guard through Pea Ridge and then enlisted as a private in a Confederate infantry battalion under John B. Clark Jr. He served in Mississippi until he received orders to accompany Johnson on recruiting service. Action on Johnson's recommendation languished until after the battle of Prairie Grove, but on December 10, Musser took command of a battalion consisting of four companies. The battalion acquired another company on December 13 and then moved with the army toward Little Rock near the end of the month. En route, two additional companies joined the battalion on January 4, 1863; Musser's unit became part of a brigade commanded by Colonel John B. Clark Jr. the same day.

After arrival in Little Rock on January 18, the battalion camped near the city in different locations, including a short stint at the arsenal. The battalion boarded the steamer *Granite State* on February 7, bound for White's Bluff on the Arkansas River. After a brief stay at White's Bluff, the battalion reboarded the *Granite State* and moved downriver once again to a camp named Fort Pleasant located atop Day's Bluff. There, the battalion shared the mission of guarding the river approach to Little Rock with other units of artillery and infantry. Musser's men spent the next four months performing routine duty at Fort Pleasant. Company G apparently disbanded, or merged into one of the other companies, in late March, as it does not appear in the battalion records thereafter.

On June 12, the battalion joined a mixed command under Colonel John B. Clark Jr. that moved to Desha County for operations against Federal shipping on the Mississippi River. The Confederates attacked a convoy of three transports and a tin-clad gunboat at Cypress Bend on June 22, severely damaging the gunboat and disabling two transports. Musser's battalion, along with other units, fired on the troops aboard the boats and inflicted serious casualties. Six days later the command launched a similar attack on transports from Gaines Landing, with unknown results. Hearing that a large Federal column had landed nearby to engage them, the Confederates returned to Fort Pleasant.

In late July, the battalion learned that the Confederate War Department had designated the unit as the 8th Battalion. On July 27, the battalion broke camp and moved with the brigade to Little Rock to oppose the advance of Major General Frederick Steele's Federal army toward the capital city. Once at Little Rock, the battalion assisted in building entrenchments north of the Arkansas River, which the troops occupied until the Confederates abandoned the city on September 10 with little fighting. After leaving Little Rock, the army marched to near Arkadelphia and established camp. The 8th Battalion ceased to exist as a separate entity on September 30, when its six companies consolidated with four of the 9th Regiment (Clark's) to create a new organization, also known as the 9th Regiment, per the provisions of Special Order No. 171, Headquarters, District of Arkansas. See the 9th Regiment (Reorganized) for the further service of the men of this battalion.

BIBLIOGRAPHY

Edwin E. Harris Correspondence. Gilder Lehrman Institute of American History, New York Historical Society, New York, New York.

Gibson, J. W. *Recollections of a Pioneer.* Independence: Two Trails, 1999.

"Richard H. Musser." In *History of Howard and Chariton Counties, Missouri,* 761–64. St. Louis: National Historical Co., 1883.

Perkins's Battalion (Formerly Perkins's Cavalry Regiment)

Lieutenant Colonel: Caleb J. Perkins

Major: Thomas B. Patton

Companies and Commanders:

Company A: (Howard, Monroe, Randolph) Frank Davis

Company B: (Randolph) Nicholas G. Matlock

Company C: (Boone, Cooper) George W. Bryson

Company D: (Audrain, Callaway) Alexander Day

Company E: (Boone, Howard) Thomas W. Todd

Company F: (Boone, Howard) George W. Rowland

This battalion was organized January 22, 1865, near Fulton, Arkansas, by consolidating the companies of Perkins's Cavalry Regiment and was paroled at Shreveport, Louisiana, on June 5, 1865, as part of the 1st Brigade, Brigadier General Mosby M. Parsons's Missouri Infantry Division. See the entry for Perkins's Cavalry Regiment for the service of the men of this unit.

BIBLIOGRAPHY

Banasik, Michael, ed. *Serving with Honor: The Diary of Captain Eathan Allen Pinnell of the Eighth Missouri Infantry Regiment (Confederate).* Iowa City: Camp Pope Bookshop, 1999.

Confederate Organizations, Officers and Posts, 1861–1865, Missouri Units. Springfield: Ozarks Genealogical Society, 1988.

Rickman, Daniel T. "Events in the Trans-Mississippi Department." *Confederate Veteran* 21 (1913): 71.

Pindall's Sharpshooter Battalion (Also known as 9th Sharpshooter Battalion)

Lieutenant Colonel: Lebbeus A. Pindall

Major: Lebbeus A. Pindall, promoted lieutenant colonel January 20, 1865; Gabriel S. Kendrick

Companies and Commanders:

Company A: (Cole, Marion, Pike, Ralls, Scotland) William C. Blanton, died February 14, 1863; Ambrose M. Hayden

Company B: (Buchanan, Platte) John S. Phillips

Company C: (Cole, Cooper, Henry) Amos F. Cake, transferred to Searcy's Sharpshooter Battalion as major ca. January 21, 1865; David A. Lilly

Company D: (Adair, Knox, Lewis, Monroe, Schuyler) Gabriel S. Kendrick, promoted major January 20, 1865; Andrew Wilson

Company E: (Monroe) Elliott D. Major

Company F: (Howard) Samuel M. Morrison

The Confederate Congress authorized a battalion of sharpshooters for each infantry brigade on April 21, 1862. The statute provided that such battalions should have not less than three or more than six companies, armed with long-range rifles of the same type. Major General Thomas C. Hindman, commander of the I Corps in northwest Arkansas, issued a circular on November 25, 1862, directing his division commanders to comply with the law if practical. Perhaps anticipating the circular, Brigadier General Mosby M. Parsons, then commanding the 3rd division, organized a company of sharpshooters on November 11 for service with the Missouri brigade he subsequently commanded. Parsons mustered two additional companies by November 29 at Camp Massard near Fort Smith and formed a sharpshooter battalion led by Major Lebbeus A. Pindall.

Nothing indicates that the soldiers possessed any particular marksmanship abilities or met any other special qualifications for assignment to the battalion. In fact, the original company consisted of men assigned from a disbanded battery and a company of partisan rangers, while the other two filled their ranks from the infantry regiments of Parsons's brigade. The battalion joined Parsons's brigade, Brigadier General Daniel M. Frost's division, upon organization. Pindall's unit marched north with the brigade on November 29 in the initial stage of the Prairie Grove Campaign. Parsons's units, along with an Arkansas cavalry brigade, occupied Reed's Mountain to guard the Cane Hill road on December 6. Late that evening, the cavalry engaged an enemy patrol; Pindall's battalion reinforced the cavalry and helped disperse the Federals. Initially deployed to protect the army from a flank attack from Cane Hill the day following, Parsons's brigade moved to the front in the afternoon. Pindall's battalion deployed on the extreme right of Parsons's line as the brigade counterattacked a charging Federal force and sent the enemy in retreat. The Confederates returned to their original position after their attack stalled, with Pindall's sharp-shooters left to screen the brigade front. Without sufficient ammunition to resume the fight the next day, the Confederates retreated toward Van Buren at midnight. The sharpshooter battalion suffered 3 wounded in the battle.

Some three weeks later, the army moved to Little Rock and established winter quarters. The battalion remained at Little Rock in garrison until late May, when it marched north to Jacksonport, Arkansas. On June 7, while camped on the White River above Jacksonport, Captain Gabriel S. Kendrick's company, formerly part of the 2nd Northeast Missouri Cavalry Regiment, joined the battalion. In late June the battalion, as part of Mosby M. Parsons's brigade, advanced with Major General Sterling Price's infantry division toward Helena, Arkansas, on the Mississippi River. The army finally arrived within seven miles of Helena on July 3, where commanders made final plans to attack the enemy fortifications. At daylight on July 4, Pindall's battalion drove in the Federal pickets and led Parsons's brigade in the assault on "Battery C" atop Graveyard Hill. Once the brigade charged forward, it quickly overcame the Federal defenders and drove them into Helena. The brigade enjoyed only short-lived success, however, for it received no support on either flank and soon experienced the full brunt of Federal firepower. Parsons's men could not long endure the fire and hastily retreated. Pindall's sharpshooters suffered 14 killed or mortally wounded, 22 wounded, and 8 missing at Helena, and mustered only 190 men present the following day.

After the defeat at Helena, the army retreated in easy stages, first to Des Arc and then to Little Rock. Parsons's brigade, including Pindall's men, constructed fortifications north of the Arkansas River in August to resist a Federal advance on the capital, but the enemy flanked the defenses. The infantry did not engage the Federals before the army abandoned Little Rock on September 10. Thereafter, the army retreated to southern Arkansas and established winter quarters near Camden, later moving to Spring Hill. In March 1864 the battalion marched with the brigade to northwest Louisiana as Major General Nathaniel Banks's Federal army advanced on Shreveport in the opening stages of the Red River Campaign. The battalion crossed the Red River and encamped south of Shreveport in late March. At that camp, General Parsons organized a division by joining his brigade with one commanded by Colonel John B. Clark Jr. under the provisions of Special Order 73, Headquarters, Trans-Mississippi Department, dated March 25. The order assigned Pindall's battalion to the 2nd brigade under the command of Colonel Simon P. Burns. It is likely that the Confederate War Department designated the battalion as the 9th Sharpshooter Battalion about this time as well.

On April 3, the division left Shreveport to reinforce Major General Richard Taylor, then opposing Banks's army near Mansfield. After a hard march, the Missourians reached Pleasant Hill on April 9, and deployed for battle that afternoon. Parsons's division held the right of the Confederate line, with Burns's brigade deployed to the left of Clark's. The brigade charged the enemy with success initially. Although receiving fire on its right, Parsons's units routed a Union brigade, killed its commander, captured two artillery batteries, and advanced into Pleasant Hill. At that point, part of Major General Andrew J. Smith's Federal corps emerged from concealment and assaulted the Confederate right. Flanked and subjected to a severe fire, the Missourians retreated in considerable disorder. By the time the Confederates rallied, night had fallen and the Federals had retreated southward. The 9th Sharpshooters lost 2 killed or mortally wounded and 8 wounded in the fight.

The division next turned northward and engaged the enemy under Major General Frederick Steele at Jenkins's Ferry, Arkansas, on April 30. In attacks made through rain-soaked fields, the Confederates made little headway against Federals protected by makeshift breastworks; after several hours of fighting, the enemy escaped across the Saline River. Pindall's battalion counted 1 dead and 4 wounded in the battle and received the brigade commander's compliments for displaying "sturdy and unwavering courage."

Parsons's division spent the remainder of the war in camps in southern Arkansas and northwestern Louisiana. On January 20, 1865, two companies recruited in Missouri during Major General Sterling Price's expedition into the state joined the battalion. After an uneventful spring, the Confederates surrendered on May 26. The men of the 9th Sharpshooter Battalion received paroles at Shreveport, Louisiana, on June 7. While the battalion was aboard the steamer *Kentucky* en route to Missouri, the boat sank on the Red River with considerable loss of life, including at least 12 of Pindall's men. During the course of the war, the rolls of the 9th Sharpshooter Battalion carried the names of some 550 men. Of that number, 17 were battle casualties, 24 died of disease, and at least 12 went down with the *Kentucky*. An original battle flag of the battalion is in the collections of the Old State House Museum at Little Rock.

Bibliography

"'Away Back in War Days': An Old Confederate Soldier Tells of the Last Company to Leave Old Howard." *Pioneer Times* 6 (October 1982): 408–10.

Bartels. Carolyn. *Bravest of the Brave: Pindall's 9th Missouri Sharpshooter Battalion*. Independence: Two Trails, 2001.

Colvert, George W. "Brief History of the 9th Missouri Sharpshooter Battalion." William L. Skaggs Collection, Arkansas History Commission, Little Rock, Arkansas.

James T. Wallace Diary. Southern Historical Collection, University of North Carolina, Chapel Hill, North Carolina.

Rosser's Battalion (Also known as 1st or 7th Battalion)

Lieutenant Colonel: Thomas Henry Rosser, assigned as post commandant at Memphis, April 20, 1862

Major: Unknown, if any

Companies and Commanders:

Company —: (Polk) Asbury Bradford

Company —: (Henry) Stephen D. Coale

Company —: (Cass, Jackson) Jeremiah V. Cockrell

Company —: (Cass, St. Clair) David Fleming

Company —: (Johnson, Macon) Ben Eli Gutherie

Company —: (Polk) Alexander Lemmon

Company —: (Jackson, Platte) Francis M. McKinney

Company —: (Jackson, Lafayette) Samuel F. Taylor

Company —: (Johnson) Owen Waddell

Although recruitment for this battalion began at Springfield, Missouri, in early 1862, formal organization did not occur until March 3 at Cove Creek, Arkansas. Most recruits came from the ranks of the 8th Division, Missouri State Guard. The battalion became part of the 2nd Missouri Brigade, commanded by Brigadier General William Y. Slack. Shortly after the battalion organized, it marched with Major General Earl Van Dorn's Army of the West to attack the enemy near Pea Ridge. Early on the morning of March 7, the 2nd Brigade deployed on the right of the Confederate line west of Elkhorn Tavern. Soon after the lines formed, the brigade received heavy enemy fire. The men quickly suppressed the fire and also repulsed a flank movement by Union cavalry. In the initial fighting, General Slack fell mortally wounded, and command of the brigade devolved on Lieutenant Colonel Rosser. A general assault by the entire Confederate force compelled the enemy to fall back; Rosser's battalion captured a bronze 6-pounder cannon of the 3rd Iowa Battery in the attack. As the day ended, the Federal line had been pushed back considerably, and the Confederates retired to the captured Federal campsite. The next morning the battalion endured a terrific barrage of artillery fire, but before it engaged the enemy, Van Dorn ordered a retreat. The known losses of the battalion at Pea Ridge amounted to 4 killed, 7 wounded, and 4 missing. Rosser's battalion retreated with the army to the vicinity of Van Buren, where it rested and drilled until ordered to Memphis, Tennessee.

For reasons unknown, the companies of Bradford, Coale, Gutherie, Lemmon, and Waddell withdrew from Rosser's unit on March 23 and joined a new battalion commanded by Lieutenant Colonel James McCown. The remaining four companies then made the long trek across Arkansas with the army to Des Arc for shipment to Memphis. At Des Arc the battalion boarded the steamer *Vicksburg* and landed at Memphis on April 17. The unit soon lost its commander, for Lieutenant Colonel Rosser became post commandant of Memphis on April 20. Temporary command of the battalion devolved on Jeremiah V. Cockrell, the senior captain. The depleted battalion camped south of Memphis until April 28, when it moved to Corinth, Mississippi, by rail. The army reorganized at Corinth in mid-May, and the battalion underwent significant changes. Two new companies joined the unit, and the men elected new field officers to form a new battalion commanded by Lieutenant Colonel Eugene Erwin. See the entry for Erwin's Battalion for the further service of the men of this unit.

Bibliography

John M. Leach Diary. Western Historical Manuscript Collection, University of Missouri–Rolla, Rolla, Missouri.

Searcy's Sharpshooter Battalion
(Also known as 1st Sharpshooter Battalion)
(Formerly Searcy's Cavalry Regiment)

Lieutenant Colonel: James Jasper Searcy

Major: John C. Moore, returned to cavalry service at date unknown; Amos F. Cake, transferred from 9th Sharpshooter Battalion

Companies and Commanders:

Company A: (Boone, Callaway) William B. Strode

Company B: (Boone, Monroe) Abel M. Johnson

Company C: (Chariton, Cole, Randolph) William E. Warden

Company D: (Chariton) Berry Owens

Company E: (Audrain, Boone, Howard) William H. Todd

Company F: (Howard) Joel H. Greene

Organized January 21, 1865, near Fulton, Arkansas, by consolidating the companies of Searcy's Cavalry Regiment, this battalion was paroled at Shreveport, Louisiana, June 5, 1865, as part of the 1st Brigade, Brigadier General Mosby M. Parsons's Missouri Infantry Division. See the entry for Searcy's Cavalry Regiment for the service of the men of this unit.

Bibliography

Banasik, Michael, ed. *Serving with Honor: The Diary of Captain Eathan Allen Pinnell of the Eighth Missouri Infantry Regiment (Confederate).* Iowa City: Camp Pope Bookshop, 1999.

Confederate Organizations, Officers and Posts, 1861–1865, Missouri Units. Springfield: Ozarks Genealogical Society, 1988.

C. Units That Failed to Complete Organization

7th Regiment (Franklin's)

This regiment appears on many lists of Missouri Confederate organizations as a regularly organized unit. Colonel Cyrus Franklin, former commander of the 2nd Northeast Missouri Cavalry Regiment, purportedly commanded the regiment. The Confederate War Department indeed authorized this regiment, but it held the issuance of regimental commissions in abeyance pending actual consolidation of the 1st and 2nd Northeast Cavalry Regiments. Both of those regiments suffered total disorganization in extensive fighting in the summer of 1862 that posed a serious impediment to consolidation. The regiments disbanded in the field in northeast Missouri; the soldiers moved to Arkansas in companies, squads, and individually. Many soldiers of the regiments spent several months as prisoners. As a consequence, no intact regiments existed to consolidate. One source states that the two cavalry units combined on April 4, 1863, to create this regiment, but a credible memoir indicates that Franklin commanded only a few squads in that time frame, and that most of them joined Pindall's Sharpshooter Battalion. It is likewise noteworthy that no infantry regiment commanded by Colonel Cyrus Franklin appears in any table of organization of the Confederate army, or in any order of battle, and no substantive records exist for such a unit. Also, Major General Sterling Price made no mention of such a regiment as part of his division in 1863 or later. Thus, compelling evidence demonstrates that the 1st and 2nd Northeast Missouri Cavalry Regiments never consolidated to form this regiment.

Bibliography

Confederate Organizations, Officers and Posts, 1861–1865, Missouri Units. Springfield: Ozarks Genealogical Society, 1988.

James T. Wallace Diary. Southern Historical Collection, University of North Carolina, Chapel Hill, North Carolina.

Boone's Mounted Infantry Regiment
(Also known as the 1st Mounted Infantry Regiment)

Commander: John C. Boone

Companies and Commanders:

Company A: Nathaniel Ferguson

Company —: John G. Provines

Company —: Rufus Ricketts

Company —: Unknown

Balance of organization, if any, is unknown.

A regiment in name only, this small command never completed a formal organization. John C. Boone began recruiting this outfit in the St. Louis environs in early August 1862. Ascertaining whether Boone possessed official recruiting authority is problematic, for little is known about his background, except that he was a grandson of Daniel Boone, the noted frontiersman. After two weeks of recruiting, Boone gathered over 100 recruits in south St. Louis County, loosely organized into four small companies. Alerted to the potential threat posed by the recruits, and anxious to end Boone's recruiting activities, Union military authorities determined to destroy the command. Union cavalry units, mostly state militia and home guards, searched for Boone's command in a wide area around St. Louis for several days. While initially unsuccessful in locating the rebel camp, the state troops eventually found Boone's recruits and engaged them twice during a matter of a few days. Union units first struck Boone on August 12 at Manchester in St. Louis County, but the recruits offered little resistance and scattered before they could be closely engaged. Thereafter, on August 18, the Schofield Hussars and 200 Home Guards surprised Boone's camp on the Meramec River in Jefferson County south of St. Louis. Their attack overwhelmed the camp; the Unionists took 49 prisoners, but a few recruits, including a slightly wounded Boone, evaded capture. Following these relatively bloodless actions, Boone ended his recruiting efforts and disappeared from the scene without completing the organization of a regiment.

Bibliography

Eakin, Joanne Chiles. *Missouri Prisoners of War.* Independence: Privately printed, 1995.

Nichols, Bruce, *Guerrilla Warfare in Civil War Missouri, 1862.* Jefferson: McFarland, 2004.

SUPPLEMENTAL BIBLIOGRAPHY

In addition to the materials cited in connection with the individual unit histories, the following sources were used in preparing this study.

Manuscripts

Peter Wellington Alexander Collection. Columbia University, New York, New York.

Applications for Missouri Confederate Pensions and Home. Missouri State Archives, Jefferson City, Missouri.

Army of the West and General Sterling Price's Division. General Orders, 1862–63. War Department Collection of Confederate Records, Record Group 109, Chapter 2, Volume 211. National Archives, Washington, D.C.

Army of the West, District of Tennessee, and General Sterling Price's Division. Special Orders, 1862–63. War Department Collection of Confederate Records, Record Group 109, Chapter 2, Volume 208. National Archives, Washington, D.C.

Brigadier General John S. Bowen's Command. Letter Book, August 1862–November 1863. War Department Collection of Confederate Records, Record Group 109, Chapter 2, Volume 274. National Archives, Washington, D.C.

Civil War Collection, Missouri, 1865–1900. Missouri Historical Society, St. Louis, Missouri.

Civil War Documents, 1862–1904. Western Historical Manuscript Collection, University of Missouri, Columbia, Missouri.

Compiled Service Records of Confederate Soldiers Who Served in Organizations from the State of Missouri. War Department Collection of Confederate Records, Record Group 109, Microcopy No. 322, Rolls 1–177. National Archives, Washington, D.C.

Confederate Muster Rolls. Missouri State Archives, Jefferson City, Missouri.

Confederate Records of the Missouri Division, United Daughters of the Confederacy. State Historical Society of Missouri, Columbia, Missouri.

Confederate States Army, Trans-Mississippi Department, 1st Army Corps, 4th Cavalry Division. Order Book, September 8, 1862–June 11, 1864. Civil War Collection. Missouri Historical Society, St. Louis, Missouri.

Confederate States of America, Department of the West. Missouri Infantry, 2d Division, 1st Brigade. Letter Book, August 6, 1862–December 1, 1863. Virginia Historical Society, Richmond, Virginia.

Index to Enrollment Cards, Civil War, Confederate. Missouri State Archives, Jefferson City, Missouri.

General John S. Marmaduke. Correspondence. Old Army Branch, Record Group 109, National Archives, Washington, D.C.

Missouri State Guard. Letter and Order Book, 1861–62. Missouri State Museum, Jefferson City, Missouri.

Missouri Volunteers, Parsons' Division. Register of Officers, 1862–65. Missouri Historical Society, St. Louis, Missouri.

Muster Rolls of the 1st–15th Missouri Cavalry Regiments, C.S.A. F1173. Missouri State Archives, Jefferson City, Missouri.

Mosby Monroe Parsons Papers. Missouri Historical Society, St. Louis, Missouri.

General Sterling Price's Command. Letters Sent, 1862–65. National Archives, Washington, D.C.

———. Letters Sent, August 1863–March 1865. National Archives, Washington, D.C.

———. Orders and Circulars, 1864–65. War Department Collection of Confederate Records, Record Group 109, Chapter 2, Volume 209. National Archives, Washington, D.C.

———. War Department Collection of Confederate Records, Record Book, 1862–63. National Archives, Washington, D.C.

Major General Sterling Price's Division. Record Book, 1863–64. Chapter 1, Volume 109 1/2. National Archives, Washington, D.C.

———. Roster of Officers, 1862–63. Chapter 1, Vol. 110 1/2. National Archives, Washington, D.C.

Service Cards of Missouri Confederate Regiments. Missouri State Archives, Jefferson City, Missouri.

W. L. Skaggs Collection. Arkansas History Commission, Little Rock, Arkansas.

Union Provost Marshal Files of Papers Relating to Two or More Civilians. National Archives, Washington, D.C.

General Earl Van Dorn's Command. Special Orders, 1862. War Department Collection of Confederate Records, Record Group 109, Chapter 2, Volume 210. National Archives, Washington, D.C.

Printed Primary Sources

Bartels, Carolyn. *Missouri Confederate Surrender, Shreveport and New Orleans, May 1865.* Shawnee Mission: Two Trails, 1991.

———. *Missouri Officers and Gentlemen: CSA Surrender.* Shawnee Mission: Two Trails, 1996.

———. *The Forgotten Men—Missouri State Guard.* Independence: Two Trails, 1995.

Castel, Albert, ed. "The Diary of Gen. Henry Little, C.S.A." *Civil War Times Illustrated* 11 (October 1972): 4–6, 8–11, and 41–47.

Eakin, Joanne Chiles. *Missouri Confederate Reports: Narrative Reports of Casualties after the Battles of Cape Girardeau, Carthage, Hartville, Lexington, Marmaduke's Expedition 1862–3, Price's Expedition 1864, Newtonia and Wilson's Creek.* Independence: Privately printed, 1995.

Estes, Claude, comp. *List of Field Officers, Regiments and Battalions, in the Confederate Army 1861–1865.* Macon: J. W. Burke, 1912.

French, Samuel G. *Two Wars: The Autobiography and Diary of General Samuel G. French.* Huntington: Blue Acorn Press, 1999.

Hewett, Janet B., ed. *Roster of Confederate Soldiers, 1861–1865.* 16 vols. Wilmington: Broadfoot, 1995–97.

———. *Supplement to the Official Records of the Union and Confederate Armies.* Wilmington: Broadfoot, 1994–2001.

Johnson, Robert Underwood, and Clarence Clough Buel, eds. *Battles and Leaders of the Civil War.* 4 vols. New York: Thomas Yoseloff, 1955.

McGhee, James E., ed. *Service with the Missouri State Guard: The Memoir of General James Harding.* Springfield: Oak Hills, 2000.

Maury, Dabney Herndon. *Recollections of a Virginian in the Mexican, Indian, and Civil Wars.* New York: Charles Scribner's Sons, 1894.

———. "Recollections of the Campaign against Grant in North Mississippi." *Southern Historical Society Papers* 13 (1885): 285–311.

———. "Recollections of the Elkhorn Campaign." *Southern Historical Society Papers* 2 (1876): 180–92.

Missouri Division of the United Daughters of the Confederacy, comp. *Reminiscences of Women of Missouri during the Sixties.* Dayton: Morningside, 1988.

Moore, John C. *Missouri.* Vol. 12 of *Confederate Military History,* edited by Clement A. Evans. Wilmington, North Carolina: Broadfoot, 1988.

Pemberton, John C. *Compelled to Appear in Print: The Vicksburg Manuscript of General John C. Pemberton.* Ed. David M. Smith. Cincinnati: Ironclad, 1999.

Ponder, Jerry, and Victor Ponder. *Confederate Surrender and Parole, Jacksonport and Wittsburg, Arkansas, May and June, 1865.* Doniphan: Ponder Books, 1995.

Schnetzer, Wayne. *More Forgotten Men: Missouri State Guard.* Independence: Two Trails, 2003.

Taylor, Richard. *Destruction and Reconstruction: Personal Experiences of the Late War.* New York: Longmans, Green, 1955.

United States Department of War. *War of the Rebellion: A Compilation of the Official Records of the Union and Confederate Armies.* 128 vols. Washington: Government Printing Office, 1880–1902.

United States Department of War, Records and Pension Office. *Organization and Status of Missouri Troops, Union and Confederate, in Service during the Civil War.* Washington: Government Printing Office, 1902.

Young, Robert E. *Pioneers of High, Water and Main: Reflections of Jefferson City.* Jefferson City: Twelfth State, 1997.

Books

Allardice, Bruce S. *More Generals in Gray.* Baton Rouge: Louisiana State University Press, 1995.

Anders, Leslie. *Confederate Roll of Honor: Missouri.* Warrensburg: West Central Missouri Genealogical Society and Library, 1989.

Baker, William D. *The Camden Expedition of 1864.* Little Rock: Arkansas Historic Preservation Program, 1993.

Banasik, Michael E. *Embattled Arkansas: The Prairie Grove Campaign of 1862.* Wilmington: Broadfoot, 1996.

Bartels, Carolyn. *Trans-Mississippi Men at War: Missouri, C.S.A.* Independence: Two Trails, 1998.

Bearss, Edwin C. *Steele's Retreat from Camden and the Battle of Jenkins' Ferry.* Little Rock: Pioneer Press, n.d.

———. *The Vicksburg Campaign.* 3 vols. Dayton: Morningside, 1985–86.

Buresh, Lumir F. *October 25th and the Battle of Mine Creek.* Kansas City: Lowell Press, 1977.

Castel, Albert E. *Decision in the West: The Atlanta Campaign of 1864.* Lawrence: University Press of Kansas, 1992.

———. *General Sterling Price and the Civil War in the West.* Baton Rouge: Louisiana State University Press, 1968.

Christ, Mark K., ed. *Rugged and Sublime: The Civil War in Arkansas.* Fayetteville: University of Arkansas Press, 1994.

Conrad, Howard L., ed. *Encyclopedia of the History of Missouri.* 6 vols. St. Louis: Southern History, 1901.

Cozzens, Peter. *The Darkest Days of the War: The Battles of Iuka and Corinth.* Chapel Hill: University of North Carolina Press, 1997.

———. *This Terrible Sound: The Battle of Chickamauga.* Urbana: University of Illinois Press, 1992.

Crute, Joseph H., Jr. *Units of the Confederate States Army.* Midlothian: Derwent Books, 1987.

Daniel, Larry J. *Cannoneers in Gray: The Field Artillery of the Army of Tennessee, 1861–1865.* Tuscaloosa: University of Alabama Press, 1984.

Denny, James M. *The Battle of Glasgow.* Independence: Blue and Grey Book Shoppe, 2001.

Dossman, Steven Nathaniel. *Campaign for Corinth: Blood in Mississippi.* Abilene: McWhiney Foundation Press, 2006.

Eakin, Joanne Chiles. *The Battle of Lone Jack—August 16, 1862.* Independence: Two Trails, 2001.

———. *Five Years of the* Blue and Grey Chronicle. Independence: Two Trails, 2002.

Forsyth, Michael J. *The Camden Expedition of 1864 and the Opportunity Lost by the Confederacy to Change the Civil War.* Jefferson: McFarland, 2003.

Gifford, Douglas L. *The Battle of Pilot Knob Staff Ride and Battlefield Tour Guide.* Winfield: Privately printed, 2003.

Goman, Frederick W. *Up from Arkansas: Marmaduke's First Missouri Raid, Including the Battles of Springfield and Hartville.* Springfield: Wilson's Creek National Battlefield Foundation, 1999.

Gottschalk, Phil. *In Deadly Earnest: The Missouri Brigade.* Columbia: Missouri River Press, 1991.

Hess, Earl J., Richard W. Hatcher, III, William Garrett Piston, and William L. Shea. *Wilson's Creek, Pea Ridge and Prairie Grove: A Battlefield Guide, with a Section on Wire Road.* Lincoln: University of Nebraska Press, 2006.

Horn, Stanley F. *The Army of Tennessee.* Norman: University of Oklahoma Press, 1953.

Ingenthron, Elmo. *Borderland Rebellion: A History of the Civil War on the Missouri-Arkansas Border.* Branson: Ozarks Mountaineer, 1980.

Jacobson, Eric A., and Richard A. Rupp. *For Cause and For Country: A Study of the Affair at Spring Hill and the Battle of Franklin.* Spring Hill: O'More, 2006.

Jenkins, Paul B. *The Battle of Westport.* Kansas City: Hudson, 1906.

Johnson, Ludwell H. *Red River Campaign: Politics and Cotton in the Civil War.* Baltimore: Johns Hopkins Press, 1958.

Joiner, Gary Dillard. *One Damn Blunder from Beginning to End: The Red River Campaign of 1864.* Wilmington: Scholarly Resources, 2003.

Lee, Fred L., ed. *Gettysburg of the West: The Battle of Westport, October 21–23, 1864.* Independence: Two Trails, 1996.

McGhee, James E. *Missouri Confederates: A Guide to Sources for Confederate Soldiers and Units, 1861–1865.* Independence: Two Trails, 2005.

———. *"Tales of the War": A Series of Civil War Articles from the* Daily Missouri Republican, *St. Louis, Missouri, 1885–1887.* Jefferson City: Privately printed, 1995.

Missouri's Sons of the South: From the Pages of the Confederate Veteran Magazine, *1893–1932.* Springfield: CBC Press, 1999.

Monett, Howard N. *Action before Westport.* Kansas City: Lowell Press, 1964.

Neal, Diane, and Thomas W. Kremm. *The Lion of the South: General Thomas C. Hindman.* Macon: Mercer University Press 1993.

Oates, Stephen B. *Confederate Cavalry West of the River.* Austin: University of Texas Press, 1961.

O'Flaherty, Daniel. *General Jo Shelby: Undefeated Rebel.* Chapel Hill: University of North Carolina Press, 1954.

Peterson, Richard C., James E. McGhee, Kip A. Lindberg, and Keith I. Daleen. *Sterling Price's Lieutenants: A Guide to the Officers and Organization of the Missouri State Guard, 1861–1865.* Rev. ed. Shawnee Mission: Two Trails, 2007.

Pitcock, Cynthia DeHaven, and Bill J. Gurley, eds. *"I Acted from Principle": The Civil War Diary of Dr. William M. McPheeters, Confederate Surgeon in the Trans-Mississippi.* Fayetteville: University of Arkansas Press, 2002.

Plaster, Daniel Joseph. *Marmaduke's First Missouri Raid: The Roles of Federal Scouts and*

Outposts in the Defense of Springfield, 1862–1863. Springfield: Benchmark, 1999.

Rolle, Andrew. *The Lost Cause: The Confederate Exodus to Mexico.* Norman: University of Oklahoma Press, 1965.

Scott, Kim Allen, and Stephen Burgess. *Pursuing an Elusive Quarry: The Battle of Cane Hill, Arkansas.* Bozeman: Kinnally Press, 1999.

Scott, Mark. *The Fifth Season: Shelby's Great Raid of 1863.* Independence: Two Trails, 2001.

Sellmeyer, Deryl P. *Jo Shelby's Iron Brigade.* Gretna: Pelican, 2007.

Shalhope, Robert E. *Sterling Price: Portrait of a Southerner.* Columbia: University of Missouri Press, 1971.

Shea, William L. *The Campaign for Pea Ridge.* Eastern National Park Service, 2001.

———. *War in the West: Pea Ridge and Prairie Grove.* Fort Worth: Ryan Place, 1996.

Shea, William L., and Earl J. Hess. *Pea Ridge: Civil War Campaign in the West.* Chapel Hill: University of North Carolina Press, 1992.

Shearer, Gary W. *The Civil War, Slavery and Reconstruction in Missouri: A Bibliographic Guide to Secondary Sources and Selected Primary Sources.* 3rd ed. Angwin: Privately printed, 2000.

Sifakis, Stewart. *Compendium of the Confederate Armies: Kentucky, Maryland, Missouri, the Confederates and the Indian Units.* New York: Facts on File, 1995.

Smith, Timothy B. *Champion Hill: Decisive Battle for Vicksburg.* New York: Savas-Beatie, 2004.

Suderow, Bryce A. *Thunder in Arcadia Valley: Price's Defeat, September 27, 1864.* Cape Girardeau: Center for Regional History and Cultural Heritage, Southeast Missouri State University, 1986.

Sword, Wiley. *Embrace an Angry Wind—The Confederacy's Last Hurrah: Spring Hill, Franklin, and Nashville.* New York: HarperCollins, 1992.

———. *Mountains Touched with Fire: Chattanooga Besieged, 1863.* New York: St. Martin's Press, 1995.

Tucker, Phillip Thomas. *The Forgotten "Stonewall of the West": Major General John Stevens Bowen.* Macon: Mercer University Press, 1997.

———. *The South's Finest: The First Missouri Confederate Brigade: From Pea Ridge to Vicksburg.* Shippensburg: White Mane, 1993.

Warner, Ezra J. *Generals in Gray: Lives of the Confederate Commanders.* Baton Rouge: Louisiana State University Press, 1959.

Weant, Kenneth E. *Deaths Reported by Missouri Confederate Regiments and Companies.* Arlington: Privately printed, 1999.

Webb, William Larkin. *Battles and Biographies of Missourians; or, the Civil War Period in Our State.* Springfield: Oak Hills, 1999.

ARTICLES

Allen, Stacy D. "Corinth, Mississippi: Crossroads of the Western Confederacy." *Blue and Gray* 19 (Summer 2002): 6–25, 36–38, 41–51.

Anders, Leslie. "Fighting the Ghosts at Lone Jack." *Missouri Historical Review* 79 (April 1985): 332–56.

Atkinson, J. H. "The Action at Prairie De Ann." *Arkansas Historical Quarterly* 19 (Spring 1960): 40–50.

———. "The Battle of Marks' Mills." *Arkansas Historical Quarterly* 14 (Winter 1955): 381–84.

Bailey, Anne J. "Texans Invade Missouri: The Cape Girardeau Raid." *Missouri Historical Review* 84 (January 1990): 166–87.

Barr, Alwyn. "Confederate Artillery in Arkansas." *Arkansas Historical Quarterly* 22 (Autumn 1963): 238–72.

Bearss, Edwin C. "The Army of the Frontier's First Campaign: The Confederates Win at Newtonia." *Missouri Historical Review* 54 (April 1960): 283–319.

———. "The Battle of Helena, July 4, 1863." *Arkansas Historical Quarterly* 20 (Autumn 1961): 258–93.

———. "The First Day at Pea Ridge, March 7, 1862." *Arkansas Historical Quarterly* 17 (Summer 1958): 132–54.

———. "Marmaduke Attacks Pine Bluff." *Arkansas Historical Quarterly* 23 (Winter 1964): 291–313.

Borland, William P. "General Jo. O. Shelby." *Missouri Historical Review* 7 (January 1912): 10–19.

Boyce, Joseph. "Missourians in the Battle of Franklin." *Confederate Veteran* 24 (1916): 101–3, 138.

Bradbury, John F., Jr. "'This War Is Managed Mighty Strange': The Army of Southeastern Missouri, 1862–1863." *Missouri Historical Review* 89 (October 1994): 28–47.

Brown, D. Alexander. "The Battle of Westport." *Civil War Times Illustrated* 5 (July 1966): 6–11, 40–43.

Brownlee, Richard S. "The Battle of Pilot Knob, Iron County, Missouri, September 27th, 1864." *Missouri Historical Review* 59 (October 1964): 1–25.

Castel, Albert. "Fiasco at Helena." *Civil War Times Illustrated* 7 (July 1968): 12–17.

———. "A New View of the Battle of Pea Ridge." *Missouri Historical Review* 62 (January 1968): 136–51.

Cozzens, Peter. "Hindman's Grand Delusion." *Civil War Times Illustrated* 39 (October 2000): 28–35, 66–69.

Davis, Steven R. "Death Takes No Holiday." *America's Civil War* (May 1993): 22–28, 71–74.

Denny, James M. "The Battle of Marshall: The Greatest Little Battle Never Fought." *Boone's Lick Heritage* 9 (September 2001): 4–13.

Ernest, Douglas J. "'A Needless Effusion of Blood': The Confederate Missouri Brigade and Hood's Invasion of Tennessee in 1864." *Missouri Historical Review* 78 (October 1983): 51–77.

Fisher, Mike. "Remember Poison Spring." *Missouri Historical Review* 74 (April 1980): 323–42.

"Gen. M. M. Parsons." *Weekly Tribune,* Jefferson City, Missouri, November 29, 1871.

Goff, William A. "The Jackson County Blues." *Westport Historical Quarterly* 9 (June 1993): 14–24.

Gregory, Ival L. "The Battle of Prairie Grove, Arkansas, December 7, 1862." *Journal of the West* 19 (October 1980): 63–75.

Grover, George S. "The Price Campaign of 1864." *Missouri Historical Review* 6 (July 1912): 167–81.

———. "The Shelby Raid, 1863." *Missouri Historical Review* 6 (April 1912): 107–26.

Hoster, Scott. " 'Jo' Shelby Goes Home to Missouri." *America's Civil War* (January 2003): 34–40.

Hughes, Michael A. "A Forgotten Battle in a Region Ignored . . . Pea Ridge, or Elkhorn Tavern, Arkansas—March 7–8, 1862: The Campaign, The Battle, and the Men Who Fought for the Fate of Missouri." *Blue and Gray* 5 (January 1988): 8–36, 48–60.

Hughey, Jeffery A. "The Last Stand of the Confederates in Missouri: The Battle of Newtonia, October 28, 1864, and Its Place in Price's Missouri Raid." *Midwest Kansas Quarterly* 27 (Autumn, 1985): 49–71.

Lee, John F. "John Sappington Marmaduke." *Missouri Historical Society Collections* 2 (1906): 22–40.

Lindberg, Kip. "Chaos Itself: The Battle of Mine Creek." *North and South* 1 (1998): 74–85.

McMurry, Richard M. "Kennesaw Mountain." *Civil War Times Illustrated* 8–9 (January 1970): 20–25, 28–35.

Matthews, Matt, and Kip Lindberg, "Shot All to Pieces: The Battle of Lone Jack, Missouri, August 16, 1862." *North and South* 7 (January 2004): 58–74.

Miller, Robert E. "General Mosby M. Parsons: Missouri Secessionist." *Missouri Historical Review* 80 (October 1985): 35–57.

Northway, Martin. "Band of Brothers: The Missouri Brigade Battled Death and Desertion to Become One of the Finest Fighting Forces in the Civil War." *Missouri Life* (June 2004): 40–46.

Oates, Stephen B. "The Cavalry Fight at Cane Hill." *Arkansas Historical Quarterly* 20 (Spring 1961): 65–73.

Richards, Ira D. "The Battle of Jenkins' Ferry." *Arkansas Historical Quarterly* 20 (Spring 1961): 3–16.

———. "The Battle of Poison Spring." *Arkansas Historical Quarterly* 18 (Winter 1959): 338–49.

———. "The Engagement at Marks' Mills." *Arkansas Historical Quarterly* 19 (Spring 1960): 51–60.

Roberts, Bobby L. "General T. C. Hindman and the Trans-Mississippi District." *Arkansas Historical Quarterly* 32 (Winter 1973): 297–311.

Robinett, Paul N. "Marmaduke's Expedition into Missouri: The Battles of Springfield and Hartville, January, 1863." *Missouri Historical Review* 57 (January 1964): 151–73.

Sallee, Scott E. "The Battle of Prairie Grove." *Blue and Gray* 21 (Fall 2004): 6–25, 45–50.

———. "Missouri! One Last Time: Sterling Price's 1864 Missouri Expedition, A Just and Holy Cause." *Blue and Gray* 8 (June 1991): 10–18, 20, 48–62.

———. "Porter's Campaign in Northeast Missouri, 1862, Including the Palmyra Massacre." *Blue and Gray* 17 (Winter 2000): 4–20, 44–51.

Sharp, Arthur G. "Battle at Lake Chicot." *Civil War Times Illustrated* 21 (October 1982): 18–23.

Shea, William L. "Battle at Ditch Bayou." *Arkansas Historical Quarterly* 39 (Summer 1980): 195–207.

———. "Blunt's Raid: The Army of the Frontier Seizes Van Burn, Arkansas." *North and South* 8 (September 2005): 20–35.

———. "Thunder in the Ozarks: The Battle of Prairie Grove." *North and South* 9 (June 2006): 13–23.

———. "'Whipped and Routed': Blunt Strikes Marmaduke at Cane Hill." *North and South* 7 (2004): 26–39.

Shoemaker, Floyd C. "The Story of the Civil War in Northeast Missouri." *Missouri Historical Review* 7 (January 1913): 63–75, and (April 1913): 113–31.

Stephenson, Jon. "Literal Hill of Death." *America's Civil War* (September 1991): 23–29.

Thompson, Joseph Conan. "The Great Little Battle of Pilot Knob." *Missouri Historical Review* 2 (January 1989): 139–60, and 3 (April 1969): 271–94.

Tucker, Phillip Thomas. "The First Missouri Confederate Brigade at the Battle of Franklin." *Tennessee Historical Quarterly* 46 (Spring 1987): 21–31.

———. "The First Missouri Confederate Brigade's Last Stand at Fort Blakely on Mobile Bay." *Alabama Review* 42 (October 1989): 270–91.

Urwin, Gregory J. W. "'Cut to Pieces and Gone to Hell': The Poison Spring Massacre." *North and South* 3 (2000): 45–57.

———. "'A Very Disastrous Defeat': The Battle of Helena, Arkansas." *North and South* 6 (2002): 26–39.

INDEX

Brown, L. B., 111
Brown, Louis T., 69
Brown, Rufus M., 51
Brown, William, 24
Brownsville, Ark., battle at, 8, 35, 66, 70, 75, 82, 85, 90, 95, 100
Bruinsburg, Miss., 182, 195
Brunswick, Mo., 116
Brush Creek, fighting at, 119, 122, 132
Bryant, Lorenzo D., 68
Bryson, George W., 125, 252
Buchanan County, Mo., 47, 93–94, 193, 217, 225, 250, 253
Buckner, James C., 102
Buffalo City, Ark., 114
Bullard, James W., 233
Bullard, W. Scott, 73
Bumbaugh, William, 144
Burbridge, John Quincy, 65, 68–70, 147, 185
Burbridge's Cavalry Brigade, 65, 69
Burke, Martin, 177
Burkholder, Jacob T., 98
Burns, Alexander F., 55, 139
Burns, Simon Pierce, 223, 225–27, 231, 236, 255
Burns's Infantry Brigade, 231–32
Burt, Henry, 94
Buster, Michael W., 214–15
Butler, Benjamin, 179
Butler, George, 185
Butler County, Mo., 106, 221, 229
Byhalia, Miss., 61
Byram's Ford, battle at, 20, 67, 71, 79, 83, 92, 105, 108, 112
Byrne, Andrew J., 181

C

Cabell, William L., 21, 110, 152
Cabell's Arkansas Cavalry Brigade, 110
Caddo Gap, Ark., 86
Cake, Amos F., 129, 253, 258
Caldwell, Josiah Hatcher, 233–36
California, Mo., skirmish at, 20, 79, 86, 101, 105
California House, skirmish at, 172
Callaway County, Mo., 47–48, 52, 68,
102–3, 116, 125, 129, 133, 150, 163–64, 169, 171, 186, 214, 217, 233, 252, 258
Camden, Ark., 15, 19, 66, 70, 82, 90–91, 104, 113, 118, 123–24, 126, 130, 154, 212–13, 219, 223, 227–28, 232, 236, 254
Camden County, Mo., 64, 69, 103
Camden Expedition, 2, 8, 82
Camp Beauregard, 178
Campbell, Charles C., 177
Campbell, J. L., 121
Campbell, Leonidas A., 64
Campbell, Leonidas C., 34, 64–65, 139–41
Campbell, Stephen J., 81
Camp Bragg, 212, 217–18
Camp Calhoun, 178
Camp Coffee, 7, 73, 94, 99
Camp Defiance, 40
Camp Fabius, 63
Camp Jackson Affair, 31
Camp Jackson, 178
Camp Massard, 211, 226, 230, 241, 253
Camp Mulberry, 30, 221
Camp Price, 179
Camp Sumter, 218
Campti, La., skirmish at, 82
Canada, H. A., 229
Cane Hill, Ark., 7, 74, 85, 89, 94, 99, 156, 215, 221, 226, 254
Caniff, Patrick, 197, 202, 238, 248
Canton, Miss., 12
Canton, Mo., 63
Cape Girardeau, Mo., battle at, 8, 70, 74, 85, 90, 95, 99, 160
Cape Girardeau County, Mo., 64, 78, 80–81, 131, 158, 206, 242
Capitol (steamboat), 48
Caroder, ———, 170
Carr, Joseph P., 244–45
Carrington, William C. P., 177, 181
Carroll, John, 210, 241
Carroll County, Mo., 98, 115–16, 127, 131, 133–34, 193, 214, 217, 250
Carrollton, Mo., 134
Carson, James, 170
Carson, James A., 229
Carter cotton gin, 56, 184, 191

Carter, George W., 74, 160
Carter, Richard H., 186
Carter, Thomas M., 185, 189
Carter, William F., 185, 189, 217
Carter County, Mo., 106, 221, 229
Carter's Texas Cavalry Brigade, 74, 160
Carthage, Mo., 26, 73, 138
Casey, John, 64
Cass County, Mo., 73, 84, 88, 98, 103,
    139, 200, 206, 217, 225, 240, 245,
    250, 256
Cassville, Ga., skirmish at, 55, 198
Cassville, Mo., 13, 16, 21
Castle Rock, Mo., 76
Catron, C. Columbus, 72
Cearnal, James T., 103, 140–41
Cecil, John, 117
Cedar County, Mo., 64, 88, 93, 118, 225
Centerville, Mo., 160
Chalk Bluff, Ark., 8, 25, 70, 78
Chalmers, James R., 60–61
Chamberlain, William M., 193
Champion Hill, Miss., battle at, xv, 5,
    17, 22, 32, 39, 49, 141–42, 182, 187,
    195, 204, 208
Champion, John R. "Rock," 14, 58, 155
Champion House, 5
Chapman, William, 148
Chappell, Edward, 15
Chappell, William C., 220, 222
Chariton County, Mo., 98, 102, 128–29,
    131, 133, 186, 193, 217, 250, 258
Chariton River, 53
Charles Town, Va., 165
Chattahoochee River, fighting at, 12, 56,
    183, 190
Chattanooga, Tenn., 23–24, 27
Cherokee Bay, Ark., 107, 160
Cherokee Spikes, 136
Chickamauga, Ga., 23–24, 27
Chicot County, Ark., operations in, 66,
    82, 91
Chiles, Richard, 47
Chinn, ———, 125
Chorn, ———, 129
Christian County, Mo., 64, 102, 200, 245
Cis-Mississippi, 36, 73, 114, 157, 159, 162,

186, 221, 246
Citronelle, Ala., 62
Clanton, William C., 65
Clardy, Martin Linn, 144–45
Clarendon, Ark., 9, 75, 86, 96, 100
Clark, B. H., 147
Clark, Frank, 64
Clark, Henry E., 37, 167
Clark, James, 77
Clark, John B., 206, 240–41, 244–45
Clark, John B., Jr., 2, 42–43, 104, 112,
    122, 167, 212, 214–15, 217–18, 223,
    227, 231, 236, 239–40, 250–51, 255
Clark, John C., 73, 156
Clark, John E., 229
Clark, Meriwether L., 28
Clark, Samuel Churchill, 10–11
Clark Artillery. See 2nd Light Battery
Clark County, Mo., 69, 214, 217, 220
Clark Dozier (steamboat), 38
Clark's Infantry Brigade, 212–13, 216,
    218, 223, 231, 250, 255
Clark's Mill, Mo., skirmish at, 65, 69
Clarkson, James J., 136–37, 215
Clarkson's Cavalry Battalion, 214
Clarksville, Ark., 241
Clarksville, Tenn., 12
Clarksville, Tex., 76, 97, 101, 110, 126,
    130, 134
Clarkton, Mo., attack on, 167
Clay County, Mo., 58, 84, 88, 98, 193,
    206, 220, 233, 240, 244–45
Claybrook, Francis M., 103
Cleburne, Patrick R., 24, 56
Cleburne's Infantry Division, 24
Cline, O. H., 106
Coale, Stephen D., 203, 248, 256–57
Cobb, John H., 80, 82
Cocke, Benjamin N., 233
Cockrell, Francis M., 22, 182, 185–86
Cockrell, Jeremiah V., 234, 240, 256–57
Coffee, John Trousdale, 93–94, 109–10,
    136, 138, 174
Coldwater River, 60
Cole Camp, Mo., 100
Cole County, Mo., 88, 103, 129, 171, 185,
    253, 258

David, J. B., 147
Davidson, John W., 146
Davies, J. F., 79
Davies's Arkansas Cavalry Battalion, 79, 145
Daviess County, Mo., 48, 193
Davis, Benjamin F., 225
Davis, Francis M., 98
Davis, Frank, 125, 252
Davis, Jefferson, 178
Davis Bridge, Miss., fighting at, 17, 39, 60, 195, 201, 203, 207
Dawson, George W., 178
Dawson, William E., 16–17
Dawson's Battery, 22
Day, Alexander, 125, 252
Day's Bluff, Ark., 216, 251
DeKalb County, Mo., 193
Demopolis, Ala., parole camp at, 6, 17, 22, 32, 39, 50, 55, 142, 183, 188, 190, 196–98, 205, 208
Denmark, Tenn., engagement at, 60
Dent County, Mo., 64, 117, 210, 220
Department of Alabama, Louisiana, and East Louisiana, 18
Des Arc, Ark., 14–15, 21, 38, 48, 140, 186–87, 194, 227, 247, 249, 254, 257
Desha County, Ark., 251
DeVall's Bluff, Ark., 75, 119, 122
Dickey, E. A., 94
Dings, William, 210
District of Arkansas, 43, 103, 123, 154, 161
Ditch Bayou, Ark., battle at, 19, 66, 71, 79, 82, 91
Dixie (song), 191
Dixon, ———, 117
Dixon's Plantation, Mo., 76
Dobbins, Archibald, 103
Dobbins's Arkansas Cavalry Brigade, 103
Dog River, 18
Doke, Fielding Y., 217
Doniphan, Mo., 75, 160
Dooley, Jesse, 77
Dorsey, Caleb W., 131–32, 152, 164, 169
Dorsey, William, 131, 169
Douglas County, Mo., 65, 69, 114, 220
Douglas, William M., 170

Douglass, James C., 186
Dowd, J. R., 147
Dowell, Elijah B., 121
Drayton, Thomas E., 217
Drayton's Infantry Brigade, 217
Dry Wood, Mo., skirmish at, 26, 30
Dubuque (Iowa) Light Artillery, 16
Duck River, fortifications at, 57, 184, 192, 199
Duffy, Robert J., 177, 181
Duncan, Jeptha, 206, 240
Dunklin County, Mo., 40, 58, 77–78, 81, 158, 203, 242
Dunn, William, 51
Dwyer, Robert D. A., 185

E

Early, Jubal, 165
Edmondson, Charles L., 178, 181
Edmondson, Robert H., 58–59, 157, 217
Edwards, William R., 73
Egypt Station, Miss., 12
E. H. Fairchild (steamboat), 15, 224, 232
8th Arkansas Cavalry Regiment, 68
8th Missouri Infantry Regiment (Union), loses flag, 183
Elkhorn Tavern, Ark., fighting at, 4, 11, 13, 16, 21, 26, 31, 42, 48, 140, 186, 194, 238, 246, 257
Elkin's Ferry, Ark., battle at, 70, 75, 79, 82, 86
Elliott, Benjamin Franklin, 73, 84–87
Elliott, Joseph P., 73
Elliott, S. M., 113
Elliott's Scouts, 84–85
Ellis, Alexander D., 217, 250
Ellison, Jesse, 77
Elm Springs, Ark., 241
Ely, Benjamin M., 51
Enfield rifles, 197
English, ———, 117
Enyart, Logan, 48, 54
Epps, Carroll, 229
Erwin, Andrew Eugene, 37, 206, 208–9, 239–41, 245, 257
Erwin, William H., 97, 101
Esselman, Joseph C., 229

Fristoe, Edward T., 113–15
Frog Bayou, Ark., encampment at, 14, 31, 48, 140, 186, 225, 238–39, 244, 246, 248–49
Frost, Daniel M., 2, 16, 21, 31, 38, 42, 59, 152, 155, 161, 221, 230, 246, 253
Frost's Infantry Division, 221, 253
Frost's Escort Company, 155, 161
Frost's Infantry Brigade, 2, 42, 152, 161
Fugate, James H., 131
Fulbright, Daniel N., 117
Fulkerson, ———, 109
Fulkerson, Phillip W., 200, 245
Fulton County, Ark., 114, 200, 220, 247
Fulton, Ark., 126, 130, 252, 258
Fulton, Mo., 169
Furnish, Lewis, 139

G

Gaines, Richard, 217, 250
Gaines Landing, Ark., operations at, 216, 251
Gainesville, Ala., 13
Gallups, Ark., skirmish at, 19
Gardner, David, 229
Garland, Hugh A., 177–78, 180–81, 183–84
Garrett, James M., 73
Gasconade County, Mo., 202, 210, 221, 248
Gates, Elijah P., 47, 54
Gause, William Randall, 192–93, 195
General Beauregard (warship), 29
General M. Jeff Thompson (warship), 41
General Order No. 6, HQ, District of Ark., 44, 103
General Order No. 18, HQ, Missouri State Guard, 161
General Sterling Price (warship), 29
Gentry County, Mo., 193
Georgia Campaign, 183
Gibbs, Thomas J., 171
Gibson, John F., 225
Gibson, Randall, 27
Gibson's Louisiana Battery (Miles Artillery), 31
Gibson's Louisiana Infantry Brigade, 27
Giddings, Julian N., 80

Gilbert, William P., 47
Gilkey, Charles A., 97–99
Gillett, ———, 117
Gillett, James H., 234
Glanville, James A., 186, 189
Glasgow, Mo., battle at, 9, 20, 67, 71, 79, 83, 91, 119, 122, 125, 127, 134, 163–64
Glenn, W. H., 77
Glenn, William H., 139
Goforth, Thomas B., 148
Gordon, Benjamin F., 72, 74
Gordon, George P., 72, 75
Gordon, John A., 178
Gordon, Silas M., 48
Gorham, James C., 13–14, 30
Gorham's Battery, 30–31
Granby, Mo., 136–37
Grand Ecore, La., 20
Grand Gulf, Miss., 4, 31–32, 39, 49, 182, 187, 195, 204, 207
Grand River, 128
Granite State (steamboat), 2, 216, 250–51
Grant, Noah, 203
Grant, Ulysses S., Vicksburg operations, 49, 60, 182, 187, 195, 204, 207–8
Graves, Jonas W., 139
Graves, Thomas A., 139
Graveyard Hill, attack on, 14, 222, 226–27, 231, 235, 254
Green, Martin E., 11, 49, 59, 65, 141, 157, 201, 207–8, 243
Greene, Henderson P., 200, 245
Greene, Joel H., 129, 258
Greene County, Ark., 78
Greene County, Mo., 64, 88, 94, 102, 139, 225
Greene, Colton, xiv, 19, 64–67, 70, 140, 147, 153, 156, 246
Greenfield, Mo., 100
Green's Infantry Brigade, 11, 141, 207, 243. *See also* 2nd Missouri Brigade
Greensboro, N.C., 33
Greenup, Campbell, 220
Greenwood, George W., 106
Greenwood, W. H., 84
Greer, Samuel W., 114
Gregg, John, 27

Homes, Benjamin, 229
Hood, John Bell, 27, 33, 56, 183, 191, 198
Hooper, James C., 93, 95
Hope, Robert A., 80
Hornback, Albert, 88
Hornet's Nest, 179
Horsehead Creek, Ark., 250
Howard, David C., 225
Howard, William, 200, 247
Howard, William J., 131
Howard County, Mo., 88, 98, 125, 127,
    129, 179, 206, 214, 217, 239–40,
    252–53, 258
Howell, Sylvanus, 99
Howell County, Mo., 200, 247
Howell's Texas Battery, 99
Hubbell, Finley L., 192
Hubble Hollow, Ark., regiment organ-
    ized at, 114
Huddleston, T. Y., 111
Hudson, John, 127
Hughes, Harry H., 214, 217
Hughes, John Taylor, 244–45
Hughes Portable Defense Guns, 36
Hulett, Amos K., 51, 68, 127, 153
Hulett Horse, 153
Hull, Edward B., 185
Humansville, Mo., 8, 100
Hunter, DeWitt Clinton, 117–20, 174,
    225–26
Hunter, Jason H., 37, 242

I

Independence, Mo., 67, 71, 76, 79, 83,
    87, 92, 98, 105, 112, 114, 134
Independence Light Artillery, 26
Independent Missouri Scouts, 106, 159
Independent Ranger Battalion, 215
Indian Territory, 9, 67, 71, 76, 83, 87,
    92, 97, 101, 105, 126, 130, 134, 136–38
Inglish, John, 139
Ingraham, Edward, 160
Iron County, Mo., 64, 106, 160, 220, 229
Irondale, Mo., 86
Irwin, Samuel, 149
Iuka, Miss., battle at, 4, 11, 17, 21, 26, 31,
    39, 48, 60, 141, 187, 194, 201, 203, 207

Ivey, Benjamin, 148
Ivey, Joel, 131

J

Jackman, Charles R., 117
Jackman, Sidney Drake, 76, 109, 114,
    119–21, 123, 134, 148, 150, 233–34
Jackman's Missouri Cavalry Brigade, 9,
    76, 109, 119, 121–22, 134, 148
Jackson Battery. See 7th Light Battery
Jackson, Dudley F., 177
Jackson, James R., 68
Jackson, Mo., skirmish at, 82
Jackson, Miss., xiv, 12, 22, 27, 39, 57,
    142, 182, 184, 192, 199
Jackson County, Mo., 21, 26, 88, 94, 98,
    125, 174, 193, 206, 226, 233–34, 240,
    256
Jackson County Cavalry, 97
Jacksonport, Ark., xiv, 31, 80, 108, 112,
    115, 121, 145, 149, 155, 222, 254
Jackway, ———, 109
James rifles (artillery), 1, 7–9
James's Plantation, La., 32
Jarratte, John, 98
Jasper County, Mo., 73, 136–37, 217, 225
Jeans, Beal Green, 97, 99, 100
Jeffers, William Lafayette, 37, 80–81, 83,
    146, 163, 167
Jefferson City, Mo., 24, 50, 71, 76, 86,
    96, 101, 104, 119, 122, 148
Jefferson County, Mo., 106, 185, 221, 260
Jenkins's Ferry, Ark., battle at, 2, 15, 19,
    66, 70, 79, 82, 86, 91, 104, 212, 219,
    223–24, 228, 232, 236–37, 255
Johnson, Abel M., 129, 258
Johnson, Benjamin A., 106
Johnson, Benjamin G., 225
Johnson, Benjamin S., 64
Johnson, Charles L., 210
Johnson, Henry S., 12
Johnson, John M., 220–21
Johnson, John Miscal, 171
Johnson, Lucian P., 47
Johnson, Matthew R., 136–37
Johnson, Waldo Porter, 200, 245–46,
    248, 250

Lewis, Levin Major, 233, 235, 237

Lewis County, Mo., 51–52, 63, 214, 253

Lexington, Mo., 10, 13, 21, 26, 30, 76, 87, 96, 101, 105, 132, 174, 234

Lexington Light Artillery, 26

Liberty Arsenal, 26

Liles, Ebenezer G., 206

Lincoln County, Mo., 131, 150, 169, 185

Lindamoore, George W., 58

Lindsay, David Herndon, 217, 250

Lineback, William T., 68, 146

Linn County, Mo., 186, 202, 217, 238, 248, 250

Little, Henry, 186, 207, 243

Little Blue River, Mo., battle at, 20, 67, 71, 79, 83, 87, 92, 96, 101, 105, 119, 122, 132, 148

Little Osage River, Mo., 67

Little Rebel (gunboat), 43

Little Rock, Ark., 2, 8, 14–15, 19, 35, 42, 66, 70, 75, 78, 82, 85–86, 90, 95, 103–4, 124, 152, 156–57, 161, 211–13, 215–16, 219, 222, 226–28, 230–31, 235–36, 250–51, 254

Little Sugar Creek, Ark., 48

Little's Division, 207

Little Teasers (artillery pieces), 34

Livingston, Samuel, 185

Livingston, Thomas R., 136

Livingston County, Mo., 193

Loan, Benjamin C., 128

Lockett, Thomas A., 171–72

Lockhart, Joseph O., 2

Locust Grove, I.T., engagement at, 137

Lone Jack, Mo., battle at, xv, 1, 7–8, 94, 98, 159, 174, 226, 234

Lost Mountain, Ga., 32

Lotspeich, Felix, 139, 142

Love, Jacob A., 221

Love, Joseph B., 111

Lovejoy Station, Ga., engagement at, 56, 183, 191, 198

Lovell, Mansfield, 179

Lovell's Infantry Division, 179

Lowe, Schuyler, 16, 21

Lowe, William M., 225

Lowry, Francis M., 121

Lowry, Thomas G., 193

Lucas, William, 21

M

MacDonald, Emmett, 16–17, 89–90

MacFarlane, Archibald A., 182, 200–201, 247

Macon County, Mo., 94, 193, 202–3, 220, 248, 256

Maddox, George T., 117

Madison County, Mo., 58, 64, 78, 80, 106, 144, 163, 220, 229

Magoffin, Elijah H., 220

Major, Elliott D., 125, 253

Major, Lucien M., 84

Mammoth Spring, Ark., 111, 247

Manchester, Mo., 260

Mankin, William, 103

Mansfield, La., 218, 255

Maria Denning (steamboat), 126

Maries County, Mo., 171, 220–21

Marines, 29, 36, 41, 243

Marion County, Mo., 51–52, 58, 103, 150, 200, 202, 238, 248, 253

Marks's Mill, Ark., battle at, 9, 75, 86, 96, 100, 118

Marmaduke, John S., 1, 7–8, 15, 19, 25, 44, 65, 69, 74, 82, 89, 95, 99, 103, 107, 112, 114, 131, 153, 156–57, 160–61

Marmaduke's Cavalry Division, 2, 35, 44, 85, 89–90, 104, 112, 114, 123, 157

Marmaduke's Escort Company, 73, 156

Marmaduke's Missouri Cavalry Brigade, 19–20, 25, 34, 37, 66–67, 70–71, 78–79, 83, 90–91, 104, 131, 153, 156

Marmaton, Kan., 138

Marshall, Mo., fighting at, 8, 75, 86, 95, 100, 105, 118

Martin, David, 84

Martin, James C., 234

Matlock, Charles, 158

Matlock, Nicholas G., 125, 127, 252

Matlock's Arkansas Cavalry Battalion, 158

Matthews, George D., 185

Maupin, William D., 47

Maury, Dabney H., 18, 27, 162

Maxwell, John H. H., 133

Maysville, Ark., 113, 137

McBride, James H., 158, 168
McBride, William, 225
McCarley, Thomas, 106
McChristy, George W., 220
McClure, James, 210
McCown, James C., 197, 202–3, 239, 248, 257
McCray, Thomas H., 107–8
McCray's Cavalry Brigade, 107–8
McCuiston, Gwinn, 193, 197
McCulloch, Robert A., 58, 60
McCulloch, Robert, 58–61
McCullough, Frisby H., 63
McDaniel, John, 221
McDaniel, Washington, 84
McDonald, James C., 51
McDonald, Robert, 36–37, 40–41, 207, 243
McDonald County, Mo., 65, 210, 234, 241
McDowell, James K., 192–93, 197
McFarland, James H., 178, 181
McGee, Henry Clay, 47
McGhee, James B., 221, 229
McGhee, Pleasant, 234
McIlwaine, William P., 193
McIntyre, Daniel H., 133
McKill, James, 225
McKinney, Francis M., 206, 240, 256
McKinney, Harvey G., 127, 203
McKinney, John C., 220
McKissick Springs, Ark., 118
McMahan, George R., 93
McNally's Arkansas Battery, 12
McNeil, John, 52–53, 110, 125–26, 129
McNeill, John Hanson, 165
McNeill's Rangers, 165
McPike, William H., 89, 154
McQuiddy, Thomas J., 139
McShane, Francis, 181, 200
McSpadden, James W., 55, 139
McWherter, John, 77–78
Meade, Benjamin F., 131, 169
Meadows, David C., 113
Medon, Tenn., 60
Memphis, Mo., 52
Memphis, Tenn., 4, 11, 14, 17, 21, 23, 26, 31, 34, 36, 38, 40, 48, 59, 62, 127,

140–41, 155, 159, 162, 177–78, 186–87, 194, 200, 243, 245–49, 257
Memphis & Little Rock Railroad, 75, 101, 119, 121
Meramec River, 104, 260
Meridian, Miss., 18, 55, 183, 190, 198
Meridian Campaign, 12
Merrick, John L., 115, 133
Mexican War, 26, 81
Mexico, exiles in, 10, 76, 87, 97, 102, 135
Middleburg, Tenn., 60
Miller, Joseph J., 68, 146
Miller, Joseph N., 217, 250
Miller County, Mo., 139, 185, 217, 221, 250
Milliken's Bend, La., 182, 204
Mine Creek, Kan., battle at, xv, 20, 67, 71, 76, 79, 83, 87, 92, 97, 101, 105, 108, 110, 112, 115, 120, 123, 132, 134, 156, 170
Miner, R. W., 113
Mirick, William G., 127, 193
Missionary Ridge, Tenn., battle at, 17, 24, 27
Mississippi County, Mo., 68, 80–81, 131, 177
Mississippi River, xiii–xiv, 2, 4, 19, 21, 24, 26, 28, 31, 34, 38, 41–43, 59, 66, 70, 82, 91, 107, 127, 141, 159, 182, 187, 194, 204, 207, 212, 216, 222, 239, 251, 254
Missouri Confederate Units: *Artillery:* 1st Field Battery (Roberts's/ Ruffner's), 1–3; 1st Light Battery (Wade's/ Walsh's), 4–6; 2nd Field Battery (Joseph Bledsoe's/Collins's), 2, 7–10, 74, 85, 123, 134; 2nd Light Battery (Clark's/King's/Farris's), 10–13; 3rd Field Battery (Gorham's/Tilden's/ Lesueur's), 13–16; 3rd Light Battery (MacDonald's/Dawson's/Lowe's), 16–18, 22, 246; 4th Field Battery (Harris's), 18–20, 25, 37; 4th Light Battery, 20; 7th Light Battery (Lucas's/Lowe's), 20–23; 8th Light Battery, 13–14, 23; 10th Light Battery (Rice's/Barrett's), 23–24; 13th Light Battery (Griswold's), 18, 25, 35; Bledsoe's (Hiram) Battery, 26–28, 42;

Oxford, Miss., 21
Ozark, Ark., skirmish at, 152
Ozark County, Mo., 65, 114, 200, 247

P

Page, James, 77
Palmyra, Mo., 53
Palmyra Light Artillery, 30
Pankey, David Y., 203, 242, 249
Paris, Mo., 52, 125
Parker, William C., 47, 54
Parrott, James M., 80
Parrott guns (artillery), 2, 4–5, 8, 12, 18,
    22, 32, 42–43
Parsons, John Denard, 28–29, 189, 206,
    242–43
Parsons, Mosby Monroe, xiv, 2, 14, 124,
    152, 168, 211–12, 218, 221–23, 226–27,
    230, 234, 236, 241, 253, 255
Parsons's Missouri Infantry Brigade,
    xiv–xiv, 14, 168, 211–12, 215, 221–22,
    226–27, 231, 234–36, 253–54
Parsons's Missouri Infantry Division, 2–3,
    15, 212, 218, 223, 227, 231–32, 236, 255;
    1st Brigade, 126, 130, 212, 252, 258; *2nd
    Brigade*, 223, 227, 236, 255
Partisan Ranger Act, 136
Patterson, Daniel P., 106, 229
Patterson, Mo., 160
Patterson, William L., 84
Patton, Aaron C., 181, 200
Patton, John, 48
Patton, Thomas B., 125, 252
Patton, Thomas J., 193
Payne, William T., 102–3
Payton, John G., 139
Peabody, Henry A., 124, 171
Peace, John M., 229
Peacher, Quinton, 125
Peach Orchard, 179
Pea Ridge, Ark., battle at, xiii, xv, 4, 11,
    13–14, 16, 21, 26, 31, 38, 48, 59, 73,
    127, 140, 155, 186, 193, 238–40, 244,
    246, 249–50, 257
Pea Ridge Campaign, 41–42
Peachtree Creek, Ga., fighting at, 56, 190
Peevey, Joseph G., 225
Pemberton, John C., 60

Pemiscot County, Mo., 178
Penny, Westly, 150
Perkins, Caleb J., 125, 252
Perry, George W., 233
Perryville, Ky., battle at, 23
Pettis County, Mo., 84, 88, 103, 185, 220
Phelan, William Gerald, 172–73
Phelps County, Mo., 64, 68, 210, 220
Phelps, James M., 106
Phillips, Edward, 81
Phillips, James, 225
Phillips, John S., 253
Phillips, Thomas J., 178
Pickett, Alexander Corbin, 220, 222
Pickler, Jesse F., 118, 136–38
Piercy, Andrew J., 136, 138
Pigeon Hill, Ga., fighting at, 33, 55
Pike County, Mo., 131, 169, 185, 217,
    250, 253
Pillow, Gideon J., 178
Pilot Knob, Mo., battle at xv, 19, 67, 71,
    79, 83, 86, 91, 96, 104, 107, 109, 112,
    114, 122, 131, 144, 148
Pindall, Lebbeus A., 252
Pine Bluff, Ark., battle at, 2, 25, 42, 66,
    70, 78, 82, 90–91, 103, 161, 212
Pineville, Mo., 117
Pinnell, Eathan A., 210
Pittsburg Landing, Tenn., 179
Platte County, Mo., 47–48, 98, 131, 139,
    206, 214, 217, 220, 225, 240, 244–45,
    250, 253, 256
Platte Valley (steamboat), 35
Pleasant Hill, La., battle at, xv, 2, 15, 212,
    218, 223, 227, 231–32, 236, 255
Pleasanton, Alfred, 20
Plum Point Bend (Plum Run Bend),
    naval engagement at, 29, 36, 41, 243
Pocahontas, Ark., 37, 65, 81–82, 107, 112,
    114, 230
Poindexter, John A., 127–28, 171, 215
Poison Spring, Ark., battle at, 3, 19, 66,
    70, 79, 82, 91, 104
Polk, Charles N., 64
Polk, Leonidas, 146
Polk County, Mo., 69, 84, 93, 139, 202,
    225, 248, 256
Pollard, Braxton, 150

Ponder, Willis Miles, 229–31
Porter, James W., 51, 68
Porter, James, 88
Porter, Joseph Chrisman, 51–53, 63, 65, 69, 81, 128, 151, 215
Porter's Missouri Cavalry Brigade, 66
Port Gibson, Miss., battle at, xv, 5, 32, 39, 49, 182, 187, 195, 204, 207–8
Port Hudson, La., 27
Potosi, Mo., 122
Pott's Hill, Ark., skirmish at, 48
Powell, Charles, 51
Powell, Isham, 125
Powell, Richard A., 111
Powell, Samuel, 23, 125
Powell's Infantry Brigade, 23
Powers, William P., 81
Powhatan, Ark., 112
Prairie D'Ann, Ark., skirmishing at, 8, 19, 70, 75, 79, 82, 86, 91, 96, 100
Prairie DeRohan, Ark., skirmishing at, 86, 91, 96, 100
Prairie Grove, Ark., battle at, xv, 1, 7, 14, 74, 85, 89, 94, 99, 156, 211, 215, 221, 226, 230, 235, 250
Prairie Grove Campaign, 159, 161, 221, 253
Prairie Grove Presbyterian Church, 230
Prairie Gun Battery. *See* Hamilton's Battery
Pratt, Jesse R., 106
Pratt, Joseph H., 10
Preston, William I., 68, 70, 146–47
Prewitt, A. T., 131
Price, Henry C., 51, 139
Price, Jesse L., 193, 197, 240–41, 244–45
Price, Miles, 169
Price, Sterling, 4, 15, 29, 43–44, 49, 51, 58, 65, 69, 103–4, 108–10, 112–14, 116, 120–21, 124–25, 127, 132, 131, 144, 148–49, 153–55, 162–63, 169–70, 193, 222, 226, 235, 238, 245, 254–55, 259
Price's Body Guard Battalion, 140, 161–62
Price's Division, 193–94, 254
Price's Escort Company, 58, 162
Price's Missouri Expedition, xiv, 9, 19, 67, 71, 75, 79, 82, 86, 91, 96, 101, 104, 107, 109, 112, 114, 116, 119, 122, 125, 129, 131, 134, 138, 144, 145, 148–49, 153, 156, 169–70, 255
Priceville, Miss., 31
Priest, John W., 221
Prima Donna (supply ship), 43
Princeton, Ark., 104
Pritchard, James Alfred, 192, 194–95
Pritchard, John N., 80
Provines, John G., 260
Pulaski County, Mo., 64, 68, 172, 210, 220
Purcell, Young, 51
Puryear, John C., 64

Q

Queen City (Union gunboat), destroyed, 9, 75, 86, 96, 100
Quesenberry, John P., 225
Quinn's Mill, Miss., 61

R

Rader's Farm, fight at, 137
Raker, David M., 233
Ralls County, Mo., 51, 68–69, 102, 127, 185–86, 253
Randall, Howard S., 64
Randolph County, Ark., 229
Randolph County, Mo., 63, 84, 93–94, 125, 127, 128, 131, 133, 193, 214, 217, 220, 252, 258
Rathbun, George S., 73
Ray County, Mo., 47, 88, 98, 131, 192–93, 225
Raymond, Miss., 27
Reaser, Jacob B., 84
Reavis, James J., 171–72
Redd, John, 116
Red River Campaign, 2–3, 15, 19, 66, 70, 75, 79, 82, 86, 91, 96, 100, 104, 118, 212, 223, 227, 236, 254
Red River, 20, 82, 218, 255–56
Reed, David, 58, 106
Reed's Bridge, Ark., skirmish at, 8, 35, 66, 70, 221, 230, 235
Reed's Mountain, 253

V

Van Buren, Ark., 1, 14, 31, 38, 42, 48,
140, 157, 186, 194, 215, 222, 225, 230,
235, 238, 241, 244, 246, 248, 254, 257
Van Buren, Mo., skirmish at, 65, 81, 147
Vandiver, Asbury, 89, 154
Van Dorn, Earl, 4, 11, 16, 29, 48–49, 60,
73, 140–41, 186, 193, 238, 247, 257
Van Dorn pattern flag, 201, 208–9, 240
Van Dorn's Cavalry Division, 11
Vasser Hill, Mo., battle at, 52
Vaughn, Joseph P., 206, 240
Vernon County, Mo., 69, 93–94, 174,
217, 225
Vicksburg (steamboat), 257
Vicksburg, Miss., xv, 5–6, 17, 22, 32, 36,
39, 49–50, 55, 60, 90, 142, 154, 179,
183, 188, 190, 195–97, 201, 204–5,
207–8, 226, 231, 235
Vicksburg Campaign, 12, 17, 24, 141,
187, 195, 208–9
Virginia Military Institute, 114, 129, 138,
146, 165
Vivien, Harvey J., 98
Von Phul, Benjamin, 2, 42

W

Waddell, James P., 24
Waddell, Owen A., 197, 202, 248,
256–57
Waddell's Artillery Battalion
(Confederate), 24
Wade, William, 4
Wade's Battery, 32, 40. *See also* 1st Light
Battery
Walker, James A., 77
Walker, James, 200
Walker, John G., 82, 228
Walker, W. B., 84
Walker's Texas Infantry Division, 82, 228
Wallace, James C., 217, 250
Walnut Creek, Mo., 53
Walsh, Richard, 4–6
Walthall, Edward C., 23
Walthall's Infantry Brigade, 23
Walton, Thomas H., 84
Ward, Samuel J., 80

Warden, William E., 129, 258
Warner, Stephen W., 233
Warren County, Mo., 69
Warsaw, Mo., 100
Washburn, Delaney S., 63
Washington, Mo., 83, 91, 104
Washington Artillery, 5th Company
(Confederate), 179
Washington County, Mo., 58, 64, 84,
122, 220, 229
Watie, Stand, 136
Watkins, William L., 242
Waverly, Mo., 116, 127–28, 156
Wayne County, Mo., 58, 106, 206, 221,
229, 242
Waynesville, Mo., 171
Weast, James J., 148
Weast, W. B., 148
Weaver, Thomas J., 114
Webb, Andrew, 78
Webb, George B., 98
Webb, John, 98
Webster County, Mo., 64, 102, 139
Weidemeyer, John M., 240
Welfley's Missouri Battery (Union), 31
Wells, John S., 185, 189
Wells, R. J., 117
West, John J., 93
Western Rangers, 161
West Point (U. S. Military Academy),
11, 178
Westport, Mo., battle at, xv, 9, 76, 87,
96, 101, 107, 119, 122, 132, 134, 149, 169
Wethers, William, 77
White, Benjamin F., 51
White, James Daniel, 14, 229–31
White, Moses J., 65, 69, 81
White, William A., 88
White River, 15, 75, 96, 100, 114, 158,
227, 254
White's Bluff, Ark., 212, 216, 250
White Springs, Ark., 85
Whitewater River, skirmish at, 160
Whitfield, John W., 17
Whitfield's Texas Cavalry Brigade, 17
Wickersham, James H., 200
Wickersham, Richard J., 102
Wiedemeyer, John M., 206

JAMES E. MCGHEE is a retired lawyer from the Missouri Department of Labor and now devotes himself to the study of the Civil War. He has written and edited a number of books focusing on the war in his home state, including *Service with the Missouri State Guard, Campaigning with General Marmaduke: Narratives and Roster of the 8th Missouri Calvary,* and *Missouri Confederates: A Guide to Sources for Confederate Soldiers and Units, 1861–1865.* He lives in Jefferson City, Missouri.